Olivia

Olivia

The biography of Olivia Newton-John

Tim Ewbank

piatkus

PIATKUS

First published in Great Britain in 2008 by Piatkus Books
This paperback edition published in 2011 by Piatkus
Reprinted 2012

A CIP catalogue record for this book
is available from the British Library.

ISBN 978-0-7499-0984-0

Typeset in Sabon by Action Publishing Technology Ltd, Gloucester
Printed and bound in Great Britain by
Clays Ltd, St Ives plc

Papers used by Piatkus are from well-managed forests
and other responsible sources.

MIX
Paper from
responsible sources
FSC® C104740

Piatkus
An imprint of
Little, Brown Book Group
100 Victoria Embankment
London EC4Y 0DY

An Hachette UK Company
www.hachette.co.uk

www.piatkus.co.uk

To my children Emma and Oliver

Contents

Acknowledgements

The author wishes to express his deep gratitude to the many individuals who have made this book possible. Heartfelt thanks go to all those who have figured in Olivia Newton-John's life who agreed to be interviewed for this book.

The author wishes to acknowledge many TV programmes as invaluable sources, notably *Enough Rope With Andrew Denton*, The Biography Channel, BBC Wales, and E! Entertainment.

Other additional important sources include *Crawdaddy* magazine, *Los Angeles Times*, *New Musical Express*, *Record Mirror*, *New Idea*, *Who* magazine, *People* magazine, *Woman's Day*, *TV Guide*, *Women's Weekly*, Express Newspapers, *Daily Mail*, *Sun*, *Daily Mirror*, *Sunday Times*, *Cambridge Evening News*, *Hello!*, *Alternative Medicine* magazine, Mike Read's book *The Story of The Shadows* and Bruce Welch's autobiography *Rock 'n' Roll I Gave You The Best Years Of My Life*.

In a book which contains many pop chart statistics, every effort has been made to ensure accuracy, and the author would like to acknowledge the Guinness book *British Hit Singles, Billboard* and the Only Olivia website.

For their co-operation help and encouragement, thanks are

due to: Roy and Liz Addison, John Airey, Brenda Barton, Julian Beauchamp, Alan Brooke, Corinna Cowie, Keith Cronshaw, Barbara Davis, Ingrid Dodd, Jane Ennis, Carole Anne Ferris, Rod and Joy Gilchrist, Justine Harkness, Stafford Hildred, Kathryn Holcombe, Clive Jackson, Paula Jones, Jerry Johns, Robert Kirby, Moira Marr, Bryan and Vicki Marshall, Fraser Massey, Nick McMahon, Zoe Nauman, Garth Pearce, Arethusa Plouidy, Alan Rawes, Keith Richmond, Alasdair Riley, Rebecca Smith, Douglas Thompson, Alison and Paul Tissington, Lynn Trunley-Smith, Paula Trewick, Joy Wade, Cynthia Warrington, Bruce Welch, Millie Koong, Steve Saunders of Paradise Wildlife Park, Bill Barr, Cindy Blanchflower, Country Music Association, William Eve, Phil Hammond, John Kay, Alan Kingston, Fiona Knight, Charles and Alicia McCutcheon, Sarita Martin, William and Samantha Mertens, Peter Morris, Claire Sefton, David Sievwright, Rosie Riley and Rob Urbino.

Special thanks are due to Simon Kinnersley for access to his insightful interviews, to Juan McShane and Debbie Bradshaw of Melbourne for their kindness, to all at Sullivan's Hotel, 21 Oxford Street, Paddington, Sydney, and to British Airways and Qantas for their comfort, care and courtesy when travelling to and from Australia for my research.

Grateful thanks to Robert Kirby of United Agents, and to Alan Brooke, Denise Dwyer, Mari Roberts, and all at Piatkus and Little, Brown Book Group.

Finally, heartfelt thanks to my mother Joy and to my two children Emma and Oliver for their love, support and patience during the writing of this book.

Prologue

Every morning as she starts to stir after her night's sleep, but before she even opens her eyes, Olivia Newton-John chooses to begin her day by offering up a simple but heart-felt prayer of thanks – for the gift of life. 'I lie there for a few minutes and think about how fortunate I am to live another day,' she says.

The enduring popularity of *Grease*, the most successful movie musical of all time, ensures that Olivia remains forever young in the minds of millions all over the world. So it may come as a surprise to many that on 26 September 2008, perennially youthful Olivia celebrated her sixtieth birthday.

No doubt special thanks were offered up by the singer on that day because, for a desperately worrying period in the 1990s, she must have wondered, in her darkest hours, whether it is a milestone which she would ever reach. 'Surviving breast cancer has made me appreciate every moment,' she now says, 'and I do feel lucky to be alive.'

Certainly, Olivia Newton-John is nothing if not a sur-vivor, and today she still radiates not only a girlish, last-ing beauty but a serenity born of the personal journey of spiritual healing she has travelled and the inner fulfilment and tranquillity she has found along the way. All of which now allows her to believe she is truly blessed, despite a series of personal setbacks any one of which many would regard as devastating, and collectively would bring most mortals to their knees.

'For me, breast cancer was a gift,' she is now able to say with utter conviction. 'I was so lucky to have survived. It left me with a lot of benefits I can now share with other people.' Through the transforming power of her own illness, from which she is so happily recovered, Olivia has gone on to help thousands of women.

Citing her own experiences, she has become an outspoken advocate for early detection. And she continues to campaign tirelessly to raise funds for a wellness centre to be built in her name at Melbourne's Austin Hospital where patients can go, before and after therapy, to pray, meditate, have a cup of tea, relax or simply talk to others in a similar situation.

The original *Grease* movie, followed by the video of the film, the DVD and the countless screenings and rescreenings by television stations around the globe, have ensured that for millions Olivia will always be the prim college cheerleader Sandy who turns into a sexy vamp in the last reel to win the heart of John Travolta. It's more than thirty years since Sandy and Danny giddily drove out of Rydell High's college carnival in an open-top pink roadster and off to a pre-Vietnam war optimistic future, but for Olivia, hardly a day goes by without somebody mentioning either Sandy or John Travolta. Successive generations have warmed to the movie in the most remarkable fashion, and every mention of the film is a reminder to Olivia of the pleasure *Grease* has given to many millions over the years. It's her legacy, and she's proud of it. But in the thirty years since she was sewn into the black skin-tight pants to knock Danny dizzy at the fairground Shake Shack, the singer's own life has undergone a transformation, which in its own way has been almost as startling as Sandy's.

Back in 1978 Olivia was one of the most successful and popular female recording artists in the world. Her records sold millions, her concerts were sell-outs and at her peak she was re-ceiving 2,000 fan letters a week. Her success made her wealthy beyond her wildest dreams and she lived in extreme, albeit un-ostentatious, comfort in her home in Malibu, California, surrounded by a menagerie of cats, dogs and horses, all of whom she adored. The years that lay ahead looked as rosy for her as Sandy's, until fate took a hand.

In those days she was under pressure from others to make hit singles, to fill concert halls, to pull in TV audiences, to promote each new album, to notch up ever higher record sales. Today she makes the records she wants to make, when she wants to make them and with the message she wants to put across. These days, performing live is a joyful experience for her. 'There are moments when you are in the light and it's just you and the music,' she said recently. 'It's a spiritual experience. You're suspended in time. It's like a meditation.'

That's a far cry from the days when she would be so wracked with nerves before a concert she felt physically ill. She was terrified of forgetting lines to songs she had sung a hundred times and the stress was tangible and unpleasant. It was a feeling of anxiety, she said, which started in her spine and settled in her stomach to the extent that she felt as though she had swallowed a block of ice.

Today, in concert, she sings without fear the songs she loves, the songs she wants to sing and for the sheer joy of using the musical gift she has been given.

Along with the fear of performing has gone the guilt she

was prone to feeling about having wealth and a nice home. 'I was slightly embarrassed because it all came to me in a way that seemed so easy,' she once said of her career. 'I did work hard for a long time, but since I always enjoyed it there was never any clawing to the top. I always had people behind me who believed in me and pushed me.'

Olivia's path to stardom was never a zealous thrust for fame. Her sister Rona, who acted as her trusty chaperone during her early chart successes, remembers driving past a vast billboard bearing Olivia's name advertising her concert at the Riviera Hotel in Las Vegas in the mid-1970s and Olivia turning to her and asking: 'Who *is* that girl?'

That girl is now a sixty-year-old woman who has had chart-topping hits in dozens of countries, who has sung for the Pope, for US presidents, and for four billion TV viewers at the opening of the 2000 Sydney Olympics. She's won countless music awards and starred in the best-loved movie musical of all time.

For the sake of a video to plug one of her records, she has been filmed lazing in a bubble bath wearing a Marilyn Monroe wig and pulling her fully clothed then husband Matt into the water. She's coped with the bankruptcy of her business Koala Blue. And she's fallen down the stairs of the royal bathroom at Buckingham Palace on her visit to receive her OBE award.

She's been a UN ambassador for the environment, and travelled the world for the nature TV series *Wild Life*, in which she's fed tigers, released a bald eagle back into the wild, interviewed Mikhail Gorbachev and ridden wild horses.

But she's also the woman who has known the joy of deep love as well as the sadness of divorce, the joys of motherhood and the despair of miscarriages, the fear of cancer but the strength to grow from it rather than weaken. She has experienced inexplicable loss with the mystery disappearance of a lover on a fishing trip, and she's felt the pain of a daughter's battle with anorexia. She's had a life-threatening illness, and by confronting the possibility of death, she has shed an innate fear of dying. She is very much alive and her life has been, and continues to be, fascinating.

Chapter 1

Olivia's Childhood

'My parents' divorce made me feel insecure. I tried to blank out what was going on and I was always the happy child trying to keep everyone else happy'

Olivia

Olivia Newton-John was born on 26 September 1948, in Cambridge, England, and there was much rejoicing in the household of her parents Irene and Brin at the arrival of their beautiful new baby girl.

Irene, who was German, and Welshman Brin, who was a master at King's College, already had a son, Hugh, and a daughter, Rona, but Olivia was very much a wanted addition to their family.

Irene, then in her early thirties, and her husband had both decided a third child would complete their family after eleven years of marriage. And for Brin, Olivia's arrival was a very special birth because he had been away in the war when his first two children had been born. He was posted to Bletchley Park in Buckinghamshire where his brilliant talent for languages was put to good use helping to crack the Germans' Enigma Code, which comprised a series of five-letter technical words detailing messages about Hitler's battle plans. Brin was also the man who interrogated Hitler's right-hand man Rudolf Hess after he parachuted into Scotland in 1941.

Olivia was born at a time when Britain was still

struggling to come to terms with the stark realisation that the end of World War Two had brought peace but not plenty. The England that welcomed Olivia into the world was a country of rationed food, clothes, petrol and tobacco. Rationing had been in force for many years as part of the war effort and, during that summer of 1948, facing a mounting financial crisis, the British government announced additional austerity measures, including a halt to motoring for pleasure and foreign holidays.

But it wasn't all doom and gloom. The country rejoiced in the news that Princess Elizabeth and her husband the Duke of Edinburgh were looking forward to the birth of their first child in November, and British cinema was revelling in the success of *The Red Shoes*, featuring the beautiful ballet-star-turned-actress Moira Shearer in a tale of a dancer torn between two men and her career. On the radio, the hit tune of the day was 'Buttons and Bows' from Bob Hope's first colour movie, *The Paleface*, co-starring a gun-toting Jane Russell as Calamity Jane.

Olivia arrived at the end of an eventful English summer largely dominated by sport. London had just successfully hosted the Olympic games despite the strictures of post-war austerity. And, fittingly for Olivia as events were to turn out, it was a group of Australians who were making their mark around the country that summer. Don Bradman's all-conquering Aussie cricketers earned the accolade of the finest team ever to play the game as they toured the English counties.

* * *

Olivia's Welsh bloodline on her father's side can be traced back to 1728; in the thirteenth-century church in St Mary Hill, a little village some twenty miles west of Cardiff, there is a 200-year-old memorial plaque commemorating several generations of the Johns who lived in the village in the late 1700s. Until very recently, Olivia's knowledge of her father's side of her family was very limited. To put that right she visited Wales in 2007 with the express purpose of discovering her Welsh roots and learning more about her ancestors.

The trip provided her with a host of surprises, not least that her great-grandfather James Newton, born in 1856, was a publican, that her prim and thoroughly puritanical grandmother Daisy had been a barmaid. Olivia also learned that her own father had been born above the family pub.

James Newton had married Elizabeth on Christmas day in 1880 in the Bethany Chapel in Cardiff, and they subsequently had a daughter, Daisy, who married a cellar boy. And it was Daisy, Olivia's grandmother, who founded the Newton-John name by adding her surname to that of her husband, Oliver John.

Although Olivia's ancestors had largely gravitated to the city of Cardiff after the late 1700s, their link with the village of St Mary Hill remained strong. Daisy's new husband was also a carpenter and he set to work converting the family's cottage and a former church into the Bell pub, which became a favourite watering hole for visitors to the horse fair held annually in the village. It was the largest fair of its kind in Wales.

During her emotional journey to Cardiff to trace her Welsh family tree, Olivia was amazed to find that Grandma Daisy gave birth to her father Brinley in 1914 over the family's new pub, the New Market Tavern, situated in a then unsavoury area of the city. The pub, in Church Street, is now part of the O'Neill's pub chain, and Olivia was further astonished to discover that she had a fourth cousin, Paul Thomas, currently working there as the manager.

Olivia discovered her musical heritage could be traced back to Daisy, who played hymns at the family piano and enjoyed singing lustily in church, which she was wont to visit as many as five times on Sundays. Olivia's sister Rona, who accompanied her on the trip to Cardiff to examine their past, remembers Grandma Daisy as thoroughly right-eous, very proper, and a strict disciplinarian who stood no-nonsense from her son. She was a stickler for decorum and good manners, particularly when it came to bad language.

Daisy instilled her love of music into her son Brinley, who went to Cardiff's Canton High School, where he shone in singing and music and became an accomplished violinist, as well as taking part in several of the school's stage productions. In the classroom, Brin excelled at languages and won a scholarship to Cambridge in 1933, where he gained a double first. And it was while he was a university student that he met and fell in love with Olivia's mother, Irene.

According to Irene, Olivia was a contented baby who showed an early aptitude for music. 'She was a very happy little girl, full of health and vitality. She started singing as soon as she could talk.'

Olivia's infant ears became accustomed to the sound of music ringing around her home almost from the day she was born. Brin and Irene would regularly take it in turns to sing to her, often in different languages, as they held her in their arms. She would be lulled to sleep by ballads sooth-ingly sung by one or other of her multi-lingual parents, or sometimes both, in English, German or French.

By the time she was fifteen months old, Olivia was capable of recognising a musical note sung to her and was able to imitate it accurately. Furthermore, by the age of two, she could vocally echo every note of a musical phrase with seemingly perfect pitch and true clarity. Such a precocious feel for music gave early hints of a life to come and Irene felt sure, even at that tender age, that Olivia would become a singer. 'But it never occurred to me she would be the kind of singer she is,' she once said. 'When I thought of singers, I thought of opera. My husband had a beautiful voice and he used to sing with my father.'

Brin had originally trained to become an opera singer, an ambition that met with the approval of Irene's father, the German Nobel prize-winning physicist Professor Max Born, who had long had a passion for opera. In fact, the professor, Olivia's maternal grandfather, just happened to have been the best of friends with Albert Einstein, whose favourite pastime apart from sailing was classical music, especially the works of Bach and Mozart. Einstein was a more than proficient violinist and he and Max Born would rope in other music-loving scientists and play string quartets together for their personal enjoyment. It was Einstein who nominated Born for the Nobel Prize in 1954, and it was in a letter to Olivia's grandfather in 1926 that Einstein made his famous remark that 'The Old One does not play dice', meaning that God does not play with the universe.

Although he was Christian, Professor Born was forced to flee the Nazis because of his Jewish heritage. He moved his family to Cambridge, where he had studied as a young man. There, his daughter Irene met Olivia's father, who was by now an honours student at Cambridge and spoke excellent German. Irene and Brin were married in 1937, soon after he had completed his studies.

Olivia never had the good fortune to meet her illustrious grandfather Max, who returned to Germany several years after the war had ended and died in 1970. Irene, who had studied mathematics at the university where he was the director, spoke fondly of him to her often, and made sure Olivia understood that she was immensely proud of him and his achievements, and that her daughter should be too.

In years to come, Irene often urged Olivia to find the time to go to Germany to see him. For one reason or another she never managed it, but she did travel to Germany in 2007 to sing at a dinner to mark the 125th anniversary of her grandfather's birth. 'He was kind, a good person, as well as a wonderful mind,' Olivia reflected. 'He helped many Jews leave Germany during World War Two.'

Brin's early ambitions of becoming an opera singer may have been ultimately unfulfilled, but his passion for music nevertheless endured. It was ever present in the Newton-John household while his children were growing up. Although Brin never achieved his personal dream, he came close to it by making a record. Unfortunately he was his own severest critic, and was mortified to discover on the playback of the recording that he had sung a wrong note. It was just one error, but being something of a perfectionist, Brin viewed this solitary vocal inaccuracy as enough of a blemish for him to shatter the record into a dozen pieces in disgust.

When he decided his bass baritone lacked the range to warrant a place among the top ranks of the world's opera singers, Brin abandoned his ambitions. He was not content simply to be one of the forty best in his field, and he chose to become an academic instead. It must have been a difficult decision for him to make, but Olivia never once heard him express any regrets. Instead, she has fond memories of her father regularly singing along to and enthusiastically 'conducting' selections from his vast collection of 78rpm opera records, stacked near the family gramophone. To young Olivia it seemed her father was familiar with every opera known to man and that he knew every note. Brin's record collection comprised mainly, but not entirely, classical music, but there was room for the odd lighter musical genre, including Tennessee Ernie Ford, best known for his 1955 US chart-topper 'Sixteen Tons'.

In church on Sundays, Olivia soon came to realise what a beautiful, strong and deep voice her father possessed when ranged against the vocal efforts of the rest of the choir and congregation. His powerful singing far outshone anyone else's, she noted, even if it caused her a little embarrassment to think that perhaps he sang too loudly for everyone's liking.

Olivia's main memories of early childhood are of walking around the Cambridge colleges and of family boat trips punting down the river Cam. Her early years were uneventful apart from a worrying few hours for her parents when she contrived at the age of eighteen months to swallow several medicine tablets she had spied on a bedroom table. When she rapidly became ill, she was rushed to hospital to have her stomach pumped.

* * *

Olivia was five years old when Irene and Brin decided to move their family to Australia, after Brin accepted a new post as dean of Melbourne University's Ormond College. Olivia's only recollection of the boat trip over from England is of her sadness and tears at somehow losing her favourite soft toy animal comforter, called Fluffy, somewhere along the way.

A large lodge house went with Brin's new post in Melbourne, and the family settled quickly and comfortably into their new life down under. From Olivia's point of view, all that was missing from their new home was a few pets. From a very early age she had developed a love of animals and, after falling in love with a neighbour's red setter she called Pauly-Orly, she was forever trying to bring home any stray four-legged animal she came across. 'It was a big campus where we lived,' she says, 'and people used to dump unwanted animals there, half-drowned cats in sacks, greyhounds that couldn't race. It was criminal.' Unfortunately for Olivia, keeping pets wasn't permitted on the university grounds and Olivia's mother had little option other than to make her take the strays straight off to the ASPCA.

When she was seven, Olivia showed an early determination to stand up for animal rights in the face of anything she perceived as cruelty. She was stung into action when she witnessed a man with a horse-drawn cart, which was used to pick up rubbish, beating his nag far too zealously. Without a thought, she shouted at him to stop and stepped forward and managed to wrench the whip out of the offender's hand. She even threatened to report him if he didn't leave the horse alone.

Such a courageous stand on behalf of a dumb animal was a sign of steely resolve to come. In future years, Olivia would put her name, her time and her energy behind anti-cruelty campaigns on behalf of creatures great and small, from dolphins to cheetahs.

Most notably, while at the peak of her post-*Grease* fame in 1978, she threatened to cancel a month-long tour of Japan unless Japanese fishermen agreed to stop slaughtering dolphins inadvertently caught in their tuna nets. Olivia was appalled that 1,500 dolphins had met their deaths in what she perceived to be such a callous and needless manner. 'Thank goodness I didn't see any of the pictures on television,' she would shudder. 'They would have made me ill.

'Animals need some kind of protection whatever and wherever they are. I'm hoping that in Japan those who were looking forward to attending my concerts might be so disappointed that they will look at the reason I cancelled and try to do something about the slaughter of dolphins in their country.'

The Japanese fishermen claimed that the dolphins were eating too many fish, reducing the size of their catches and therefore their income. But Olivia was by then the most popular singer, male or female, in Japan and so her threat had precisely the impact she hoped for. The slaughter ceased and Olivia's threat was rescinded. It was a resounding victory for the singer and made her realise just what she could achieve on behalf of God's defenceless creatures.

* * *

While Olivia was growing up, Brin and Irene proved to be loving but firm parents. Irene was meticulous about tidiness and cleanliness and brought the family up on health foods long before it was fashionable – yoghurt, sour cream, and a plentiful supply of fruit and vegetables were staple fare. None of the children was allowed comics, and they learned that work came first, and only when it was done was there time for pleasure. It was a work ethic instilled into Olivia at an early age and that stayed with her throughout her life.

On her recent trip to Wales to find out more about her father's family, Olivia's visit to the Canton High School in Cardiff provided her with a clearer understanding as to why her father imposed boundaries of behaviour upon his children. The school her father attended is now Chapter Arts

Centre, and enough of the original architecture remained for Olivia to see that there used to be separate entrances for boys and girls. And, in records kept by a former pupil, it emerged that using the wrong entrance or walking past litter and not picking it up was punishable by a caning. 'So that's why he was a disciplinarian,' said Olivia of her father as she was shown round her dad's old classroom.

Tall and slim, there was an imposing, aristocratic air about Brin that warranted respect, and Olivia says she was even quite frightened of her father when she was a child, particularly when she'd be daydreaming and he suddenly called out to her with his penetrating voice. Nonetheless, he was a tremendous source of security.

Olivia was ten when her world was shaken to its foundations by the break-up of her parents' marriage and subsequent divorce. It not only had an immediate and profound impact upon her, but it scarred her for life and had a major bearing on her attitude towards marriage and commitment in relationships for decades to come.

Six years after her parents' divorce, her sister Rona was divorced as well and Olivia said many years later: 'It left me afraid of marriage because I'd seen so much divorce. There's hardly a member of my family who hasn't been through it and I guess I've been affected by all that. If you've never seen a relationship that lasts for ever, you tend to believe it's not possible.'

In years to come, Olivia would come close to marriage more than once but she was always fearful of such a step and only finally married at the age of thirty-six. 'Of course nobody ever wants divorce to happen to them,' she explained, 'but I became a bit hung up on it. I was so determined to make the right choice in marriage.'

As her fame grew throughout her twenties and early thirties, Olivia gave countless interviews to the press and it was a rare interviewer who did not ask her when she was going to get married and settle down. Olivia never ducked the question and generally cited her parents' divorce as the reason why she was remaining resolutely single.

Olivia was very close to her father and she suffered a tremendous sense of loss when it became clear that her parents could no longer go on living together and that their marriage was coming to an end. 'I can still remember the terrible shock I felt when my father said he was moving away,' she recalled in a recent interview. 'He was very upset when he told me.'

The shock Olivia felt was compounded by the realisation that her father was moving not to somewhere close by but to a new home many hundreds of miles away and in another state in Australia. He was to take a new post as a university vice-chancellor in Newcastle, a coastal town some two hours' drive north of Sydney in New South Wales. 'After that I saw my father maybe once or twice a year during vacations,' Olivia remembers sadly.

Olivia's outwardly sunny nature hid her true feelings, as inside she felt wounded, hurt and insecure. She tried to blank out the ensuing upheaval in her family life. 'I was always the happy child trying to keep everyone else happy,' she said.

Divorce in the mid-1950s in Australia was viewed in a very different way from how it's regarded today. In some sections of Australian society it was still frowned upon as not the done thing, scandalous even, and Brin's high-ranking university position unfortunately made his separation and divorce from Irene more of a talking point locally than most.

The large majority of Olivia's friends had happily married

parents and it made her feel she was the odd one out. 'I kept hoping they would get back together again,' Olivia says.

Following the divorce, Irene stayed put in Melbourne and moved with her children into a small flat. 'I had to go with my mother but didn't want to leave my father,' Olivia would later explain. 'But I had to cope with my feelings quietly. I kept things to myself. I didn't want my mother to know that I was disappointed. I guess it must have shown because teachers used to take me out. One of my English teachers used to take me to the zoo so that I would not have to go home to an empty house. My mum couldn't help it. She had to be out at work all day.'

In an era when it was far from usual for women to work by choice, Irene was forced to take a job as a public relations consultant. She was by now over forty and was having to go out and work for the first time since her marriage. It was a financial necessity if she was to pay the bills, but she resented the fact that her job meant her youngest child was often forced to let herself into an empty flat with her own key when she came home from school. She hated the very idea of Olivia as a latchkey kid but it was case of needs must.

Although Olivia has written some fine songs in her time, it is only comparatively recently that she has become a prolific songwriter. But some twenty years after being hit so hard by her parents' separation, she was moved to put her feelings about divorce into words in the song 'Changes', which she wrote for her album *If You Love Me Let Me Know*. She wrote of weekly outings, gifts and picture shows which could not make up for the absence of a father, his voice, his touch, his manly sound. Olivia actually wrote the song for a friend but the sentiments she expressed in 'Changes' welled up from her own memories.

When Olivia's brother Hugh went off to university and Rona dropped out of school early at fifteen to follow her dream of becoming an actress and then soon got married, Olivia felt her father's absence ever more keenly. 'Being alone is hard to cope with,' she noted. 'Maybe that's why I channelled all my energies into music. It helped me not to feel so alone and to accept what had happened.'

* * *

With her keen ear for music, Olivia enjoyed tuning in to the radio in Australia to listen out for her favourite singers, who included Joan Baez, Dionne Warwick, Ray Charles and Nina Simone. 'More than anyone else they were the people I listened to in Australia. I listened to the radio and I knew every pop song. I sang all the time for my family and friends, but if they asked me at school to get up and sing, I was always too shy.'

Olivia's reluctance to push herself forward was partly due to her embarrassment over having a double-barrelled surname. It made her feel self-conscious and it automatically set her apart from the other girls. Many was the time she dearly wished she was simply called Claire Smith or had some other surname less fanciful than her own. Her natural shyness, however, coexisted with a strong innate desire to perform.

The first tangible signs that Olivia might be destined for a career in the public eye came when she was twelve. Rona entered Olivia for a local cinema's contest to find a Hayley Mills lookalike, a girl who resembled the young British actress who was then making a name for herself as a child star in films like *Tiger Bay*, *Pollyanna* and *The Parent Trap*. Olivia duly won but, although she went on to become president of drama at her school and take part in many school productions, she was never going to be Australia's answer to Hayley – in her heart she was much keener on music than acting.

The Hayley Mills experience did, however, lead to an appearance at the local Melbourne theatre as a cherub in the religious play *Green Pastures*, but music took on a new meaning for her when her mother bought her an acoustic guitar when she was thirteen. She began to learn a few basic chords and soon mastered enough to accompany herself on 'Where Have All The Flowers Gone?'. Olivia even managed to write her first song at thirteen, called 'Why Does It Have To Be?'.

By the following year, Olivia was interested enough in singing to form a folk group with three other girls, two of whom, she later laughingly recalled, were tone deaf. They called themselves the Sol Four, a name they all agreed sounded ultra-sophisticated and avant-garde because it included the French word for 'sun'.

'We were awful!' Olivia later conceded. Dressed in hessian jackets, black polo necks and desert boots, the girls thought they were the epitome of beatnik cool as they trilled the folksy favourites of the day like 'Down By The Riverside', 'Tom Dooley' and 'Michael Row The Boat Ashore'.

The Sol Four made time to rehearse after school and at the weekends Olivia sneaked out to join the other three for appearances at local folk and trad jazz clubs. But audiences were often distinctly underwhelmed by Sol Four's vocal efforts (unsurprising given half of them were tone deaf). Olivia remembers it was not uncommon for the group's performances to be greeted by derisory boos or a shower of coins. The quartet eventually disbanded, but not through lack of vocal talent. Irene decided that Olivia was spending

far too much time on Sol Four because her homework was
starting to suffer.

Olivia remained undaunted and looked ahead to the day
when she might perhaps become a singer full-time. Both
Irene and Olivia's father had mixed feelings about her lean-
ings towards a singing career. Both harboured hopes that
she would eventually go on to university, though she was
not a pupil who stood out academically. 'I don't think I was
very noticeable. I was always the youngest in my class and
felt that everyone knew what was going on and I didn't.'
Irene was also shrewd enough to appreciate that Olivia's
burgeoning talent for singing needed nurturing, so she
packed her off to the best vocal coach in Melbourne for
lessons.

Olivia went along just to please her mother. She returned
home after the first lesson unimpressed and complaining
that the coach had put her through some scales and then
asked her to project her voice in a way she felt was unnatural. The teacher was of the opinion that Olivia had the
right vocal range for opera but felt she needed to sing out
more forcefully. Olivia herself was unhappy that he was
trying to change the soft and gentle manner in which she
sang and she returned home disconsolate. Olivia never
went back for a second lesson. 'I always had a mind of my
own,' she says.

Apart from music, animals continued to be an abiding
passion in Olivia's life. 'There was a period when I considered being a vet. But when it came to the point I found I
just couldn't discipline myself to the necessary studies,' she
said. Much to her disappointment, the size of her mother's
flat meant it was impractical to keep a pet. Instead, Olivia
started saving up for a horse and even considered becoming
a mounted policewoman once her schooldays were behind

her. With a child's logic, she reasoned it would at least be a job in which she would get to have a horse she could call her own and go riding every day as well as get paid for it.

But there were no mounted policewomen in Australia at that point, and by the time Olivia was fourteen, she was becoming more interested in boys than spending all her spare time riding, though her shyness continued to manifest itself. She was so self-conscious about wearing a swimming suit in front of boys that she refused to be on the school swimming team. She had innocent crushes on a couple of boys, including the captain of the football team, but was too reticent to do anything about it.

High school dances, she remembers, were torture because she wasn't a natural dancer and felt she might fall over at any moment. She was too self-conscious about her gangly frame to enjoy herself on the dance floor. Boys did not figure in Olivia's life with any real significance until indirectly through Rona she met a handsome young man called Ian Turpie. Then she knew this would be something very different.

Born in Melbourne in 1943, Ian was some five years older than Olivia and considerably more mature. He had been destined for a career in showbusiness from the moment he was given a place at the age of ten at the highly rated Hector Crawford Drama School. Soon he was catching the eye as a juvenile actor in theatre and in radio drama productions. By the age of sixteen he had already built up an impressive body of work in musicals and in Australia's National Theatre Productions, which included a production of Shakespeare's *Macbeth*. Additionally, Ian had developed a passion for music and became a decent singer-songwriter who could be found accompanying himself on guitar in trendy Melbourne circles.

One day a friend told Ian he should check out 'this chick singer in this coffee lounge', referring to Olivia who was appearing occasionally at an establishment run by the boyfriend of her sister Rona. He did so, and his reaction was: 'Pure voice. Perfect pitch. Exceptionally good-looking.' She looked as though butter would not melt in her mouth, but he was astonished to hear that Olivia included in her repertoire a thoroughly bawdy song that ran:

> *Cats on the rooftop, cats on the tiles,*
> *Cats with the clap and cats with piles*
> *Cats with their arseholes wreathed in smiles*
> *As they revel in the joys of fornication.*

Just a reminder of this coarse ditty is enough to make Olivia blush still.

As well as her occasional appearances, Olivia would sit by the stage to listen to other folkies singing and strumming and she was thrilled when one day Ian invited her up on stage to join him. The union proved to be harmonious in every way and Ian lost no time in asking Olivia out. Much to Irene's disapproval he took her to a drive-in movie for their first date and Olivia says that predictably she saw nothing of the movie.

Ian was something of a celebrity at the point where he met Olivia, and when romance blossomed between them she could not help but be flattered that someone so well known could be interested in her, particularly as she was just fifteen and still at school. She recognised, too, that she could learn much about the world of showbusiness from this man, her first serious boyfriend, and she was eager for him to teach her more of the guitar. Together their voices blended well when they sang their favourite folk and country songs made popular by the likes of Joan Baez, Bob Dylan and The Springfields.

Around the time she was falling for Ian, Olivia was already making her first appearances on television, spurred on by both Ian and Rona. Her TV debut came as an amateur singer appearing on a show called *Kevin Dennis Auditions*, a forerunner of shows like *New Faces* and, more recently, *The X Factor*.

The programme owed not a little to America's TV hit *The Gong Show* in which amateur acts went through their paces until they were sent packing by the sounding of a gong. Some of the entrants on the US show barely got to sing a note before they were humiliatingly gonged off, but *Kevin Dennis Auditions* turned the tables by allowing performers to showcase their talents long enough to collect gongs according to their entertainment value before they were hooked off. To her delight, Olivia, accompanied by Ian Turpie on guitar, managed the maximum three gongs for her rendition of 'Summertime', and Evie Hayes, a local actress and TV and vaudeville star who was one of the judges, was impressed enough to phone up Olivia's mother, offering to manage Olivia's career. Irene rejected the idea and said that Olivia was still at school and still far too young to consider being a professional singer. And besides, she said, if anyone was going to manage Olivia it would be her mother.

But there was no doubting that Olivia's ability to sing was now starting to point her towards a professional career. She made her first paid-for appearance on a TV show called *Sunny Side Up* and sang 'Melody d'Amour' wearing an outfit made for her by her mother.

Before long she was being offered a wide variety of work

in television and the odd film despite still being at school, and Irene effectively became her manager. She fielded the offers in a thoroughly supportive but protective manner, once turning down a movie role in New Zealand for her daughter mainly because she could not accompany Olivia as her chaperone.

A turning point for Olivia came after Ian Turpie took over as host of *The Go!! Show*, a programme that had been successfully launched to court a youth audience and which was loosely modelled on pop shows like *Oh Boy!* and *Ready, Steady, Go!*, which had proved so successful in the UK.

Olivia became a regular guest singer on *The Go!! Show*, usually miming to two numbers per programme, which she had pre-recorded at the TV studios in Melbourne. She sang the occasional duet with her MC boyfriend but largely performed solo cover versions of the hits of the day by American and British artists, backed by a house band called The Strangers, who performed in smart matching suits. The band included a young guitarist and lead singer by the name of John Farrar, who would later play a significant role, as songwriter and arranger as well as record producer, in shooting Olivia to stardom.

The Go!! Show featured almost exclusively local singers and performers and among them was another promising young songstress, called Pat Carroll, who was also destined to play an important role in Olivia's early career as well as even-tually becoming her business partner, treasured lifelong friend and, initially, dance teacher. 'When Olivia came along the first time Ian Turpie put her on, she couldn't dance,' Pat remem-bers. 'So the producer came to me and said: "You've got to help her learn to dance. She can't move."'

Another TV break presented itself when Olivia was

asked to fill in on the kids programme *The Happy Show*, replacing one of the presenters, known as Lovely Anne, who was leaving to get married. For the show's younger viewers Olivia took on the mantle of Lovely Livvy for two months over the Christmas school holidays. The show went out live five afternoons a week and Olivia's job was to present items, sing and give away toys to kids. She acquitted herself well and proved popular.

Soon she found herself working, again with Ian Turpie, on *Time For Terry*, which gave her an early grounding in the discipline needed for performing on television. She had to learn songs quickly and go on to perform them, sometimes live, to a tight schedule. While Irene shrewdly handled Olivia's fledgling career, Ian Turpie was equally supportive. He believed in his pretty young girlfriend and felt she had an exceptional singing voice which could take her a long way in showbusiness.

He encouraged her at every turn, and at the urging of her sister Rona, Olivia went in for the local heat of Johnny O'Keefe's talent contest *Sing, Sing, Sing*, and, again accompanied by Ian Turpie on guitar, went on to win the entire competition. Olivia clinched victory by singing 'Anyone Who Had A Heart', the Burt Bacharach–Hal David ballad which had been a hit for Dionne Warwick in America and a number 1 for Cilla Black in the UK. The song has always been a favourite of Olivia's and she would record her own version for her 2005 CD *Indigo: Women Of Song* some forty years later.

Olivia's triumph in the *Sing, Sing, Sing* talent show carried with it the prize of $300 and a return trip to England. It also presented her with a dilemma. 'I entered that contest for fun. I never thought I'd win. But before I knew it, I had indeed won and I was still at school with choices to make.' Because of her schooling and other commitments, Olivia could not take up the offer of the trip immediately.

Now, however, it was time to choose between finishing her schooling or pursuing her career. The dilemma prompted a local paper to print two pictures of Olivia, one in her school uniform and the other in a party dress, under the heading 'School Or Stardom?'.

Olivia chose the latter. She sought advice from one of her teachers at University High, Mr Hogan, who told her that if she was thinking about singing then she was not going to concentrate on her work in the classroom and wouldn't pass her matriculation. If she really was serious about going for a career as a singer and her heart was in it, then she would be better off leaving. Olivia has thanked him ever since for encouraging her. Olivia's gut feeling was that it was time to put her schooldays behind her. Latterly she had had to cope with a fair amount of teasing from fellow pupils jealous of her increasingly frequent television appearances.

Olivia's father was disappointed at Olivia quitting school at such a young age. Her brother Hugh had studied hard to go on and become a brilliant doctor, which was what the family had hoped for. But Rona had broken the family's academic pattern by leaving school at fifteen to become an actress, and now Olivia was following a similar path.

Among the work coming her way was a small part in a film called *Funny Things Happen Down Under*. It was essentially a children's musical about a group of kids in the small village of Wallaby Creek in the outback who face losing the barn in which they play and sing. To save it, they must raise two hundred dollars before Christmas Day and, in an effort to find the money, they accidentally invent a formula that will make sheep grow coloured wool, which they try to sell to foreign wool buyers.

The film gave Olivia the chance to sing one song, 'Christmas Time Down Under', and to work alongside her first love once more. Ian Turpie landed a part in the movie playing the movie's bad boy Lennie, out to impress with his sports car.

By the spring of 1965 Olivia's profile was such that cosmetic company Pond's snapped her up to promote a new skincare range. 'Exciting young beauty, Olivia Newton-John, has the fresh, natural look of Angel Face,' proclaimed one promotion, accompanied by photographs of Olivia at a record shop looking immaculate with flawless skin, at an ice-cream parlour, window-shopping, performing with guitar in hand at a club and heading home after a dinner dance.

Having made the important decision to finish her schooling, Olivia was having to face another of even greater consequence. Time was running out for her to take up the offer of the trip to England she had won. Her heart told her to stay in Australia with Ian. She was a teenager madly in love for the first time and the thought of leaving Ian, even temporarily, was too much for her to bear. But Irene, who would accompany her to England, had other ideas.

Irene was concerned that Olivia's romance with 'Turps', as he was known to his friends, was intensifying too fast. Olivia was still so very young and, although Irene liked Ian very much and could see how fond Olivia was of him, she was determined that her youngest daughter would not make the mistake of marrying anyone at such a tender age. Irene felt Olivia still had a lot of growing up to do and she insisted that going back to England would expand her outlook on life. She pointed out to Olivia that she was fresh out of school and there was a whole new world ready for her to explore.

Olivia fought against it. All her friends were in Australia, she argued, and not being at all ambitious, she couldn't see how going to England would further her career. She simply wasn't interested. To her, singing was just something she happened to do quite well and which she thoroughly enjoyed. Success had come so easily to her that she didn't have the drive to want to try her luck in another country.

But Irene was adamant. She was a strong woman, she would not be swayed and she prevailed. To Irene's relief there was never any question of Ian Turpie joining Olivia on the trip as his own TV commitments prevented it.

At the end of January 1966, after a tearful farewell in which Ian and Olivia swore undying love to each other, mother and daughter packed their bags and prepared to leave Australia and board the ship bound for England. Olivia was heartbroken. But, as she has openly conceded in the fullness of time, Mother really did know best.

Irene was a proud guest among a large and cheering audience in October 2002 when Olivia was given a lifetime achievement award and inducted into the Australian Recording Industry Association's Hall of Fame at ARIA's sixteenth awards ceremony in Sydney. In her speech at the event, Olivia graciously thanked her mother from the stage for encouraging her to see the world and to leave Australia to make her mark. 'You needed to do that in those days to be accepted here,' she said.

2

London

*'The British don't like their girl singers to be too good,
they think it smacks of emancipation'*

Rock writer Nik Cohn

Ever since they had left England for Australia nearly twelve years before, Brin and Irene Newton-John had often talked about returning one day. And while Olivia may have been seething on the voyage over at her mother's insistence on dragging her away from Ian Turpie, Irene was looking forward to spending time in London.

Mother and daughter arrived in February 1966 to find an England in which Harold Wilson was calling for a general election which was to return him to power, Watney's was putting a penny on a pint of beer increasing the cost to 1s 8d, and the BBC was announcing plans to broadcast television programmes in colour the following year. *Doctor Zhivago* was the big hit at the cinema, and the rising star of the modelling scene was a six-and-a-half-stone Cockney called Lesley Hornby, whose waif-like appearance earned her the name of Twiggy and a fee of ten guineas an hour. Top of the UK singles charts was Nancy Sinatra with the witty 'These Boots Are Made For Walking'.

On arrival in the capital, Irene rented a small flat for £9 a week for herself and Olivia in Perons Court, Hampstead village, north London. Irene quickly adjusted to their new surroundings but Olivia found it desperately hard to settle. She missed the sunshine of Australia, moaned that England was rainy and cold and, much to her embarrassment in later life, she naively complained that London's buildings were so old! 'I was completely horrified by Britain. I love it now, but as a teenager who'd grown up in Australia, I thought it was the greyest, dingiest place I'd ever seen, and that everything in it was old and dismal.'

Olivia spent nights crying into her pillow, pining for Ian and trying to figure out a way to escape back to his arms. She felt miserable without him and spent anxious moments wondering whether her faraway lover boy was staying faithful.

Back in Melbourne, Ian was doing his best to prove that their romance could stand the 10,000-mile separation. 'Turps wants to Go!! down the aisle' was the provocative headline in the *TV Times* issue of April 1966, above a photograph of Olivia nestling cosily in Ian's arms by the banks of a river. The gist of the article was that Ian wanted to marry Olivia before the year was out. He was quoted as saying: 'I don't know how Olivia feels, she hasn't really said. But I'm genuine when I say I'd like to become engaged to her as soon as she comes home.'

Ian's public declaration of his love for Olivia was music to her ears when news of it reached her after eight weeks away from her boyfriend. But it also made her miss him even more, and on more than one occasion she sneaked out of the flat for a surreptitious visit to a travel agent and managed to book herself an air ticket back to Melbourne. But with a mother's intuition, Irene guessed what she was up to, and went round to the travel agent to ask if her daughter had called in. When they confirmed Olivia had indeed booked a flight to Australia, Irene promptly cancelled the ticket each time. 'I thanked her many years after, but at the time I was furious,' says Olivia.

This booking and un-booking procedure went on for two months until Olivia realised it was pointless to continue. Irene was insisting absolutely that she stay. 'I even ran to a lawyer,' Olivia says, 'to see if I could be made a ward of court. I was very angry, I was in love and my hormones were going crazy. But my mother thought I was too young for romance. She was right, of course.'

Olivia may have been too preoccupied at that point with nursing her teenage heartaches to appreciate fully the golden opportunity her trip to London was presenting. But Irene was European, she was well travelled and worldly, and she recognised full well the benefits of travel, particularly in a city like London, which was steeped in history and bursting with culture. Irene kept telling Olivia she didn't know how lucky she was to be there. 'Again, she was right, of course,' Olivia said, on adult reflection. 'I think she wanted to get me away from my boyfriend, but she also wanted to broaden my horizons.'

In addition to the cultural benefits for Olivia of staying on in London, Irene harboured hopes of her daughter gaining a place at the Royal Academy of Dramatic Art, recognised as London's premier drama school. 'She had dreams that I'd go to RADA and study and do all these intelligent things,' says Olivia. 'But of course I had my own dreams.'

Olivia's first live singing performance in the UK made for an inauspicious start. She was booked into a little known dive called The Poor Millionaire's Club, where she was permitted to sing three songs as a fill-in before the main act, a folk singer, took to the stage.

Her prize trip to London eventually led to a one-off record deal with Decca and she recorded a number written by American singer-songwriter Jackie de Shannon called 'Till You Say You'll Be Mine', which was released in May 1966. Olivia's was a rather brash version of the song; the B-side, 'For Ever', suited her gentler, folksy feel far better.

To make an impact, every new recording artiste needs at least a modicum of promotion and exposure, but Olivia's debut disc had virtually none. This was perhaps unsurprising since Decca already had a very pretty, blonde, highly marketable girl singer on their label whose folksy singles were doing very nicely in the charts on a regular basis. What's more, her private life frequently kept her, and therefore her records, in the headlines. She went by the name of Marianne Faithfull.

Olivia's debut disc didn't stand a chance. Decca, who also had another promising songstress, called Lulu, on their label at the time, chose not to get behind 'Till You Say You'll Be Mine' and in those days all-important radio play was hard to secure. There was no network of commercial radio stations as there is today, and the launch of the BBC's Radio 1 pop music channel was still one year away. *The Light Programme*, the BBC's main entertainment radio channel, offered precious few opportunities for new pop records to get an airing. The pirate radio stations, like Radio Caroline and Radio London, which operated from ships offshore and therefore outside the country's broadcasting regulations, were gaining a committed teenage audience. But these stations tended to play only records that were in the Top Forty.

Olivia's first record also happened to be issued at a time when pop groups were dominating the UK charts. Family favourites like Ken Dodd and The Bachelors still managed to register hits, but the beat boom had spawned dozens of four-man guitar-dominated combos, and many of them were still successfully riding the wave created by the all-conquering Beatles with The Rolling Stones, The Who and The Kinks not far behind.

But if Olivia needed encouragement, she only had to scan the charts to find that a handful of British girl singers were nevertheless capable of making their mark. It appeared there was a place in the charts for girl singers, and she was heartened to see that each one who succeeded was very different from the others.

Essex girl Sandie Shaw was slim, coltish, short-sighted, dark-haired, and declined to wear shoes on her feet when she sang her hits with a natural ache in her voice. Cilla Black was a giggly Liverpool redhead who radiated next-door mateyness and whose vocal delivery could shake the rafters of the largest theatre when her throat tackled a middle eight at full throttle. Lulu was a bouncy, no-nonsense pocket dynamo from Glasgow, all restless energy as she belted out her rasping, bluesy vocals. Marianne Faithfull, Olivia's rival on Decca, was a classy, convent-educated daughter of an Austrian baroness, with tumbling blonde hair, a perfect face, an angelic, virginal look that belied her interest in sex, and a penchant for singing in a tremulous whisper with an enigmatic smile.

Among the most highly rated vocally was Dusty Spring-field, blonde and beehived with over-kohled panda eyes and a rich, bluesy, huskily soulful voice that earned her the tag 'the white Aretha Franklin'. And then there was Shirley Bassey, the girl from Tiger Bay, whose powerful, dramatic and emotional vocal delivery, vibrant personality and daring concert gowns made her a cabaret favourite as well as a regular in the hit parade, as the charts were then called.

In time Olivia would get to know them all, but faced with such formidable and varied competition, she was going to find it difficult to create a niche for herself, and she knew it. Not that she was overly bothered. At that point she still lacked ambition; she was dreaming of the house with the picket fence, children and animals in the yard.

Olivia's version of 'Till You Say You'll Be Mine' sank without trace, unnoticed except by one reviewer, who said the record sounded as though it had been recorded in a bathroom and that she would be better off being an air hostess. The record made no impression on the charts whatsoever.

Olivia's early attempts to get herself noticed with live appearances on the club circuit were just as disappointing. At one particularly seedy nightclub she was shocked to the core when a male singer swore in front of her. When she politely asked him to moderate his language, he rounded on her and forcefully told her in plain Anglo-Saxon what she could do if she didn't like it. His outburst reduced Olivia to tears.

On a personal level, however, life improved considerably for the homesick teenager when Pat Carroll suddenly got in touch from Australia to pass on the exciting news that she too was coming over to England. Pat had also won a talent contest, on radio, and, like Olivia's, the prize was a trip to London. It was just the fillip Olivia needed. She went out to the airport to welcome her good friend off the plane from Melbourne, and accompanied her back into town to check out where Pat would be living during her stay. Accommodation was provided as part of Pat's prize, but when the girls were shown the room Pat had been allocated, it proved to be hardly the Ritz. 'It was so crummy,' Olivia remembers, 'so we said she could come back and stay with me and Mùm.' Pat was duly made at home at Perons Court.

Olivia now had a trusted friend with whom to explore what London had to offer. And a whole new world started to open up for her when, with Irene's approval, she and Pat eventually moved out of the Hampstead apartment and into a rented flat in Shepherd's Bush on the other side of London, which they shared with two budding young actresses. For the first time Olivia was living away from home, away from Irene's eagle eye, with all the freedom that entailed. A flat with four pretty girls trying to make it in showbusiness inevitably attracted more than its fair share of male visitors, which made for some lively evenings and eventful, fun-filled weekends.

Olivia herself had plenty of male admirers but her thoughts loyally stayed with Ian Turpie whenever she went on a date. After her wretched first few weeks in London she was now starting to enjoy herself in the city she had originally thought was so dreary. With Pat as a companion, she began seeing London in a new light, and the capital was shining brightly in what was turning out to be a momentous year.

* * *

In the summer of 1966, England was enjoying the feel-good factor after winning the World Cup at Wembley. The Beatles still so ruled the world that John Lennon ventured the opinion they were now more popular than Jesus – the Fab Four were making it clear that youth culture was here to stay. London was where it was at for all that was cool and all who were hip, so much so that America, in the form of its prestigious *Time* magazine, dubbed the capital 'Swinging London'. *Time*'s issue of 15 April 1966 told an international audience: 'In this century, every decade has its city ... and for the Sixties that city is London.'

There was plenty of evidence that the capital was indeed doing its best to live up to its Swinging London billing, and rarely can there have been a more exciting place and time for people in their teens and twenties to start spreading their wings. The baby-boom generation was coming out to play – and with a sense of live-for-now fun, liberated style and a freedom that previous generations of teenagers had never enjoyed, particularly the girls, partly due to the introduction of the contraceptive pill.

Olivia needed no convincing that London was now the fashion capital of the world: hemlines rose daringly above the knee after Mary Quant invented the mini-skirt, and trendy boutiques sprang up in the King's Road, Chelsea, in Kensington and Carnaby Street selling pop art clothes in which 'dolly birds' could colourfully dance the night away to the sound of the latest beat groups in clubs like the Scotch of St James, the Bag O'Nails and the Cromwellian. As for the young men, they had shoulder-length hair and wore Afghan coats, bell-bottomed trousers and Cuban heels.

The in-crowd were artists like David Hockney, models like Jean Shrimpton and Twiggy, named Woman of the Year in 1966, photographers like David Bailey, rock stars like Mick Jagger, and young actors like Michael Caine and Terence Stamp, all dedicated to their individual art and dictating the hip young style to a whole new generation along the way. England's pop music scene was thriving as never before.

In time, a chance for Olivia and Pat to break into the

much-envied Swinging London in-crowd presented itself
after they met up with an old friend from Australia, Athol
Guy. Athol was a member of the Australian harmony vocal
group The Seekers, who had become hugely popular in
England. Olivia and Pat knew the band well from having
moved in much the same music circles in Melbourne, where
The Seekers had first got together. The girls were familiar
with the group's remarkable success story since the band's
move to England – and they were genuinely thrilled for
them.

Athol and his bandmates, Bruce Woodley, Keith Potger
and Judith Durham, all hailed from in or around
Melbourne, and Olivia could remember the excitement
they generated in the local press in 1964 after they set out
to work their passage to Britain on board an ocean liner.
Soon after stepping ashore, The Seekers won a spot on
Sunday Night At The London Palladium, then Britain's
top-rated TV entertainment show, and a record deal
followed with Tom Springfield, brother of the celebrated
Dusty. Tom had written a song called 'I'll Never Find
Another You', which launched The Seekers as the ideal
group to fill the gap in the market left by the break-up of
his own group, The Springfields, the year before.

The Seekers recorded in a similar tight harmony vocal
style to The Springfields, which owed a great deal to folk
music and not a little to pop. They sang tuneful melodies
with Judith Durham's crystal lead voice as their instantly
recognisable trademark. 'I'll Never Find Another You'
soared to number one in the charts, followed by 'A World
Of Our Own' which reached number three, and 'The
Carnival Is Over', which was also a chart-topper.

These three massive hits were quite a contrast to the
predominance of beat groups at the time, and Athol, keen

to help two fellow singers from Melbourne, felt there was room for a female vocal duo to make their mark on the UK music scene. He therefore suggested Pat and Olivia team up and try to make a go of it as a double act. They both sang well, he said, they both appreciated and could hold a melody, they were both great-looking girls and they would look good together, Pat's dark looks contrasting agreeably with the blue-eyed fair complexion Olivia had inherited from her mother. The girls had already sung alongside each other back in Australia and, perhaps most importantly of all, they were really good friends. It was good timing, too. The folk purists who appreciated the kind of straightforward songs Pat and Olivia enjoyed singing were outraged that Bob Dylan had just 'gone electric' on his tour of Britain. Pat and Olivia's musical approach would go down well with the folk music fraternity.

The girls considered Athol's idea was well worth a try. Olivia's solo career was clearly not taking off at this point. After the dismal showing of her first record, Decca appeared to be in no hurry for her to record for them again. Teaming up professionally was also a case of needs must for Olivia and Pat, who were discovering that the downside to flat-dwelling was, of course, there was a fridge to be filled and their share of the bills and rent to be paid. Athol felt that teaming up would give them not only a means of earning a crust, but also a chance to have some fun and maybe make a name for themselves all at the same time.

Pat took the initiative and put the idea to her agent at the Sir Bernard Delfont agency, one of the most powerful in British showbusiness. 'I said: "I've got this girl and I really want us to be a double act." And they said: "That's OK . . . if you split your wages." So that's what we did.' Very generously, Pat agreed to give half her usual performance fee of

£18 to Olivia, a selfless gesture the latter has never forgotten down the many years they have remained friends. Pat's generosity was all the greater for the fact that of the two budding songstresses, Pat was by far the more focused and motivated at that point. Pat remembers that, to Olivia, it was still all a bit of a lark. 'It was hard for me at first,' Pat said, 'because I was always the one who was ambitious. She never was really.'

Faced now with the imminent prospect of work, the duo chewed over several names but decided to call themselves simply Pat and Olivia. Pat set to work designing and making outfits, matching pink mini-skirts as well as pretty blue velvet mini-dresses with little frilly white collars; Olivia was pressed into sewing the hems. Olivia found sewing tedious but she knew she needed to make a contribution to Pat's designs in view of Pat's big-hearted gesture towards her.

Bookings quickly started to come their way, courtesy of Sir Bernard Delfont's many business contacts and outlets in the British entertainment industry. If they were to perform successfully on stage together, the girls needed to work out a repertoire of songs with dance routines to go with them. Rehearsing their act in the flat proved to be unsatisfactory. They had no means of playing back their vocals as they tried out their harmonies, and they had to rely on their own ears to spot any weaknesses. But they had no other option than singing along together in the flat, holding Coke bottles as imitation microphones while they worked out various dance moves.

Embarrassingly, the first time they went on stage together they got into a tangle. They'd spent two weeks rehearsing in the flat but had completely forgotten that proper stage microphones, unlike Coke bottles, had electrical leads attached. On stage they kept tripping over them, but despite this technical hitch, the reaction from the audience was generally favourable. The menfolk clearly approved of the way the girls looked. Both of them were blessed with good legs and Pat's home-made mini-dresses showed them off to advantage.

The girls were soon given a helping hand by Des O'Connor, then forging a showbusiness career as a singer as well as a comedian. They appeared with Des on the same variety bill at the Prince of Wales Theatre in London, and he reckoned they could go places as a vocal double act provided they practised their harmonies. He suggested they call themselves The Poppettes, but they preferred to stay billed as Pat and Olivia. When Olivia told Des they had no practical way of rehearsing their vocals, he took them out shopping in the electrical stores in Tottenham Court Road and generously forked out £12 to get them a tape recorder.

Encouragement came at times from unexpected quarters. They were thrilled when the inimitable French singing entertainer Maurice Chevalier popped backstage on one occasion to offer compliments and wish them well.

Despite beginning to rub shoulders with the stars of the day, the sex, drugs and rock 'n' roll lifestyle of the 'Swinging Sixties' somehow passed them by. It's said that if you can remember the 1960s then you weren't really there – the implication being that you weren't really a part of the sixties unless you were habitually too high at the time for banking anything but the haziest of memories. 'Turn on, tune in, drop out,' was Timothy Leary's message for the psychedelic era. Olivia says: 'I was quite naive then, and although people were doing drugs around me, I never seemed to notice. I floated through on this little cloud of everything being lovely.' On the road, the girls had fun, but they made sure they looked out for one another and steered each other away from trouble. But it was their basic common sense, and sheer naivety, which essentially kept them away from rock's debauched excesses.

Life for Pat and Olivia wasn't always plain sailing. The girls' most memorable booking, for all the wrong reasons, turned out to be an invitation to perform at the Raymond Revue Bar. The two of them had been appearing at the perfectly respectable Celebrity Club for £25 a week, and Raymond Revue Bar was a sister club which, in their ignorance and innocence, the girls treated as just another booking. The alarm bells began ringing, however, when they found themselves picking their way through neon-lit alleyways in the heart of Soho, past sex shops, sleazy members-only cinemas showing dubious foreign films and hookers in hot pants lingering in doorways, to get to the venue.

The Raymond Revue Bar was no run-of-the-mill club and, as Olivia and Pat rapidly discovered, certainly no club for two teenage girl singers unless they were prepared to take most, if not all, of their clothes off for the male clientele.

Back in 1958, Paul Raymond had caused a sensation when he opened his Revue Bar as the first legal nude cabaret in town. 'Mr Soho', as he was known, had neatly side-stepped the existing law over nudity in theatres by making his own theatre a club where girls could disrobe in front of the club members out of reach of the authorities. Raymond, who went on to earn the title of porn baron, became a familiar figure himself in Soho, pulling up in his Rolls-Royce outside the club, and stepping out with a trademark fur coat draped around his shoulders to mingle with members who paid good money to see his gorgeous girls.

The Raymond Revue Bar was infamous in its day, but somehow its notoriety had failed to reach the ears of two young girls fresh in from Melbourne.

The penny didn't drop until Olivia and Pat stepped inside the venue. 'It was a well-known strip club in the middle of town, but I really had no idea until I looked round a corner and there was a girl swimming around in a fish-tank with just a mermaid bottom on and nothing else,' says Olivia, laughing at the memory. 'We thought this was kind of strange, but thought nothing more of it, being young and naive as we were. But when we went on to do our show in our pretty little pink mini-dresses, there were a couple of guys sitting there in raincoats.'

It didn't take long for both the management and Pat and Olivia to realise that it had all been a horrendous mistake. On stage the girls gamely went through their set list of song-and-dance numbers in front of a handful of disbelieving men. The girls were as pleased to get off the stage as the disgruntled punters must have been to see the still fully clad backs of them. 'I don't think they liked us at all,' said Pat. 'We were very cute and innocent, we were too young and we had too many clothes on!'

The whole sorry experience came to an end when Paul Raymond paid the girls a visit backstage. 'He came in,' Olivia laughingly recalls, 'gave me £40, and said: "Thank you very much, but you don't need to come back. I don't think it's going to work out for you here!" The manager thought he had booked two strippers who could sing.'

The girls were soon able to look back and have a good giggle about it. 'That was kind of the crummiest place we played,' Olivia says, 'and it's hilarious when I think of it now because we had no idea what was going on.'

Fortunately there were plenty of other gigs lined up in

authentic music venues. The two girls played ballrooms, pubs, bars and clubs, singing cover versions of hits of the day by such as The Beatles and Dionne Warwick, and they worked into their act a few simple dance routines to numbers like 'The Locomotion', which had been a hit for the American singer Little Eva four years before. On occasion they travelled in a minibus to the north of England to appear at working men's clubs, where they found audiences could be far tougher than down south.

Inevitably there were lean times, and the travelling, in particular, proved a drain on their finances. 'I used to budget down to the last penny,' Olivia remembers. 'We shared the rent, everything, with the other girls. We had a kitty for food, and Pat made clothes for the stage. We didn't have very much money because we didn't work every week and we used to have to travel to shows and pay our own expenses. We were very careful, but we never ran short.' The girls became used to such a frugal existence that they managed to make £50 between them last for a two-week holiday on the Continent, and still come home with some change.

Eventually, as Pat and Olivia honed their act and word spread, they warranted higher billing and were paid higher fees accordingly, and they were thrilled to be booked eventually as a support act for The Seekers. Athol Guy was especially pleased his protégés seemed to be doing well.

Another high spot for the girls was being hired as the opening act for popular English ballad singer Matt Monro for his concerts in South Africa.

Television bookings for Pat and Olivia followed and they made appearances on light entertainment programmes such as *The Dick Emery Show*. But any progress the girls were making was tempered by the knowledge that Pat's visa was due to run out at the end of the year. Olivia had no such problems; she had retained her British passport, and would not obtain an Australian passport until 1994.

Pat's visa worries made for an uncertain immediate future: Pat and Olivia's booking agent was understandably wary of arranging work for them more than a few weeks ahead for fear Pat might not be available unless she succeeded in securing a visa extension allowing her to stay in England.

Pat did in fact manage to win a month's reprieve on the strength of a booking to entertain British troops in Cyprus where two very pretty mini-skirted girls went down a storm with the squaddies. But it looked increasingly likely Pat would have to return to Australia at the end of the year, which would leave Olivia in a quandary.

To stay in England or to return home became even more of a dilemma for Olivia after she and Pat were booked to appear for a week at Bournemouth on a bill topped by Cliff Richard and The Shadows. There Olivia met a famous guitarist by the name of Bruce Welch – and he fell in love with her more or less at first sight.

3

Bruce Welch

'She was a stunning blonde, very good-looking with a bright and bouncy personality'

Bruce Welch of The Shadows

Olivia Newton-John had no idea she was talking to one of Britain's most successful and best-known guitarists when she first said hello to Bruce Welch of The Shadows at a concert venue in Bournemouth in the late summer of 1966.

Bruce was on stage busy checking all the gear in preparation for another sell-out concert by Cliff Richard and his famous backing band, of which Bruce was a prominent member. But Olivia simply didn't recognise him as she made an interested appraisal of the inside of the theatre where she was booked to appear with Pat Carroll on the same bill as Cliff. The diligent way the casually dressed man on the stage was carrying out his detailed inspection of the equipment prompted Olivia to think he must be an electrician or a member of the road crew. Little did she realise that the man in front of her was the composer of Cliff's smash hit 'Summer Holiday', a song she had sung as a duet with Pat on TV back in Australia.

Bruce's reaction to meeting Olivia for the first time was somewhat different. He thought she was stunningly beautiful and it was pretty much love at first sight.

'He seemed quite nice,' Olivia later recalled of the man

who would become the most important figure in her life, both personally and professionally, over the next five years, 'and after we'd been introduced he didn't waste any time in asking me out. I knew of The Shadows, but Hank Marvin with his distinctive glasses was the only one I recognised.'

Bruce was somewhat amused that the beautiful girl he'd just met had no idea who he was. There weren't too many teenage girls who did not recognise him after the eight years of phenomenal pop success he had enjoyed with The Shadows. Bruce decided straight away that he and this young girl should get to know each other a great deal better.

Like Olivia, Bruce had come through a difficult childhood. But his had been deeply unhappy. He was born in the coastal town of Bognor Regis in Sussex in 1941; his mother and father split up when he was small and his mother died of TB when she was only thirty-two. Bruce was brought up in Newcastle by his aunt Sadie, who lived with her Indian boyfriend above the fish and chip shop he owned. The first time Bruce could remember seeing his father was when he was eight years old and then he didn't see him again for another nine years.

Bruce was seventeen when he discovered that he had been born illegitimate, and he admits it gave him a chip on his shoulder. He found out the truth when he tried to obtain a birth certificate in order to wed his sweetheart, Anne. Bruce later changed his name by deed poll to his mother's maiden name.

Music had always played an important part in Bruce's life. At an early age he was given a ukulele, which he learned to play. He listened to popular records of the day on a wind-up gramophone, went to see America's top singing stars like Johnny Ray and Slim Whitman at the

Newcastle Empire and, like many thousands of teenagers in the 1950s, he was swept along on the rock 'n' roll wave that hit Britain in the shape of Bill Haley and Elvis Presley.

Bruce knew very early on that he wanted a career in music and he saw a chance to gain a foothold when the skiffle craze swept Britain, spearheaded by Lonnie Donegan, the UK's undisputed King of Skiffle, who had a string of catchy singalong hits.

Skiffle had a simple, homespun quality to it. Thousands of skiffle groups sprang up with a basic guitar sound complemented by the rhythmic finger-tapping of thimbles on a wooden washboard or the bass-like plucking of a cord stretched taut over a broomstick and a tea chest. Skiffle offered everyone a chance to join in and Bruce needed no second invitation. He went out and bought himself a guitar for £4 19s 6d and, after meeting up at the local grammar school with a musically like-minded lad called Brian Rankin, later to change his name to Hank Marvin, they formed a group and called themselves The Railroaders, principally because they used to meet at a café next to Newcastle's Central Station.

Soon, both aged just sixteen, they headed south to London to seek their fame and fortune. They lived from hand to mouth in a boarding house in Finsbury Park, north London, and ended up drawn to Soho to the 2i's coffee bar, whose cramped cellar offered skiffle groups and budding rock 'n' roll singers and musicians a chance to showcase their talents.

By this time, Bruce and Hank were moving on from skiffle and were being heavily influenced in their own guitar playing by the music of Elvis Presley and Buddy Holly. Now inseparable friends, they complemented each other well as guitarists and their voices blended tunefully for Everly Brothers-style harmonies. One night at the 2i's they were spotted by John Foster, who happened to be looking for a guitarist to back a promising British rock 'n' roll singer he was managing by the name of Cliff Richard.

Foster offered Hank the job, but Hank loyally said he would only go on the tour if his friend Bruce went too. Foster agreed, signed them both up on the spot and within weeks Bruce and Hank found themselves backing Cliff on his first UK tour to scenes of wild audience hysteria. Soon they became one half of Cliff's permanent backing quartet The Drifters, before changing their name to The Shadows.

Now, as Bruce, ever the perfectionist, made his pre-concert sound checks at Bournemouth and retuned his guitar for the umpteenth time, he could look back on eight years of unparalleled international success. He'd played on Cliff's string of hit records, enjoyed smash hits as The Shadows in their own right, and performed at sell-out concert tours at home and abroad, as well as in pantomimes and in movies like *Summer Holiday*. Bruce had also proved himself to be a prolific songwriter of chart hits for both Cliff and for his own band. Among the hits he'd co-written were chart-toppers like 'Please Don't Tease', 'Bachelor Boy' and the theme song from 'Summer Holiday'.

Olivia may not have recognised him, but Bruce Welch was a very famous, hugely successful star. He was also a married man.

Bruce had first met pretty Anne Findley by the jukebox at the famed 2i's. He chivalrously went to her rescue when a speaker shook itself loose from its mounting on the wall due to constant reverberations and happened to fall on her. Soon Anne and Bruce were going steady. 'And in those days you married your steady girlfriend,' said Bruce.

In August 1959, at the very young age of seventeen, and with Cliff Richard as his best man, Bruce married Anne. Two years later, after he began to reap the financial rewards of his songwriting and his general success with The Shadows, Bruce and Anne bought a lovely cottagey house in north Harrow for the then splendid sum of £6,000.

Cliff and The Shadows had hit the big time almost immediately they had got together. They had started at the top and, despite Beatlemania, they were still a very big attraction in 1966 at the time when Pat and Olivia were added to the bill as a support act for the summer concerts by the seaside in Bournemouth. From the wings Olivia watched Cliff and The Shadows go through their thoroughly professional paces on stage, bringing the screaming audience to their feet. She witnessed at close quarters how the singer and his band worked their magic. Now she was left in no doubt that the man she thought was an electrician was indeed a star.

When Bruce later managed to get Olivia on her own to chat to her for a few moments, he promptly asked her out. He realised how young and innocent she was when Olivia said she wouldn't mind going out with him but only if her friend Pat came along too. Pat Carroll duly played gooseberry on their first date, but it was nevertheless the start of what was to become Olivia's first real love affair.

Olivia eventually agreed to another date with Bruce, and this time she was happy to go out with him without a chaperone. The delivery to her door of a dozen roses beforehand not only took her breath away but clearly showed the romantic feelings Bruce had towards her. And when he arrived to pick her up, he was behind the wheel of his Rolls-Royce. Olivia could hardly have been more impressed. 'I'd never been out in one before. He took me to dinner at a fancy restaurant and then we started going round to expensive nightclubs, another and another, all over town.

'Everywhere we went we drank champagne, glass after glass, champagne on top of champagne, and we danced. It was quite a night for a teenager who had never been exposed to such things and I'm sure I'll never forget it, mostly because I drank too much, got sick and threw up all over his beautiful car . . .'

At the age of twenty-four, Bruce Welch was seven years older than Olivia, he was far more worldly, and decades ahead of her in terms of life's lessons. Bruce himself had not had a drink until he was twenty-one and he forgave the teenage Olivia's over-imbibing on their first date and her eventual 'chunder'. It was just a shame his beloved Rolls had caught the brunt of it.

Bruce was tall, solidly built, dark, good-looking, plain-speaking with a strong personality, and Olivia found him very attractive. He was dedicated in his work as a well-travelled songwriter and guitarist – with Cliff he had toured the USA, South Africa and Australia as well as several European countries. He had made a success of his chosen profession and he enjoyed the acclaim and the rewards that came his way.

Given his extraordinary success and his standing in the music business, it's not difficult to see why Olivia looked up to Bruce. She was even a little in awe of him. Besides Olivia's obvious good looks, he adored her bouncy person-ality, and their passion for music was a common bond. He liked the way Olivia sang and her interest in music in general. She might not have had the strongest voice, he realised, and yet he noted she had a good ear for music.

As their relationship developed, Olivia was happy to accompany Bruce to gigs by Cliff and The Shadows, and to concerts where The Shadows themselves were the stars. They had had a string of instrumental hits, such as 'Apache' and 'Wonderful Land', and were in big demand as a headline attraction even without Cliff. Olivia was so supportive of her new boyfriend she even helped out willingly as an emergency spotlight operator during a week's residency for The Shadows at Darwen in Lancashire.

Once she had hooked up with Bruce, Olivia's own life was pretty much dictated by his. 'I guess you could say I was detached,' she commented. 'We had our own little group of people, Cliff and The Shadows, Pat and me, and a few other musicians.'

But in November, just when Bruce and Olivia's budding romance might have blossomed into a full-blown love affair, Olivia decided to head home to Australia for Christmas, much to Bruce's dismay. They had been seeing each other for just a matter of weeks but Bruce was already smitten.

The problem was Pat Carroll. Pat's visa expired at the end of 1966. And after much deliberation, Olivia chose to go back to Melbourne with her great friend. Together they had made an encouraging start in England as a singing duo, and there was every chance they could build on this experience back in Australia. Olivia was also anxious to find out whether she and Ian Turpie still felt the same way about each other. With Bruce now on the scene and clearly enamoured with her, she needed to sort out her own feelings and find out where she and Ian both stood and whether they still had a future together.

Even putting aside any personal feelings about Bruce, it was still a difficult decision for Olivia to make. By leaving London she would be passing up the chance of a giant leap up the showbiz ladder: Bruce was urging her to audition for the role of Cinderella in a Christmas pantomime. The Shadows would be starring in the panto with Cliff at the London Palladium for a winter season, and the role of Cinders was up for grabs.

By now Olivia had got to know Cliff reasonably well and they clearly liked each other very much. If Bruce hadn't been so quick off the mark when they had all first met at Bournemouth, Cliff would most certainly have asked her out. Olivia was exactly Cliff's kind of girl and a girl he would have most certainly been proud to take home to his adoring mum Dorothy, who vetted all her son's girlfriends before they could get too close to her boy.

Olivia appreciated Cliff was kind and polite to her, encouraging about her singing, and there was even talk about the possibility of Olivia providing back-up vocals on one of his recordings. Most certainly Cliff would not have been averse to Olivia as his Cinders.

After Cliff's first big hit 'Move It', his management had moved him away from wild rock 'n' roll into movies and pantomime in the belief that rock was a passing fad and that the way to ensure a long career was to turn him into an all-round family entertainer. Pantomime was a sure way to reach that family audience and, with Bruce and Hank Marvin coming up with catchy, brand new songs written specifically for each new Christmas show, Cliff and The Shadows had proved a sell-out panto attraction for the previous two years. With TV favourites Terry Scott and Hugh Lloyd added to the Cinderella cast as the Ugly Sisters, and even a baby elephant due to make a novelty appearance, the show was a guaranteed box-office hit from the moment it was announced.

Bruce felt sure Olivia would stand a good chance of

winning the part of Cinders. He stressed what a notable showbiz break it would be for her if she clinched it. She'd be appearing opposite a huge star in Cliff, who would be playing Buttons, and Bruce himself would be on stage much of the time as one of the Brokers Men to help her through and support her.

Cinderella would also mean ten solid, well-paid weeks of work for Olivia and a vital springboard to a possible solo career now Pat was heading home. All in all it was a tempting opportunity, but Olivia displayed her typically Libran trait of being unable to make up her mind while seeing every point of view. In the end she stood firm. She felt she wasn't ready for such a big step. She didn't feel confident she could pull it off, and she was determined to fly home.

Bruce was sad to see her go and seriously wondered whether he would ever see her again. It left him facing tricky times both personally and professionally because Olivia was leaving him at a time when he was feeling vulnerable. His new love was going home to her old boyfriend, growing friction among the members of The Shadows was making his professional life uncomfortable, and the band's very future with Cliff was looking uncertain anyway as the singer was seriously contemplating giving up his showbusiness career completely in the new year.

Cliff had recently declared himself to be a committed Christian in front of a crowd of 25,000 at a rally by the American evangelist Billy Graham at Earls Court. Now, Cliff doubted whether he could combine his career with his Christian beliefs and commitments. If Cliff quit showbusiness, where would that leave Bruce and the other members of The Shadows?

* * *

Just as Bruce had predicted, the Cinderella panto at the London Palladium proved another runaway success, with young actress Pippa Steele seizing her chance to make an eye-catching Cinders. Towards the end of the panto's run, Bruce happened to meet up with John Ashby, the manager of The Seekers, who informed him that a friend of his from Australia was back in town and that she would be very happy to hear from him. Bruce wasted no time in getting in touch with Olivia and meeting up with her. He was thrilled to hear her teenage romance with Ian Turpie back home had petered out. It had run its course and was now well and truly over. Olivia and Ian both knew they had changed. Their lives were on different paths now.

Olivia may have become a free agent, but Bruce emphatically was not. Not only was he still married to Anne, but they had a six-year-old son to consider. He knew he was falling for Olivia and, when Anne found out about his new love, Bruce had a desperately difficult decision to make about their future.

He has freely admitted that when it came to girls, he had been 'the naughtiest Shadow'. It was wrong, of course, said Bruce, because he was married. But Olivia was different. 'The moment I met Olivia it was over. Until then it had just been one-night stands, but with her it was different. I told my wife what had happened and that our marriage was finished.'

According to Bruce, his wife tried to talk him out of leaving but he decided he couldn't live without Olivia. When the final split from Anne became inevitable, he left the marital home in Stanmore and moved with his new young girlfriend into a rented flat overlooking Lord's cricket ground in St John's Wood in north London. Their flat was high up on the ninth floor and offered a fine view of the most famous turf in the whole of England.

Having been cosseted at home with Irene for the past seven years, apart from a brief spell with Pat in the Shepherd's Bush flat, Olivia's domestic and culinary skills left something to be desired. Peter Vince, The Shadows' recording engineer, could testify to that.

One night after a recording session, Bruce and Olivia invited Peter and his wife back to their flat for something to eat. In a humorous account of the evening, Peter said they were all starving by the time the lift had reached the ninth floor; Olivia fixed everyone a drink and brought out a couple of bowls of cheese footballs for the four of them. But as time went by, it became clear to Peter that Olivia had no intention of getting busy in the kitchen. After two hours of devouring cheese balls, Peter knew for sure that he and his wife were not going to be properly fed. When a third hour passed with Olivia and Bruce, then in the first flush of an exciting love affair, passionately wrapped up in each other on a mattress on the floor, he felt it was time to go. He left wondering how Bruce didn't waste away with all that exercise and no food other than cheese balls.

Inevitably, Bruce's social life had for some years revolved around the world of showbusiness. The guitarist was a popular man and his circle of friends included fellow musicians, songwriters, actors and actresses and important people in the record business. He knew his way around London's showbiz scene and Olivia was happy for Bruce to set their social agenda. Wherever they went, everyone seemed to know her boyfriend. He was welcomed with open arms at the London clubs he took her to, especially drag artist Danny La Rue's club in smart Hanover Square in the West End, where showbusiness folk regularly congregated and lived it up until the small hours. Bruce seemed to have an automatic entrée even to clubs he wasn't a member of, Olivia noted. Fame certainly opened doors.

Olivia was wide-eyed at some of the people she was introduced to, not least Beatle Paul McCartney, who was a good friend of Bruce's. 'We went round to Paul's house one day and he said: "I've just written this song," and he started playing "Lady Madonna". At the time I didn't even realise what I was hearing. I was thrilled to meet Paul and all, but I had no sense of what was really going on at the time. Now when I look back, I know it's amazing that I was there at the time he wrote that song.'

Bruce was a dedicated musician, and Olivia soon came to learn about his degree of perfectionism. Just by observing him at work, she learned a great deal about the importance of a thoroughly professional approach. She accompanied him to concert venues and saw Bruce was a stickler for time-keeping and made sure that when he went on stage his shoes were finely polished and his suit immaculately pressed. She patiently watched her boyfriend endlessly checking and rechecking his guitar was in tune in the long hours leading up to his going on stage. He was meticulous about this. Such attention to detail inevitably led to tension when others around him failed to meet his high standards and there were times when Olivia felt it her place to chase after him and calmly coax him to return after he had stormed out pre-concert and driven off in a huff in his E-type Jaguar.

In time, Bruce and Olivia were able to move out of their flat overlooking Lord's and relocate to a house in Hadley Common near Totteridge in the north of London, which Bruce bought from Jerry Lordan, the musician who had written The Shadows' first smash hit, 'Apache'.

Olivia's joy was apparent to all who knew her. She radiated contentment. She was living in a lovely home with a lover who adored her, and her happiness was complete when Bruce, knowing her fondness for animals, bought her a red setter she named Geordie, followed by another they called Murphy. She had dreamed of the house with a picket fence, a garden and pets to pamper, and this was just about it.

The couple were still getting to know each other, however, and to spend more time with Olivia, Bruce decided he would leave The Shadows in the not too distant future. The band's ten-year association with Cliff was coming to an end. Bruce planned to take on the job of looking after The Shadows' music publishing interests. That would entail regular trips into the West End of London to the group's Savile Row office, but it would free up his evenings and weekends for quality time to be enjoyed with Olivia, rather than him asking her to traipse around the country or abroad on tour whenever The Shadows' schedule demanded. As a member of such a famous group with a devoted female fan following, Bruce had enjoyed some wild times, but now he wanted to nurture the love he and Olivia had for each other.

Bruce had been touring or recording more or less continuously for ten years and he had seen what frequent and long separations, coupled with female temptations on the road, could do to relationships. He and Olivia were madly in love and he wasn't going jeopardise their relationship.

As luck would have it, some months before he left the band The Shadows were booked to tour Australia, and Olivia accompanied Bruce down under for the duration. She was able to introduce her boyfriend to family and friends and show him the sights of her hometown. At one of the Melbourne concerts, Olivia's old friends The Strangers from *The Go!! Show* were the support act, and

Bruce was particularly impressed by the brilliant musicianship and vocals of the band's lead guitarist John Farrar, especially his falsetto.

Pat and Olivia had always liked and admired John, and Olivia was pleased Bruce held him in such high esteem after watching and hearing him at work. Olivia had often talked to Pat in glowing terms about John back in the days when they were in England. In fact she'd frequently said that Pat ought to marry him. She reckoned Pat and John would be just perfect for each other.

* * *

On 24 June 1968, shortly after Bruce and Olivia got back home to England after their trip to Australia, Bruce's divorce came through. His adultery was cited as the cause and Olivia was named as 'the other woman', which inevitably made headlines in the newspapers both in England and Australia. 'My divorce was because of her,' Bruce has said, 'although she didn't wreck the marriage. I fell in love with her, but there had been lots of women before her.' Bruce revealed in his autobiography that they had to arrange for a private detective to observe Olivia and him together in order to speed up the divorce process. 'Looking back it was very seedy,' he commented.

The outcome was, of course, that Bruce was now free to wed Olivia, but although the couple had every intention of marrying at some future date, Bruce was all too aware that she was still only nineteen. He felt it would be a mistake to rush her into marriage – and that suited Olivia, not to mention her mother Irene. Olivia was in love with Bruce but she would have been an extremely reluctant bride if Bruce had pressured her. Olivia had seen enough of broken relationships in her family to know that it would be wiser to wait.

Bruce's divorce, piquantly, came through just as he was finalising his plans to leave his bandmates. He wanted to get the timing of his departure right, with the least inconvenience to the other members of the group. The Shadows were committed to one more major winter season at the London Palladium at the back end of 1968 and he felt that would be a fitting time for him to exit. In the event, Bruce and the other members of the band all agreed they would call it a day as The Shadows when the season's allotted run came to an end.

At the London Palladium on Saturday, 19 December 1968, with great fanfare, Hank Marvin, Bruce Welch, drummer Brian Bennett and bass guitarist John Rostill played together as The Shadows for the last time. For Bruce and Hank, the two original members who had been Shadows all the way through for a decade, it was an emotional moment when they took their final bow and bade farewell. They were given a thunderous ovation, and it would be two years before Bruce would appear on a stage again.

* * *

The year 1969 found Olivia and Bruce happily devoting time to decorating their nest in Hadley Common. And when Bruce made his regular forays into town to spend time in The Shadows' office listening to new songs, Olivia had Geordie and Murphy to keep her playful company or to accompany her on long walks.

There was even time for the couple to take a winter break together and travel up to Edinburgh by train. Olivia insisted on taking the dogs with them and they all enjoyed a pleasant uneventful stay until their return journey. With Geordie and Murphy safely locked up in the guard's van, Bruce took off his jacket and settled back in his seat next to Olivia in the heated carriage. When the train slowed down to pull into Newcastle, Bruce began looking out of the window and pointing out various buildings he recognised and recounting to Olivia some of his teenage escapades in the city where he was brought up. But after the train had finally come to a stop in Newcastle Central Station, Bruce got the shock of his life. Through the window he saw Geordie and Murphy haring past along the platform. Obviously they had somehow managed to get out of the guard's van.

Bruce was out of his seat in a flash. He leaped out of the train on to the platform, leaving Olivia wondering what all the kerfuffle was about. Bruce was horrified to find there appeared to be no sign of the dogs and in a panic he grabbed a porter and asked if he'd spotted them. The porter pointed in the direction of the front of the train, and Bruce, in his shirt sleeves, raced off. His heart was in his mouth when he realised the dogs must have run down the slope at the end of the platform on to the track and across the Tyne railway bridge. With no thoughts to his own safety, Bruce jumped down on to the track and raced along it, calling out the names of Olivia's beloved pets. Olivia meanwhile was still sitting in her seat, largely oblivious to all the drama that was unfolding.

Bruce's pursuit took him some 250 yards across the bridge into Gateshead, where he paused to catch his breath in the freezing cold. There was no sign of the pets anywhere. The dogs had simply disappeared and he was totally distraught. He was turning disconsolately to make his way back up the track to rejoin the train and dreading telling Olivia the awful news when he looked up to see that the train had started to resume its journey south. It was pulling out of the station and heading straight towards him, with the startled driver sounding his hooter as a warning for the trespasser on the tracks to get out of the way immediately.

Bruce was forced to press himself flat up against the bridge to allow the train to pass him by safely. As each carriage rumbled slowly past him he scanned its every window for signs of Olivia, only to catch sight of her finally, still sitting comfortably in her seat . . . with Geordie and Murphy happily reclined in her arms. Bruce didn't know whether to laugh or cry. One thing he did know was that he was going to have an extremely difficult time making his way home. He had no money on him, it was bitterly cold and his jacket was still on the train that was rapidly disappearing into the distance on its way to King's Cross. After explaining his predicament to station staff, he later managed to catch a slow train back to London and a reunion with Geordie and Murphy, with Olivia asking: 'What happened to you?' Bruce could have cheerfully throttled all three of them.

The Newcastle nightmare was but a blip in the cosy domestic existence the couple were enjoying. In her contentment, Olivia was not overly bothered that her own musical aspirations as a singer were taking second place to Bruce's career, until Cliff Richard came through with his promise to ask her to provide some background vocals on the B-side of one of his singles.

Both Cliff and The Shadows had been managed very shrewdly by Peter Gormley, an Australian who had arrived in England in 1959 to launch the career of a singer by the name of Frank Ifield. Ifield was born in Coventry, but after the war he moved with his parents to Australia where he began his singing career. Tall, fair-haired and good-looking, Ifield arrived back in the UK in 1959 and Gormley steered him to major stardom three years later with the help of a million-selling chart-topper, 'I Remember You'.

Olivia's own Australian background meant there was an obvious affinity with Gormley, and after hearing her sing he believed she had what it takes to be a successful recording artist. He was prepared to offer her his expertise in management, and Olivia gratefully accepted. Gormley's alliance with Cliff and The Shadows would turn out to be hugely beneficial for Olivia. As a first step she would be invited to duet with Cliff on a song called 'Don't Move Away', to be recorded as the B-side of Cliff's single 'Sunny Honey Girl'. It would be the first time Cliff duetted with a female singer on record, but by the time the single was released in January 1971, Olivia had bigger fish to fry.

Not long after Gormley had signed up Olivia, one of America's most successful and powerful hotshots in the music business got in touch with him to enquire about a girl he had vaguely heard about on the UK music scene called Olivia Newton-John. His name was Don Kirshner. He was putting together 'a dynamite film and music' concept and was on the lookout for a pretty girl who could sing. Olivia was most certainly good-looking and she had a lovely voice, Gormley told him. 'Right,' said Kirshner, 'when can I meet her?'

4

Toomorrow Never Comes

'When you see the Toomorrow group, it's impossible to dislike them. They're young, with-it, and have the looks and appeal of "today" and tomorrow. They are undoubtedly the best-looking pop group ever brought together'

Music Mogul Don Kirshner

Back in the spring of 1969, the cream of America's pop music and showbiz journalists were invited to a party at the Rockefeller Centre's plush Rainbow Grill in New York. Don Kirshner and Harry Saltzman had something important they wished to announce to the world's press: the formation of a new Anglo-American pop group called Toomorrow – and Olivia Newton-John would be its lead singer.

The very names Kirshner and Saltzman were enough to guarantee a good turnout of writers for the press conference, and they were eager to hear what the two men had to say. As co-producer of the series of James Bond films, Canadian-born filmmaker Saltzman's stock could hardly have been higher in the movie business, and Kirshner's pedigree in the music industry was equally impressive.

A native New Yorker, born the son of a Bronx tailor, Kirshner had first attempted to engineer an entrée for himself into the music business during a spell working as a bellhop at a hotel. While carrying the bags of Frankie

Laine, he cheekily attempted to sell a song he had written to the then hugely popular singer. Laine turned it down but told him how he could go about getting the song made into a demo disc. Kirshner was on his way.

In 1957 he met and befriended a budding singer and musician called Robert Cassotto, later to change his name to Bobby Darin. Kirshner helped Darin secure his first recording contract, which paved the way eventually for great international success. Then, still in the early days of rock 'n' roll, Kirshner formed Aldon Music with musician Al Nevins, and in May 1958 they opened an office on Broadway which became a phenomenal hit factory.

Realising that the people writing songs were all too often grown-ups taking a random guess at what teenagers wanted to hear, Kirshner signed up young, unknown songwriters he believed in, and who were willing to work for him for $150 dollars a week or less, and coaxed from them hit after hit about teenage love. Kirshner's talented team of songwriters included the husband and wife duos Barry Mann and Cynthia Weil, and Gerry Goffin and Carole King, as well as Neil Diamond, Neil Sedaka and Howard Greenfield.

By 1962 Aldon Music had no less than eighteen songwriters on its staff and new songs flowed by the hour from the keys of upright pianos installed in cubicles in their offices on the fifth floor of 1650 Broadway. During this four-year period of frenzied creativity, Kirshner's team composed and published dozens of big hits. They included 'Up On The Roof' for The Drifters, 'Breaking Up Is Hard To Do' for Neil Sedaka, 'Will You Love Me Tomorrow?' for The Shirelles, and one of the most played radio songs of all time, 'You've Lost That Lovin' Feelin'' for The Righteous Brothers. On their first album The Beatles even covered 'Chains', a catchy Aldon song written by Carole King and Gerry Goffin, which had originally been a hit for The Cookies.

The emergence, however, of the Lennon–McCartney songwriting partnership in The Beatles, Jagger and Richards in The Rolling Stones and the general trend towards singer-songwriters composing their own material, persuaded Kirshner to diversify. He sold Aldon's back catalogue of songs to Columbia Pictures in a multi-million-dollar deal and Columbia also installed him as musical director of Screen Gems, a division of the company producing television and films.

In this capacity, Kirshner's next move was to mastermind the music for a new band called The Monkees, a rock quartet brought together specifically for the creation of a television series chronicling the zany life of a pop group. The TV series was inspired by the antics of The Beatles in their first movie *A Hard Day's Night*, and the plan for The Monkees' TV programme was to follow that simple formula – the music would sell the show and the show would sell the records.

The plan worked like a charm. Audiences instantly warmed to the group as they got into all sorts of bizarre scrapes, rescuing maidens in distress, falling foul of dastardly villains and playing pranks on themselves and the world while pausing every now and then for a song.

Under Kirshner's guidance, The Monkees simultaneously had a hugely successful career on record. Their discs, heavily promoted and carefully co-ordinated with the TV series, resulted in massive hits for 'The Prefab Four', as The Monkees were known because they were so obviously a manufactured group. Kirshner was able to give The Monkees songs like 'I'm A Believer' written by such an established songwriter as Neil Diamond.

Thanks to Kirshner's influence, Davy Jones, Peter Tork, Mike Nesmith and Mickey Dolenz as The Monkees enjoyed hit singles and two number-one albums. But when rifts opened up between the group's four young Monkee-men and Kirshner over the style of music they were record-ing, Kirshner switched his musical attention to a cartoon group called The Archies. He had made millions from The Monkees, but two-dimensional characters, he now reasoned, would be far easier to manipulate. For a start, they would not answer him back.

The Archies was an animated TV show about the comic book adventures of a teenager called Archie and his pals, and Kirshner, as musical supervisor, found the perfect slice of bubblegum pop to match the cartoon creation. It was a song called 'Sugar, Sugar', and he put together a studio group and issued their record as by The Archies. 'Sugar Sugar' proceeded to sell an incredible ten million copies, topping the charts in America and in the UK where it stayed at number one for eight weeks. Kirshner, known as 'the man with the golden ear', had done it again.

Now, in 1969, Don Kirshner had joined forces with Harry Saltzman on yet another project combining movies and music. To the world's music press gathered at the Rockefeller's Rainbow Grill, they announced with great confidence the formation of a four-member 'multi-media' rock band called, with the deliberate mis-spelling, Toomorrow.

Covering the event, *Rolling Stone* magazine caustically reported: 'The clichés were as plentiful and as expensive as the hors d'oeuvres. Should Tomorrow ever come, the complete package would eventually include three "musical adventure" films for United Artists, a series of records on the Calendar label to be distributed by RCA Victor, numerous TV appearances, and the usual Licensing Corporation of America plastic product tie-ins.'

It was not hard to understand *Rolling Stone*'s scepticism. Unveiled as the members of Toomorrow were four youngsters almost totally unknown in either the film or the music business. They comprised Olivia Newton-John, Karl Chambers, Vic Cooper and Ben Thomas, and all were trumpeted as the chosen ones after a 'six-month worldwide talent hunt'. They were four very different personalities with four very different backgrounds and chosen specifically to appeal to four different audiences.

They were, Kirshner enthused, 'a smorgasbord . . . the best-looking total group that ever existed'. And, he claimed, Toomorrow 'can be the biggest thing in the history of the business'. As for Olivia, Kirshner dubbed her 'the Julie Andrews of the future, the girl next door . . . only groovier'.

The three boys had already been chosen and signed when Saltzman's and Kirshner's search for a girl singer to complete the group reached London. Initially the hot favourite was Susan George, a stunning, sexy, blonde young English girl with a promising career as an actress ahead of her. Susan was primarily an actress but she could also sing, and she was on course to be the female face of Toomorrow until one of Krishner's many music industry contacts in London tipped him off about a girl called Olivia Newton-John.

Kirshner says he knew as soon as he met Olivia that she was right for the new group he had in mind. 'I'll never forget it,' he said. 'I walked into Peter Gormley's London office one day and there was this kewpie doll in knee socks. I knew she could be the darling of millions!'

Once he had heard her sing, Kirshner realised she also

had a decent voice to go with her good looks. 'I knew with some double-tracking that we could get a great, sweet sound out of her,' he said, and arranged for Olivia to go for an audition with Saltzman at his Mayfair office in London. Saltzman proved to be as enthusiastic about Olivia as Kirshner. He took such an instant liking to her that she walked out of his office with a firm offer of the leading female role in the Toomorrow project. She was informed this would start with a film to be released worldwide the following year with a soundtrack album to accompany it. After that, the world could be her oyster, Kirshner kept telling her.

'I walked the streets of London with Olivia just telling her how incredible she was gonna be,' he recalled. 'Talent is the key to her success,' he declared, 'but there's a powerful magnetic quality about her, something that immediately gets under your skin and you can't shake it. And I loved her three names. Unusual, it sticks with you, and the bit about her grandfather winning the Nobel thing; very marketable press stuff.'

Kirshner says he knew for sure Olivia possessed a rare magnetism when, just to please her, he found himself spending an entire afternoon visiting a string of pet shops across London searching for a special kind of dog food as a gift for Olivia's red setter Geordie. Kirshner had been invited to dinner with Olivia and Bruce and he wanted to present Olivia with a special treat for her pooch. 'Funny way to spend an afternoon,' Kirshner mused, 'but I finally found it. It's crazy, but that's the kind of effect she has on you.'

* * *

The hyperbole for Toomorrow soared to extraordinary heights. Harry Saltzman said the whole concept was to 'fill a void for fourteen-year-olds to thirties' left by the break-up of The Beatles. Ben Thomas, a Georgia-born singer-guitarist, was described as 'what you might get if you crossed Paul McCartney with Gary Cooper'. It was hoped that he would generate 'the same kind of excitement as James Dean'. Karl, a former drummer with Gladys Knight and The Pips from Philadelphia, admitted that he was chosen because he was seen as a combination of Bill Cosby and Sidney Poitier. And Vic, who had played backing keyboards for Tom Jones among others, apparently won his berth in Toomorrow on the strength of being not only a fine keyboards player but English, handsome, funny and able to do impressions of James Cagney and James Stewart.

'When you see the Toomorrow group, it's impossible to dislike them,' Kirshner enthused. 'They're young, with-it, and have the looks and appeal of "today" . . . and tomorrow. They are undoubtedly the best-looking pop group ever brought together.'

According to Kirshner, the Toomorrow project was principally going ahead because The Beatles had 'become big business, leaving behind their image as exciting, real people', and because 'the world of pop was facing a tedious and vacuous future'.

It was little wonder that *Rolling Stone* magazine labelled the launching of Toomorrow as '. . . the greatest barrage of bullshit in many years', particularly as the quartet of untried unknowns had yet to produce a single note together.

As the only girl in the group and its lead singer, much of the attention inevitably focused on Olivia. Naturally she was flattered by Kirshner's confidence in her and the big build-up he kept giving her to the press. In view of Don Kirshner's remarkable track record in the music business, and Harry Saltzman's equally notable movie achievements as co-producer of the James Bond films, she had no reason to doubt that the Toomorrow project would be anything other than an unqualified success. Kirshner and Saltzman thought so too. They were confident enough to offer their principal stars exclusive five-year contracts. With solid financial investment from the two moguls, Olivia could look forward to five years of guaranteed work from Toomorrow.

Bruce Welch was thrilled for his young girlfriend. She had passed up the opportunity to star with Cliff Richard in *Cinderella*, but this one looked too good to miss. Toomorrow appeared to be a wonderful break for her, and lucrative too.

Money seemed to be no object with the Kirshner–Saltzman partnership – a budget of around £1million was to be allocated to the first film – and Olivia was to be paid an annual Toomorrow retainer of £10,000, a huge sum back in 1969. The duo also paid for her to have singing lessons as well as general pampering. She was sent to leading London hair salon Leonard's in smart Upper Grosvenor Street in London to have blonde streaks put in her hair. And when she turned twenty-one, the birthday gift from Kirshner and the Toomorrow team was an expensive gold key to wear around her neck – a nod to the traditional twenty-first birthday notion of gaining the key to the door. Thirty-eight years later Olivia would present the key to her own daughter Chloe on her twenty-first birthday. Bruce and Olivia's relationship was strengthened by the announcement of their engagement that same night. Bruce bought Olivia a large pearl engagement ring set in silver with diamond chips, to add to a black opal ring set in diamonds that he had given her as a token of his love.

When Olivia flew to the United States for the very first time for preliminary Toomorrow meetings, she took her sister Rona along as chaperone. But on arrival in New York, they discovered they had arrived too early. Due to a mix-up, the Toomorrow team weren't expecting Olivia for another week. No problem, the girls were told, just take off for a week's holiday in Florida together and all expenses would be paid. Kirshner and Saltzman duly picked up the bill without a murmur for their young star's unscheduled vacation with her sister in the sunshine state. For Olivia and Rona, it was in every respect the warmest of welcomes to America.

Soon Olivia was making regular trips with Bruce across the Atlantic to New York in connection with the Toomorrow project. They travelled first class, stayed in the very best hotels and were given the red carpet treatment, all at the film company's expense.

Olivia insisted Bruce travelled with her as often as his own work allowed. Now they were fully committed to each other and officially engaged she was determined the extraordinary showbiz break that had come out of the blue would not jeopardise their relationship. For his part, Bruce had been fully supportive of her leap into Toomorrow, even though nothing quite so unexpected had ever figured in their plans for cosy domestic bliss together. He found it ironic that after giving up touring with The Shadows as a way of spending more time at home with Olivia, she was now the one flying off, often leaving him behind on his own.

First up for Olivia and the other three members of Kirshner's hot new showbiz property was a sci-fi musical called, of course, *Toomorrow*, written and directed by Val Guest, a distinguished and experienced British filmmaker. He seemed a perfect choice for such a vehicle, having directed the sci-fi hit *The Day The Earth Caught Fire* as well as Cliff Richard's first movie musical *Expresso Bongo*.

The *Toomorrow* movie would be made at Pinewood Studios in England, and Olivia and the three boys would portray four students attending the London College of Arts and living in Chelsea with Olivia as the 'den mother'. To pay their way through college they form a pop band, and together they create a stimulating and original musical sound, thanks to the invention by organist Vic of a new instrument called a 'tonaliser'. This instrument has the unexpected consequence of bringing them into contact with visitors from another world. Its sonic vibrations cause an extra-terrestrial, played by established British character actor Roy Dotrice, to beam the group up into space to entertain the Alphoid population. It transpires that the Alphoid inhabitants need Toomorrow's vibrant beat to cure them of a mysterious malady – sterility of sound. But when the Alphoids realise their environment is wrong for the group, they allow them to escape back to Earth.

One huge sound stage at Pinewood was given over to the Alphoid space ship, and Olivia had the satisfaction of singing at the famous Roundhouse music venue in north London for a pop festival scene. But filming was anything but a smooth ride for her. She struggled to overcome her Australian accent, and it didn't take her long to realise that she was in the movie to look pretty as much as for her voice. The wardrobe she was allocated indicated she would be expected to show plenty of leg as often as possible. The boys in the group would attract a female audience and Olivia was expected to look cute and sexy to redress the balance.

Tight little shorts or micro-skirts were the order of the day, and Olivia burst into floods of tears when she learned that at one point the script called for her to seen in her underwear. She refused and, rather than argue the point, Val Guest relented. On the whole it seemed that Val Guest handled Olivia's inexperience on a film set as sensitively as possible. Indeed, dealing with Olivia's anxiety and modesty were the least of Guest's problems. As he later outlined during a *Guardian* lecture he gave at the National Film Theatre in London in 2005, the veteran director had far more important things to worry about.

He explained to the NFI audience that the film's production was beset with fundamental difficulties. Harry Saltzman had put up the money for the movie, but he had also put his interest in the Bond films up as collateral. 'Then halfway through the film, we realised this was chaos,' Guest told his audience, 'because Cubby Broccoli [Saltzman's partner on the Bond films] had broken with him and was suing him because part of their contract was that they couldn't put up the Bond films as collateral for anything. So, Harry's bank went, the film went. We finally finished it somehow, and then I put a clamp on it being shown. And then we lifted the clamp so it could be shown at the London Pavilion. It just had an opening there. And that really was almost the end of *Toomorrow*.'

Prior to the film's release, Bruce Welch got to see an early preview and was utterly dismayed at what he saw and heard. 'The film was a disgrace,' he said in his autobiography, *Rock 'n' Roll I Gave You The Best Years Of My Life*. 'It was reminiscent of so many of the low budget pictures that were made during the early sixties, and the biggest letdown of all was the music. It was all so lightweight. There were no hit songs – the numbers were naive and instantly forgettable.' Instead of going for songwriters with a proven track record as hit-makers, Kirshner handed the job to some relatively inexperienced writers signed to his publishing company and, of course, the chances of success were not so good.

Bruce was so worried about the damage the film could do to Olivia's embryonic career that he went so far as to arrange for a private screening of *Toomorrow* for several of his music industry pals to see if they could at least salvage it musically. Bruce's devotion to Olivia was evident from the calibre of songwriting professionals he called in. They were among the UK's very best and the most prolific hit-makers: Roger Cook and Roger Greenaway, whose output included 'Home Lovin' Man' for Andy Williams, 'Something's Gotten Hold Of My Heart' for Gene Pitney and 'You've Got Your Troubles' for The Fortunes; Mitch Murray, who had written the chart-topper 'How Do You Do It?' for Gerry and The Pacemakers, and Les Reed who wrote Tom Jones's massive hit 'It's Not Unusual'.

It was a brave and gallant gesture on Bruce's part to assemble such songwriting talent on a rescue mission, but it was futile. It soon became obvious that any musical changes would mean some major reshooting of several key scenes and the cost would be prohibitive.

Despite Guest's efforts, in the run-up to its scheduled UK opening, the beating of the drum for *Toomorrow* continued apace. The movie's distributors, the Rank Organisation, promised: 'The film launches the supergroup with the sound of the seventies in a contemporary story which is as fresh and compelling as tomorrow's date. Each individual member of the combo – Olivia, Karl, Vic and Ben – radiates those unique qualities of built-in excitement, personal magnetism and a powerhouse of potent musical talent. Together they ensure that *Toomorrow* provides out-of-this-world entertainment for the young-at-heart filmgoers of today.'

One of the press handouts said of Olivia: 'Livvy has buttery skin, big, big, very round grey-green eyes, stands 5ft 6ins and weighs 98lbs.' She dug 'Baez, horse riding, Mac Davis, Redford, Bruce Welch, McQueen, Streisand, Feliciano, steak and salad, Hank Marvin, Beatles, wine, Bacharach and her red setter named Geordie.'

Another reported: 'She is five feet and six inches tall, weighs 115lbs, and has dark blonde hair and grey-green eyes. Olivia sings and "sort of" plays the guitar. She loves to wear micro-miniskirts (sometimes 18 inches above the knee) and loves animals of all kinds.'

Bruce and Olivia flew to America for a starry New York launch and were back in London to attend the UK premiere. *Toomorrow* the movie finally opened at the London Pavilion cinema in Piccadilly Circus, but quickly vanished, accompanied by a lawsuit between Harry Saltzman and Val Guest. 'What can I say but it was terrible and I was terrible in it,' Olivia much later told the music press. 'They kept telling me I had to project so I went through the whole movie shouting.'

The movie did briefly surface later in the UK, but its very limited screenings ensured that the multi-media Toomorrow project got off to the worst possible start. Without the movie to guarantee cross-promotion, the records by Toomorrow the pop group failed to make any sort of a dent in the charts. Two singles and a soundtrack album was the sum total of the group's output, and during their two years together they played not a single concert.

Don Kirshner has said that he began to lose interest in the whole Toomorrow project when he saw it was all going in the wrong direction, and it was no surprise when the venture that had promised so very much was quietly wound up and consigned to history.

'The film opened and closed within a week,' Olivia said. 'They called us into the office and told us that we were all being released from our contracts. And that was that. I suppose I was disappointed. It had all seemed too good to be true at first. I thought it was all going to be terrific. Then we were told that it was all over.

'We knew it would end eventually, but the guys in the group were shattered. We didn't realise it would be over so soon. Mr Saltzman just called us into his office and told us it was over. The group had been together for two years and we'd done nothing. Just rehearsed a lot and did auditions for big businessmen.'

Olivia and the other three members of the group had been signed to exclusive five-year contracts and their release at least enabled them now to press on with their careers as solo artists. 'I wasn't desperately unhappy,' Olivia later reflected about the whole experience. 'It didn't destroy me that it wasn't as perfect as I imagined it would be. I was into other things, I was engaged to Bruce Welch and I was having a lovely life.'

Olivia's image and career might have been so very different if *Toomorrow* the movie had not proved to be such a disaster. She might never have gone on to solo success. Mass audiences never got to see her as the singing young student looking cute and sexy in her little shorts and those micro-skirts daringly '18 inches above the knee'. Overall, the entire Toomorrow venture was a desperate letdown for the four young co-stars, especially for Ben Thomas, whose actress girlfriend Susan George had been pipped to the lead role by Olivia, and whose own big break had now come to so little after promising so much.

The records had flopped, the movie was barely seen and Olivia came away vowing to stay clear of films for the foreseeable future. Failure was hard to swallow and the whole enterprise had been a harsh lesson. Nothing at the start had pointed to such an unhappy outcome.

Frustratingly for Olivia's fans, *Toomorrow* the movie has rarely seen the light of day since its limited release, and it's thought that very few prints are still in existence. There was a rare showing of the film at the Egyptian Theatre in Los Angeles in 1970, which Olivia attended with her sister Rona, after a copy was tracked down in England and flown out to LA for the special screening. With the passing of time the film's inaccessibility has given it considerable curiosity value among film buffs.

* * *

During Olivia's involvement with Toomorrow, Bruce Welch began to get restless spending his time behind a desk on behalf of Shadows Music. He started tossing a few ideas around with Hank Marvin and they talked of the possibility of teaming up to perform as a duo but without calling themselves The Shadows. In the course of their conversation, the name of John Farrar cropped up. The guitarist had left a lasting impression on them both in Australia and they decided to call him up and invite him over to England. It was a telephone call that would have a major bearing on Olivia's success as a singer – John was just emerging as a highly talented songwriter and, in time, he would go on to write and produce many of Olivia's biggest hits.

John arrived in London in August 1970, and Hank and Bruce immediately took him off to Portugal with a view to spending some time working on new songs together. They all gelled so well during this working holiday that they agreed to team up to record and perform as a trio, Marvin,

Welch and Farrar, as soon as they returned to England.

Olivia was especially pleased when John pitched up in London. The bonus for her was that by now the girl in John's life was Olivia's erstwhile singing partner, Pat Carroll. Just as Olivia had predicted, John and Pat proved to be very good for each other and Olivia was thrilled when the couple decided to get married. And now that John Farrar was planning to base himself in England with his new wife, it meant Olivia would be seeing a lot more of her great friend Pat – but not as a regular singing partner. Pat had no alternative but to cheerfully accept that Olivia had forged ahead with her solo career and there was to be no real opportunity to team up again as a singing duo.

5

If Not For You

'We just looked at each other and there was this lightning flash'

Lee Kramer on meeting Olivia for the first time on a beach in Monte Carlo

Once Olivia was released from her Toomorrow contract, her manager Peter Gormley saw the importance of rapidly distancing her from the doomed project. He wanted any lingering whiff of Toomorrow's failure to be dispelled as quickly as possible. Gormley personally had seen nothing in Toomorrow to shake his firm belief in Olivia's talent, and he and Bruce Welch realised that the best way of drawing a line under the whole Toomorrow disaster was to find Olivia suitable songs to record for a debut LP that would give her the chance of a hit and put her on the map.

Together with John Farrar, they picked out a handful of outstanding American country songs for the album, including Kris Kristofferson's 'Me And Bobby McGee' and 'Help Me Make It Through The Night', Tom Rush's 'No Regrets' as well as Canadian singer-songwriter Gordon Lightfoot's classic 'If You Could Read My Mind'.

Among other numbers that came up for consideration was Bob Dylan's 'If Not For You', one of the strongest tracks on Dylan's *New Morning* album released in 1970. George Harrison had also recognised 'If Not For You' as the pick of the bunch on Dylan's new LP, and the Beatle had recorded his own version with a distinctive slide guitar backing for a track issued on his solo album *All Things Must Pass*.

Peter Gormley heard Harrison's rendering of 'If Not For You' and suggested Olivia might like to record it. Olivia was far from convinced it would suit her, but John Farrar and Bruce Welch won her round. They would take care of everything in the studio, they assured her. John, by now showing a remarkable ear for harmonies and musical arranging, would take on the responsibility of the song's arrangement and Bruce would mastermind Olivia's vocal performance. Surrounded by experienced professionals who were also friends who loved her and believed in her, Olivia was hardly in the mood to turn down their choice of 'If Not For You'.

During the studio recording, John Farrar seized on George Harrison's slide guitar sound as the dominant force in the backing and took a similar approach to cushion Olivia's soft vocal. John had always enjoyed music with a country tinge and there was undeniably a touch of Nashville about the finished recording.

By the end of the studio session everyone was happy with the outcome, even Olivia. 'I didn't think it was my type of song at all,' she admitted, 'and I had a little bit of trouble being convincing in putting it over. But everyone else was so enthusiastic that I came round to liking it eventually.'

'If Not For You' was chosen as Olivia's first single from the album. It was released early in 1971, and by the middle of March it had reached the Top Ten in the UK charts, eventually peaking at number seven. After the false dawns with Decca and Toomorrow, Olivia had finally achieved some tangible success. Bruce, Peter and John were all delighted for her.

Olivia's personal delight was tempered by the fact she knew this success would now turn her life upside down. And so it proved. Her chart hit heralded a sudden non-stop whirlwind of activity. Soon Olivia was given a part in a fifty-minute film caper with Cliff Richard for BBC TV called *Getaway With Cliff*, and in October she was added to the bill for Cliff's three-week run at the London Palladium. Conveniently the run also starred Marvin, Welch and Farrar. By this time, Olivia had also followed up her initial chart success six months earlier with another smash hit, a contemporary reworking of the traditional American country song 'Banks Of The Ohio'.

The song was as old as the hills and was first recorded way back in 1936, but Olivia's catchy version brought it up to date, helped by some resonant bass vocal refrains from Mike Sammes. Peter Gormley was a country music fan and Olivia felt entirely comfortable when it was suggested she record 'Banks Of The Ohio'. She had frequently included the song in her set list on her club engagements and it had always gone down well. She was, moreover, well acquainted with country music after listening to the Tennessee Ernie Ford LPs she had, as a child, found nestling between her father's opera albums.

'Banks Of The Ohio' entered the UK Top Ten at a time when 'If Not For You' had also started to make a dent in the charts in America, where the great Bob Dylan even professed approval of Olivia's version of his song. 'If Not For You' finished up as a creditable Top Thirty US hit and also made the charts in South Africa, Ireland, Canada, Israel and across the Continent.

Hard on the heel of her hits, television, too, was now beckoning in a major fashion. Olivia had already made a guest appearance on Cliff's BBC-TV series *It's Cliff*

Richard! earlier in the year where she'd been so nervous that Cliff held her hand to stop her shaking when they duetted together. But now, buoyed by the confidence of an international hit record, she was ready for bigger things and she was signed up as a resident guest star on Cliff's new thirteen-week BBC-TV series, *It's Cliff Richard!*. Cliff's show, which started in January 1972, became required family viewing and the weekly TV exposure for Olivia helped her to secure a third consecutive UK hit with a cover version of George Harrison's 'What Is Life?'.

In addition to appearing in Cliff's TV show, Olivia was also starring in the West End in a revue called *Paris To Piccadilly* with French singer Sacha Distel. She had her own fifteen-minute solo spot in the show, joined in the half-time finale, and later sang a duet with the French charmer.

Distel was strikingly good-looking and regarded as a sexy heartthrob in Britain. He had gained quite a reputa-tion as a lover after embarking on a high-profile affair with French screen sex kitten Brigitte Bardot. In the UK, Sacha came to prominence when he had a Top Ten hit in 1970 with 'Raindrops Keep Fallin' On My Head' and, although he didn't sell huge quantities of records in Britain, he was always a popular performer and an interesting guest on any TV show. He sang well, played guitar, oozed Gallic charm and melted English female hearts with his obvious sex appeal and his soft French accent.

Olivia was only too aware that the audiences who turned up to the show at the Prince of Wales Theatre were predominantly female and were there to see sexy Sacha. The adoration emanating from the stalls for the chanteur was almost tangible. Despite her hit records, she had to accept that she was very much a minor addition on the bill. 'At first it was frightening to go out and see so many women looking at you,' she told *Australian Women's Weekly*. 'I mean, they could hate me. Women in an audience can get very resentful towards female artists on stage.'

Then one night, at the end of March 1972, Olivia arrived home, unusually past midnight, after appearing in concert, and coolly announced to Bruce she was breaking off their engagement and that their five-year love affair was over. Bruce was not only devastated, but also nonplussed. He'd had no inkling that anything was amiss between them. He pleaded with Olivia to give him some sort of explanation. According to Bruce, she was unable to do so, and the more he tried to prise the reason out of her, the more she clammed up. All she made clear was that they were finished. Olivia was adamant it was over, a fait accompli.

Faced with an unyielding Olivia, the following morning Bruce felt he had no option but to move out of the house at Hadley Common that had been such a happy home for them both. He never went back. With a heavy heart and still shell-shocked by such an abrupt, unforeseen ending to his relationship with Olivia, he moved into a flat he had bought some years before in the middle of Soho, just a stone's throw from the London Palladium.

Bruce was still very much in love with Olivia and he couldn't get her out of his mind. At home in his flat he played her records just so he could hear her voice, and at night he found he couldn't stop his feet from taking him to the Prince of Wales Theatre where Olivia was appearing in concert. There he would forlornly watch her on stage and mourn the love he had lost. He was in complete torment. 'I went haywire,' he said. 'I had nothing to live for.'

Having never had a drink until he was twenty-one, Bruce now started hitting the bottle in a big way to drown his sorrows. 'My world just fell apart,' he recalled. 'It took me two full years to get over it. After a while I would sit at home and drink a bottle of brandy a day on my own – not just once, but day after day, so I put on weight.'

And when the house at Hadley Common was sold, he increasingly felt desperately alone and that he had nobody to turn to – no parents, no grandparents, no relations; his ex-wife Anne had moved away to Majorca with their son Dwayne after the divorce.

'Having no family hits hardest when things are really bad, like when Olivia and I broke up,' he said. 'The sense of isolation and loneliness can be overwhelming. Sometimes I sat and talked to myself because there was simply no one else.'

Bruce's misery was complete when he discovered towards the end of May that Olivia had been having an affair with a famous singer, believed to be Sacha Distel, and he was unfortunate to find them together at the flat Olivia had moved into in St John's Wood, round the corner from her sister Rona.

The break-up for Bruce was painful enough, but on a professional level it could hardly have come at a more inopportune time either. He was in the middle of producing an album for Olivia and was also scheduled to go on a Marvin, Welch and Farrar tour. He felt that in the circumstances he could hardly continue to work on Olivia's album and handed over production duties to John Farrar. And given the amount he was drinking, Bruce felt he wouldn't be in any fit state to undertake any sort of a tour with John and Hank. He says that at his lowest point he was downing two bottles of brandy a day as well as wine.

In July, heartbroken and at the end of his tether, Bruce decided life no longer held anything for him, and he was ready to end it all. With typical precision, he informed friends that he was going away for the weekend and cancelled his milk and newspaper orders before swallowing some barbiturates and drinking copious amounts of brandy. The last thing he remembers, he says, was the view from the window of his flat, high up above Soho, of a vivid red evening sky stretching across London's rooftops. The next thing he knew, he was waking up in the Middlesex hospital after coming out of a coma.

For all Bruce's meticulous planning, he had forgotten one small thing – to cancel the window cleaner. The care-taker of Bruce's block had let the cleaner into his flat with a master key and, after finding Bruce comatose on the floor, he had called an ambulance in the nick of time.

Bruce remained in hospital for several weeks, during which time Olivia visited him twice. She had career commitments she could not break, including the filming for the BBC of a Cliff Richard comedy thriller called *The Case*, and a tour with Cliff of the Far East in which Hank Marvin and John Farrar would also feature, but augmented by former Shadows bassist John Rostill and drummer Brian Bennett.

For Olivia, the tour of Indonesia, Hong Kong and Japan was a welcome change of scenery from the pressures that had been building up around her in London. Her career was moving at a hectic pace and her private life had been in turmoil, but now she was touring with a twelve-strong group she regarded almost as family and she felt relaxed in their company.

The Japanese, in particular, were bowled over by Olivia's blonde beauty and radiant smile, and she easily charmed the hotel managers into granting her request that all the musicians in her party should sample the delights of staying in authentic Japanese suites. As a tight-knit group of

A hair-raising start to life in the public eye.

(*Above left*) Olivia as a young girl.

(*Above right*) Olivia's father, Professor Brin Newton-John.

(*Below*) Teenage Olivia, before she was groomed for pop stardom.

Waving hello to a first taste of UK success as singing duo Pat and Olivia in 1965.

Pat Carroll married Olivia's prolific hit songwriter John Farrar and the couple remain among Olivia's closest friends.

Ian Turpie was Olivia's first love and early music mentor.

Wide-eyed at the
cultural explosion in
London in the
Swinging Sixties . . .

. . . and full of the
joys of a British
springtime in
England in 1972.

Sitting pretty with the other members of the ill-fated Toomorrow pop group. (*Left to right*) Ben Thomas, Vic Cooper and Karl Chambers.

Sitting in with Ben Thomas on an audition to find a drummer for Toomorrow, touted as 'the best-looking total group that ever existed'.

(*Left*) Bruce Welch of The Shadows was Olivia's record producer and songwriter as well as her fiancé in the early 1970s.

(*Below*) Cliff Richard gave Olivia an early break on his top-rated BBC TV show *It's Cliff Richard!* and, forty years on, is still a treasured friend.

(*Above*) Olivia's bid to win the 1974 Eurovision Song Contest for the UK gets a lift from Brighton bobbies on the Sussex coast.

(*Below*) Boyfriend Lee Kramer became Olivia's manager to help launch her career in the United States in the mid-1970s.

Rocking the boat: Olivia's clutch of country music awards upset some of Nashville's traditionalists.

friends as well as British musicians far away from home, they all tended to stick together, sightseeing, going out to eat or playing cards or charades while drinking saki. On one window-shopping expedition, a fabulous Japanese wedding gown in white satin and beautifully embroidered in gold caught Olivia's eye. Cliff Richard spotted Olivia pausing to stop and stare at the beautiful dress in the window. It had no price tag on it; just a note to say it was second-hand.

Olivia's twenty-fourth birthday was approaching and Cliff resolved to secretly buy the gown for her as a present. Back at the hotel, he told the others of his plan and swore them to secrecy. He also told them that Olivia must be escorted by at least one of them on any future shopping expeditions to steer her away from that particular shop. He felt that Olivia had been so taken by the dress she was certain to go back for another look and possibly try to buy it.

Cliff's plan worked like a charm and, as Olivia's birthday fell on a day when they would all be flying home, he also arranged for a large birthday cake to be smuggled on to the aeroplane along with bottles of champagne – and the dress.

The airline took steps to make sure all twelve in the party were seated together and, at the appointed moment, the captain made a special birthday announcement to all the passengers, who broke into applause. 'Poor Olivia!' said Cliff. 'She was in one big, happy, tearful state when I sprung my special surprise – the wedding gown. She was too thrilled even to speak for a while. Finally she collected herself, thanked us and we toasted her with champagne and each had a slice of birthday cake.'

During the Far East tour, Cliff, who has never married,

frequently found himself in interviews having to deny, quite truthfully, that he had any romantic interest in Olivia. From day one he had had a soft spot for her, but he was at pains to point out that his gift of a wedding dress was not a gigantic hint. 'It was for Olivia to wear on stage and not in church,' he stressed.

Olivia and Cliff never had a romance as such, but there's no doubt that he was exceptionally fond of her. 'She has more sex appeal in her little finger than the whole of Madonna,' he once said, and he remains to this day a very close friend. There was a time when Cliff kept framed photographs of Olivia both at home and in his office, and Cliff's late mother Dorothy maintained that Olivia could have been the perfect girl for the bachelor boy. 'There was only one girl we thought had a chance with Cliff,' Dorothy once said. 'That was Olivia. Knowing all the girls he's been out with and knowing him, I think that was his chance. If he was going to marry, she would have been the girl.'

That may just have been wishful thinking on Dorothy's part. Setting the record straight, Olivia stated on TV that the possibility of an affair never arose. 'It was just never the right time, the appropriate time,' she said of Cliff. 'He was my friend, and I think sometimes when you work with someone a long time and they become your friend, that's how it stays. There'll always be a chemistry between us and we always really liked each other and still do. There'll always be that closeness, but it just wasn't meant to be, I guess, in that way.'

* * *

Once back in England, Olivia spoke to Bruce on the phone from time to time and, since Peter Gormley was manager of them both, it was inevitable their paths would cross in Peter's office. It made for some awkward moments. 'Our careers were really entwined at that time,' says Bruce. 'We had the same office, the same manager and I was producing her records. I couldn't get away from it. She always seemed to be in the office if I came in.'

A determined Bruce, however, was winning his battle with the brandy after being discharged from hospital in October, and he was happy for Olivia when, towards the end of the year, she found herself with a big hit record in America. 'Let Me Be There', written by John Rostill, was a song that Bruce found for Olivia, and it represented a major breakthrough for her in the US when it reached number six in the American singles chart. Olivia could hardly believe it, especially as 'Let Me Be There' proved to be a failure in Britain. While it soared up the America charts, curiously it sold only around 8,000 copies in the UK.

As a seasonal goodwill gesture, Olivia invited Bruce to spend Christmas with her. And although the festive reunion was not enough to effect a lasting reconciliation, Bruce now felt more positive about the future. He bought himself a house in Hampstead High Street, in north London, and he was looking forward to working again and getting his life back on track.

Olivia began the new year by taking her cover version of John Denver's 'Take Me Home, Country Roads' into the UK charts. At first it looked as though the record was not going to be a hit and Olivia despaired of it making even the Top Fifty. But it turned out to be what the record industry calls a sleeper. 'It started selling slowly, over Christmas it did well but compared to everybody else not well enough. Then all the rush on everything else died down and it took off, which was just great,' she said.

'Take Me Home, Country Roads' was Olivia's fourth UK hit in the space of twenty months and, coupled with her growing reputation in America, it was obvious to Bruce that, given the right US management of her career, she could be on the brink of becoming a very big star. When John Denver heard she'd covered his 'Take Me Home, Country Roads', he invited her over to America to appear on his TV special. Olivia filmed her segment in an igloo specially built in the snow in Colorado in the depths of winter. But thanks to the magic of filming it was warm enough within the igloo for dozens of butterflies to be introduced to flit around inside. Steve Martin, yet to become a top comedy actor, played the banjo on one number with a butterfly inadvertently perched on his nose throughout.

Bruce still harboured hopes that Olivia would return to his arms and in April, while they were enjoying a friendly tête-à-tête together at a Hampstead teashop, Bruce was overjoyed when Olivia suggested they should get back together and try again. Bruce says he didn't ask what had happened to her lover. He really didn't want to know. All he cared about was that Olivia was happy to have him back. 'Olivia's lover was a married man,' Bruce has revealed, 'and I believe that she always hoped he would leave his wife to be with her one day.' Bruce surmised that when it became clear that wasn't going to happen, Olivia had ended the affair.

One year after Olivia had dropped her bombshell on Bruce that their relationship was over, she moved back in with him and they made every effort to make it a loving reconciliation and to pick up the pieces. But it was in vain. They lasted together just eight weeks. 'Every time we made love, all I could focus on was Olivia in the arms of her lover,' Bruce revealed in his autobiography. 'No matter how hard I tried, I still kept seeing the two of them together. When I told Olivia about it, we both broke down and cried together. There was nothing I could do about it.'

The end finally came in June 1973, when Olivia went off to the south of France for a holiday with a girl friend, Greek-born actress Chantal Contouri, whose family, like Olivia's, had moved to Melbourne when she was a little girl. Bruce later flew out to join Olivia for one last-ditch attempt at a lasting reunion, but within a couple of days they both knew it was over. The spark between them was no longer there and he flew back to London leaving Olivia to continue her holiday with her good friend Chantal. This time the break-up was final.

* * *

Many years later, Bruce was to say:

> I thought Olivia and I were the perfect couple. But looking back I can see that I was a bit of a Svengali. Because we both had the same careers, I didn't want her to make the same mistakes as I'd made. I knew how to short-circuit them, and in the end I gave her a hard time. I would make her do things over and over again in the studio and she would end up in tears. I would tell her what to do, who to talk to, what to wear, even how to move on stage.
>
> In the end I overdid my role in her life. I didn't give her room to grow, it was all a little ridiculous. I was seven years older than her and I became over-protective.
>
> When it was over I remember it all being blissful – but friends had to keep reminding me that it had in fact been pretty stormy. It was a puppy love kind of relationship.

Despite their parting of the ways on a personal level, Bruce Welch would continue to play a significant professional role in Olivia's burgeoning recording career over the next eighteen months, both as producer, song-finder and song-writer. Olivia even recorded Bruce's 'Please, Mister, Please', which was inspired by the couple's painful break-up. Bruce co-wrote it with John Rostill and developed the song's theme about a song on a jukebox that brings back too many painful memories of a lost love. 'Please, Mister, Please' would go on to provide Olivia with yet another million-selling Top Ten hit in America in the summer of 1975, peaking at number three.

Sadly for John Rostill, he would not live to see Olivia succeed so spectacularly in the USA with three of his songs: 'Let Me Be There', 'Please, Mister, Please' and 'If You Love Me (Let Me Know)'. Just a few months after Olivia's holiday in France, on 26 November 1973, Bruce turned up at John's home in Radlett, Hertfordshire, ready to join him for a music session at the eight-track studio John had built on the first floor of his house. But when he went upstairs to the studio, Bruce found that the door appeared to be jammed by something on the inside and he was unable to open it.

Bruce fetched a ladder from the garage and from the top he peered through the studio window. There he could see that the door was blocked by John's piano, but he was shocked to see that John himself was lying motionless at an odd angle with his bass guitar still in his hands. It transpired his good friend had been electrocut-ed; he had been dead for several hours. John's death at the tragically young age of thirty came as a huge shock to Bruce, and to Olivia who had got to know him well. She was deeply saddened; she had much to be grateful to him for, and Bruce had lost not only a writing partner, but a treasured friend.

* * *

Within days of Bruce flying back to London from the south of France, Olivia had continued her holiday by moving on to Monte Carlo to spend some time exploring the principality, swimming in the Mediterranean and topping up her tan. She was ready to put the recent emotionally turbulent few weeks behind her and simply relax and enjoy the Riviera's balmy climate. She hit the beach every day with Chantal to laze in the sun and, as she stretched out on the sand relishing the peace and quiet and enjoying the warmth, the last thing the very newly single Olivia Newton-John was prepared for was a new love to surface, quite literally, from the waves rolling in towards the shore.

The man in question was a wealthy, young English businessman and self-confessed playboy who went by the name of Lee Kramer. Striding athletically out of the shallows, he walked up the beach and directly into Olivia's life. Gazing admiringly at the beautiful blonde girl soaking up the sun in her bikini, he was immediately smitten. 'We just looked at each other and there was this lightning flash,' said Lee of the moment he fell for Olivia Newton-John. 'It was a classic romance on the French Riviera!'

6

Atlantic Crossing

'We think Olivia is beautiful and a lovely singer. We hope we can be as successful as her in the UK'

Abba's Agnetha Faltskog after winning the Eurovision Song Contest in 1974

Olivia Newton-John wouldn't be the first or the last pretty young girl to fall giddily in love with a rich and handsome playboy on the shores of the French Riviera. But when she met Lee Kramer in Monte Carlo in the summer of 1973, it was the start of a very great deal more than just a holiday romance.

Lee was tall, blond and blessed with good looks and, although at twenty-one he was three years younger than Olivia, he exuded a worldly self-assurance and a confident maturity. Olivia found him enormously attractive from the outset. And the attraction was mutual.

Already wealthy from a shoe import business he had started up when he was just a street-smart seventeen-year-old, Lee regularly spent long weekends in the south of France, where he kept a boat in order to cruise the Med in style and call in at the many resorts and lively hotspots that dotted the coastline.

He first set eyes on Olivia after dropping anchor several hundred yards offshore because there was no pier available at Monte Carlo where he could tie up his speedboat. A strong swimmer, Lee dived overboard to swim to the beach and he emerged from the sea where Olivia was sunbathing with Chantal. It was no chance meeting – Lee was a cousin of Chantal's fiancé – but fate was certainly playing a hand.

'As I was coming out of the water, there was this beautiful, tanned, blonde-haired girl with the biggest eyes I have ever seen in my entire life,' Lee recounted to *Crawdaddy* magazine. It was the start not of a holiday fling but a romance that was to blossom and endure with far-reaching repercussions for them both.

Up to this point in his life, and by his own admission, Lee had never taken any girl very seriously. But Olivia was different from the kind of girls he had dated thus far. He was instantly smitten.

Lee's only disappointment was to learn that Olivia had just a couple of days left of her holiday before she was due to fly back to England. But they made the most of their time together and he left Olivia in no doubt about his strength of feelings for her, even after such a short time, when he cut short his own stay and wangled a seat next to Olivia on the plane. Olivia could not fail but to be impressed.

They chatted happily all the way during the flight and, once back in London, Lee took her out for a meal at a little-known Chelsea restaurant, tactfully chosen in an area well away from the kind of places Olivia used to frequent with Bruce. Soon Lee and Olivia were a couple madly in love and inseparable.

Lee's background could hardly have been more different from her former boyfriend Bruce Welch's. Lee had enjoyed a privileged upbringing with a father who had become wealthy through owning shops, flats and other property in London. As a lad, he was sent to good schools to gain a decent education, but at fifteen, with a thirst for adventure, Lee decided to leave school to see something of the world. He spent time on a kibbutz in Israel before travelling around Africa and ending up getting a job as a lifeguard in Durban in South Africa.

On returning to England, determined to be his own boss, he launched a shoe company with a brother and business boomed in highly lucrative fashion when he began importing cowboy boots into Europe. Lee's business acumen would eventually prove a major asset to Olivia's progress as a singer in America.

Lee arrived in Olivia's life just at a time when her singing career was taking off in a major way, particularly in the USA. By the time the couple were due to spend their first Christmas together, 'Let Me Be There' was becoming a huge hit in America. They decided to fly over to spend Christmas in Miami, where they met up with singer Helen Reddy and her then husband Jeff Wald.

Helen and Olivia had a natural affinity. They were both from Melbourne and, like Olivia, Helen had earned her big break as a singer through a talent contest sponsored by an Australian television station. She beat 1,358 contestants to win the prize of a trip to New York, $400 cash and an audition with Mercury Records. Like Olivia's start in London, Helen sang where she could, even at a veterans' hospital for a fee of $25. But it all paid off when she topped the US charts in 1972 with 'I Am Woman' and went on to become a major singing star, astutely managed by her husband Jeff Wald.

Jeff had been a talent agent for the powerful William Morris agency and therefore had a firm grasp of the way singers were groomed for stardom in the US and the steps that needed to be taken to achieve it. An engaging and persuasive man, Wald told Olivia that if she was serious about building upon the chart success of 'Let Me Be There' and her other hits in the US, then it was imperative she base herself in America. By moving to America she would be on the spot and readily available for guest TV appearances, concerts, chat shows, personal appearances and radio interviews to promote her records. America's entertainment industry dwarfed Britain's, he pointed out, and Olivia would be crazy not to make the transition to cash in on the way America was now embracing her records.

Wald's reasoning made sense. As Cliff Richard had already discovered to his dismay, out of sight frequently meant out of mind for English stars as far as the American public were concerned. For all his many UK hits, Cliff was still a little-known artiste in the United States. Had he chosen to make a concerted effort to spend six months at a time in America, Cliff might well have achieved his dearest wish of establishing himself in the land that gave the world rock 'n' roll.

After Christmas, Olivia flew back to England with major decisions to make. Any long-term uprooting to America would have to wait at least until the spring of 1974 because she had been nominated by the BBC as the UK's contestant for the Eurovision Song Contest, to be held in mid-April. That was one commitment she simply could not break. She was also intent on buying herself a house in London, and just before the Eurovision contest she purchased a detached three-bedroom house in Hampstead, north London, with a large garden.

Ever since its inception, the UK has enjoyed a love–hate relationship with the Eurovision Song Contest. Launched in 1956 to find a song for Europe, the competition was won in its inaugural year by Switzerland with 'Refrains'. It

was a fitting title as the UK, or *Royaume-Uni* as the UK
was to become known annually at the contest, actually
refrained from entering.

Over the years the contest has gone on to give the world
such memorable lyrical masterpieces as songs entitled
'Ding Ding A Dong', 'A-Ba-Ni-Ba', 'La La La' and the UK's
own 'Boom Bang-A-Bang', which, incredibly, spurred Lulu
to a shared winner's spot in 1969. Eurovision has always
attracted ridicule on many counts: its poor quality of songwriting, Norway's propensity for garnering '*nul points*', its
oddball, often strangely garbed performers singing utterly
unfathomable words for international juries, and voting
that has frequently proved utterly illogical or blatantly
tactical politically.

But despite the Eurovision Song Contest being regarded
in some quarters as a joke, Olivia's manager Peter Gormley
recognised that the contest could be a wonderful international showcase for an artiste of real talent and worth.
Despite the stigma attached to it, the programme always
pulled in a huge TV audience in Britain, and Gormley had
had no hesitation in putting Cliff Richard forward to sing
for the UK twice in previous years.

In 1973, Cliff had come third in the contest with a song
called 'Power To All Our Friends' and he was seen performing
the song by a TV audience of more than three hundred million
in thirty-two countries. Even though Cliff didn't win, massive
record sales in a dozen different countries was the end result.
Gormley hoped it would be the same for Olivia at the concert
in 1974, to be held in Brighton on the Sussex coast, after she
was selected by the BBC.

As in previous years, the nation's songwriters were
invited to submit their offerings and a BBC panel whittled
the four hundred entries down to a final half-dozen. The

pre-selection process then involved Olivia performing a different song each week for six weeks on Jimmy Savile's *Clunk Click* TV show. The nation was finally invited to vote for the song Olivia would take forward into the Eurovision Song Contest itself.

Each week Olivia was allowed to choose a different outfit to wear for each song – trouser suits in satin, jersey and crepe for the faster numbers, and dresses, two in jersey and one in organza, for the ballads. Her personal song favourite was a ballad called 'Angel Eyes' and she was secretly hoping it would win the public's vote. Instead, a singalong, oompah-oompah song called 'Long Live Love' about the Salvation Army band was the one the nation plumped for. Disappointingly for Olivia, 'Angel Eyes' was beaten into second place by some 7,000 votes.

Putting her heart and soul into a song she didn't much care for was never going to be easy. But Olivia gave a decent enough performance on the night of 16 April at Brighton's Dome Theatre. She looked pretty enough, too, in a long, flowing baby-blue dress, but she appeared somewhat old-fashioned compared with the two sexily dressed girls who fronted an unknown Swedish group – they were called Abba, and went on to win. Olivia had studied Abba in rehearsals and had no doubt they would emerge as winners: 'Of course they were going to win,' she said. 'Their song was so different and so terrific and they were so bright and alive.'

Abba's colourful and joyful rendering of 'Waterloo' romped home as the 1974 song for Europe and Olivia tied for fourth place. The press tried to make out that Olivia had snubbed the official BBC after-party and that she was sobbing over her failure to win – neither of which was true. She was certainly disappointed not to have won but honest enough to admit: 'I was never really happy with the song I had to sing. It's not the one I'd have chosen. I'd have preferred a nice ballad.'

By making no secret of her lukewarm feelings towards 'Long Live Love', Olivia came in for a good deal of resentment and criticism from the press and the British public. Record sales indicated, however, that she had a valid point. Despite choosing 'Long Live Love' as the UK's entry, the nation didn't back up its choice of song for Europe by rushing out to buy the record. 'Long Live Love' managed to finish up no higher than number eleven in the UK charts, hardly the runaway hit that Eurovision habitually produced as a matter of course for the UK's contestant. A song about the Sally Annie band may not have provided Olivia with the success she hoped for, but she never forgot the organisation's good work. Twenty-five years later she recorded the carol 'The First Noel' for a CD called *Spirit of Christmas*, whose profits went to the Salvation Army.

* * *

With the certainty of hindsight, Olivia's losing out to Abba was a blessing in disguise. If she had won the Eurovision Song Contest, she might have concentrated on furthering her career in Europe rather than in America, which was beginning to beckon ever more warmly and invitingly.

One month after Eurovision, Olivia found herself with a Top Five US hit on her hands with John Rostill's composition 'If You Love Me (Let Me Know)'. It was her highest Stateside chart position to date, and when she was flown to America to make a guest TV appearance on a Dean Martin show, Olivia had a glimpse of what could lie in store for her on the other side of the Atlantic.

This latest US chart success now posed her a difficult dilemma. It came at a time when she had just acquired a new lover in Lee, who was London-based, and a new house to go home to in the capital, and yet the lure of America was becoming impossible to ignore. One major concern for Olivia when she considered any move to America was who would manage her career in the US. Peter Gormley had guided her successfully thus far in England. But he was also skilfully handling Cliff Richard's career from his London office, and it was inconceivable that he would switch his management operation base across the Atlantic just to launch a lesser artiste in a country whose entertainment scene he was much less familiar with.

It was Lee Kramer who came up with the answer. He realised that if Olivia went off to America he would quite probably lose her – unless he went with her. He was fully pre- pared to do just that and, since he was now the person in Olivia's life who loved and cared about her most and was with her all the time, he proposed that he should not only accompany her but become her manager in the USA as well.

News of a shoal of attractive offers from America prompted by the huge sales of 'If You Love Me (Let Me Know)' persuaded Olivia that she must wait no longer. 'I remember Helen Reddy saying, "You've really got to do it,"' she said. 'I decided to go. It's every entertainer's dream to make it in America, I've no doubts about that.

'When I decided Helen and Jeff were right, I briefly moved into the Sunset Marquis hotel in West Hollywood. When I arrived to check in there were a dozen red roses waiting at the desk for me. They were from Glenn Frey [of the Eagles]. The card said: "Welcome to America." I wasn't even sure who the Eagles were but I've always had a soft spot for Glenn because it was such a nice thing for him to do.'

Olivia's less than happy Eurovision experience and the British perception that she was not much more than 'that girl on the Cliff Richard show' were contributing factors in her decision. In the UK she lacked credibility, and it was not lost on Olivia that America's record-buyers seemed much more receptive to her than their British counterparts.

'Let Me Be There', for example, was released twice in England but still failed to interest the public, whereas Americans bought the record in huge numbers. 'They took to me,' Olivia explained, and her new single 'I Honestly Love You' proved the point and vindicated her decision to concentrate on establishing herself more fully in the States. A lovely ballad written by Australian Peter Allen and American Jeff Barry, 'I Honestly Love You' shot to number one in the US charts in August 1974 but didn't even make the Top Twenty in England.

Lady Luck was perching on Olivia's shoulder when she recorded 'I Honestly Love You'. The song came to her by a circuitous route; Peter Allen had originally intended to record it himself. That he didn't do so until after Olivia had a hit with it was down to Jeff Barry, a songwriter who had written number-one hits for artistes ranging from The Archies to Manfred Mann to The Dixiecups. Barry was scheduled to produce Allen's new LP but, when he deemed that the material to hand lacked any obvious hit, he felt he had to come up with one himself.

'I had this song called "I Honestly Love You" that I thought would be great for a man to sing,' said Barry. 'So Peter and I wrote the song and made a demo. Then someone at the publishing office was going to see Olivia with new material and she loved it. She loved it so much she wanted to record the song. So we decided to let her cut it instead of Peter. No one thought it was going to be a single. The label didn't want to put it out, but radio demanded it.'

Admitting to her good fortune, Olivia said: 'I flipped out when I heard it. But I was terrified that I would find out it had already been done.' As Jeff Barry predicted, once radio stations seized upon it as the standout track of Olivia's album *If You Love Me Let Me Know*, demand from listeners ensured her US label MCA issued it as single. Peter Allen didn't get around to recording 'I Honestly Love You' until several years after it had given Olivia her first number-one hit in America.

Olivia watched with mounting excitement as 'I Honestly Love You' moved up the charts and eventually reached the top spot. From this lofty position she could look down and see, two places below her in the charts, one of her original singing idols from her schooldays: Dionne Warwick. To crown a memorable 1974, soon afterwards her album *If You Love Me Let Me Know* climbed to number one in the US LP charts. Olivia had to pinch herself to make sure she wasn't dreaming.

Particularly pleasing for Olivia was the knowledge that America had seemingly taken to her because of her voice rather than her looks. The Americans knew little of her and had seen even less and yet she was top of the charts. In England she had always had the feeling that her looks had been a major contribution towards her success. 'If I were less attractive, maybe they would pay more attention to my talent,' she was stung into saying of her detractors. 'They always think you're playing on your looks. It's just how I was made. But that old all-beauty-and-no-brains thing is still in existence.'

To build on this welcome from America's record-buying public, concert appearances were needed and Lee and

Olivia decided it would be best for her to play small venues and colleges first in order to gain a foothold. With John Farrar she flew to the US just four days before her first concert to meet the band who would back her. 'I was absolutely terrified because I'd never worked in the States before,' Olivia remembers.

In Minneapolis Olivia worked solidly with her hired musicians for two days of rehearsals but she was unhappy with the results and decided she had no option but to fire them. It was a brave move under the circumstances, and it was only on the night before her first concert that she was able to hire a replacement band. Together they rehearsed for six hours, starting at eight in the evening and finishing at two in the morning, before Olivia was satisfied that together they could put on a credible show the following night.

Next day Olivia and the band piled into a tour bus at 10am to head for the gymnasium in north Dakota where she would appear live in the US for the first time. In England Olivia had always favoured wearing dresses at her concerts, but for a college gig in a gymnasium she decided to put on jeans. As ever, Olivia was gripped by pre-concert nerves, but the tension was eased when the MC urged the audience to give the singer from England an extra warm welcome as it was her first-ever US gig. 'And the whole audience stood up and cheered,' Olivia recalls. Thus began an American love affair with Olivia Newton-John that has never waned.

Olivia's first three-week low-key tour of universities and colleges took place around the time she registered her first massive US hit 'I Honestly Love You'. But the warm reaction gave her a pleasing taster of what she might accomplish on American soil. With successful record releases at regular intervals, Olivia was gradually able to build up her live appearances in carefully chosen venues.

Fortunately The Oneness, the band of all-American musicians from Minneapolis and Minnesota she had recruited, proved to be a versatile bunch. They essentially favoured heavy jazz and wrote their own material in the Chick Corea vein, but they were talented enough to comfortably double up on different instruments to provide the appropriate backing for Olivia's repertoire, which varied from country rock numbers to ballads.

Olivia travelled with the band in a customised air-conditioned bus fitted with stereo and television, and her only complaint about going on the road in America was that she never stopped long enough in any one town to see something of it.

Olivia progressed to the concert circuit of hotel venues where she performed in towns like Reno, Lake Tahoe, Miami and, for the first time, in Las Vegas, where she was the support act for Charlie Rich. Charlie was a country music star best known in the UK for his 1974 smash hit 'The Most Beautiful Girl', which also reached number one on the national pop charts in America. Unlike the more stuffy country music traditionalists, who were beginning to question Olivia's authenticity as a country singer, Charlie was impressed enough by her to buy Olivia a beautiful heart-shaped pendant with an opal, Olivia's birthstone, in the centre as a mark of his appreciation.

* * *

By the middle of 1975, Olivia had notched up five Top Ten hits in a row in the US. Her breakthrough came in December 1973 when 'Let Me Be There' peaked at number six in the singles chart, and six months later she went one better with 'If You Love Me (Let Me Know)'.

Two number ones followed with 'I Honestly Love You', and 'Have You Never Been Mellow', and her next single 'Please Mister Please' reached number three. She was enjoying a remarkable run of chart success.

While hit singles helped to establish Olivia, confirmation of her true popularity came with the warmth with which her albums were received in America. At a time when teenagers were leaning towards progessive rock, heavy metal, and long, drawn-out guitar solos, Olivia's soft, clear vocal delivery proved most appealing to more mature American record-buyers, particularly when she put a new slant on hits by other established singers and songwriters.

Shrewdly guided first by Bruce Welch and then by John Farrar in her choice of melodic material, Olivia's LPs included a varied selection of tuneful folk and country ballads – Tom Rush's 'No Regrets', Chip Taylor's 'Angel Of The Morning', Beatle George Harrison's 'Behind That Locked Door' and 'If' by David Gates. Olivia was also not averse to throwing in the odd surprise – on her album *Clearly Love* she included her own distinctive version of 'Summertime Blues' by America's fifties rocker Eddie Cochran. Another adventurous choice was her version of The Beach Boys' 'God Only Knows' on the LP *Long Live Love*.

As a hugely popular recording artiste, Olivia was now a solo star who warranted elevation to headline status. Lee Kramer was able to field a host of money-spinning offers for his girlfriend and eventually she was booked into the Riviera Hotel in Las Vegas for a season.

Backed by an orchestra and her own six-piece rhythm section, Olivia played to packed houses and to critical acclaim for a show that featured a carefully balanced selection of numbers. Her set list included a Beatles song 'Good Day Sunshine', her version of the big Hollies hit 'The Air That I Breathe', and the nostalgic 'As Time Goes By', in addition to her own string of hits.

'She's well on her way to being the biggest hit of the year among first-time headliners,' said Dennis Hunt in his review for the *Los Angeles Times*. The critic went on to note the response from male punters going wild for her in the front rows: 'If the men in the audience get any more enthusiastic than they did towards the end of one of Newton-John's midnight shows last week, the Riviera is going to have to place some security guards in front of the stage.'

In 1978 Olivia was to return to the Versailles Room at the Riviera Hotel, by which time she was even bigger star thanks to *Grease*. And there was pandemonium one night when, just as she was winding up her act, a man jumped up on stage and started jiving away. It was John Travolta, and the crowd went wild as Olivia and John boogied their way through their massive international hit 'You're The One That I Want', and then followed this up by duetting on another *Grease* favourite, 'Summer Nights'.

By his own admission, Lee Kramer found himself out of his depth when he first took charge of Olivia's career in America. He was still just twenty-one, knew nothing of showbusiness and confessed he was in turmoil for the first year he was at the helm. But he was willing to learn fast – and he knew he had to if his relationship with Olivia, both on a professional and personal level, was to survive.

The opportunity to cash in on Olivia's astonishing and largely unexpected chart success was wide open, and Lee had to plan a productive course that would be acceptable to them both. Inevitably American showbiz sharks were circling the hottest new female singer to emerge in years, hoping to grab a piece of the action. Some seemed to delight in trying to stir up trouble between the couple. Olivia's record success was propelling her into the big money league and Lee had to endure jealousy, contempt and even ridicule – how could a shoe importer with no prior knowledge of showbusiness possibly successfully manage the career of a singer who was starting to sell millions of records and be in huge demand as a concert attraction?

Nevertheless, Olivia and Lee's relationship flourished, with sporadic hiccups. It was not helped in its early stages by Lee Kramer's family being unimpressed by his romancing a girl who was in showbusiness. It was unsettling for Olivia, and it was a long time before Lee was able to persuade his father even to meet his girlfriend, let alone get to know her.

In America, the couple were each in their own way under pressure to succeed. 'It's very difficult for a guy to get involved in my career,' Olivia explained to one interviewer. 'The guys in my life have had their own thing, but they can't help but get involved in what I do because it consumes so much of my time.

'It takes a strong man to take second place. It's Mr Newton-John a lot of the time. They have to have a good sense of themselves to take it. A lot of men are frightened by me, by what I represent and my success. It's very difficult for me to have a relationship. But it's very important for me to know one person and to trust one person.'

Lee had enough business acumen and drive to succeed in what were initially unfamiliar surroundings. But his great strength was that nobody loved and cared for Olivia more than he did, and his duties in caring for her were many and varied, not least ensuring her safety. An intruder once managed to get into Lee's office and, while maniacally shouting Olivia's name, he proceeded to pour petrol all over the floor and prepared to set light to it.

On another occasion, just before one of Olivia's concerts, Lee discovered a letter on her dressing table containing a threat to her life. Cranks and over-zealous fans are an occupational hazard for famous singers. Lee told *Crawdaddy* magazine that as a general rule he tried to stop mail reaching Olivia before a show, even if it meant having to open up personal letters. It was a necessary procedure for safety and peace of mind. 'Yet one also doesn't like keeping anything from artists – they have to deal with life and whatever goes on in their world,' said Lee. In this instance, it was felt Olivia had to be informed of the danger. Fortunately the man who had written the menacing letter had also chosen to write down the number of the row he was sitting in, and Lee was able to locate him and have him taken out by security and dealt with.

Olivia's introduction to California had been less than friendly. During her first night in Los Angeles, at the Westwood Marquee hotel, she heard gunshots in the street below. But she was soon able to rent a house in Trancas, around half an hour from Malibu, an area much favoured by Hollywood stars. Eventually the financial rewards accruing from her massive record sales enabled Olivia to splash out $400,000 on a rambling ranch-style house set in four acres in the Malibu mountains, which offered glimpses of the Pacific Ocean. There she lost no time in surrounding herself with the kind of large menagerie of pets she had always dreamed about, including five horses, an Irish setter, a cat and three Great Danes, one of whom she had taken pity on after it was discovered locked in a house where it had spent a week without food or water.

Olivia liked to exercise and groom the horses herself and be involved with the animals as much as possible. But eventually she found it necessary to hire a girl to come in six days a week to look after the horses. It was no surprise when the singer's accountant pointed out to his client that she was spending more money on caring for her animals than on anything else. Olivia felt it was worth it. Most mornings, sometimes even before dawn, she could be found running along the beach with her dogs bounding along beside her, and whenever she was home she tried to find time to ride out for a couple of hours in the hills behind her house. Her superstar status even meant that when she was doing shows in Las Vegas, she could lease a jet to fly back home to her Malibu base each day to go riding.

While Olivia was finding personal contentment in her new surroundings, her fortunes as a singer and recording artist continued to soar. America's top three music publications, *Billboard*, *Record Mirror* and *Cash Box*, all listed her as the best-selling female album artist of 1975. She had scaled a peak she had never dreamed possible.

7

Country Matters

'We don't want somebody out of another field coming in here and taking away what we've worked so hard for'

Country singer Johnny Paycheck after Olivia was voted Female Vocalist Of The Year, 1974, by the Country Music Association

Ever since the mid-1950s, Nashville, Tennessee has been the home of country music, and it's a town that prides itself on being one of the friendliest in the United States.

The first million-selling country song was released as long ago as 1927, and Nashville's Country Music Hall of Fame proudly projects the down-home, folksy, musical image of real country music: often impoverished, rurally raised musicians sitting on the back porch guitar-picking and singing sad songs, surrounded by family members who are steeped in the traditions of country living and will never forget their humble roots or battling through the hard times.

Nashville has always insisted country music is a distinctly American art form and it prefers its country music heroes and heroines, such as Hank Williams, Loretta Lynn and Dolly Parton, to have experienced the rough, harsher side of life before finding success and fame. The legendary Hank was born with a spine defect which was aggravated when he was thrown from a horse at the age of seventeen, and he died a lonely death from heart failure at the desperately young age of twenty-nine in the back of a taxi, with only a bottle of whisky for company, on the way to a gig. Dolly Parton is one of twelve children born to farmers who were so poor they had to pay the doctor in corn meal to attend the birth of their fourth child. Loretta Lynn, a one-quarter Cherokee coal-miner's daughter, was raised in a shack during the Depression and married a serviceman at the age of thirteen.

With such struggles chronicled for everyone in Nashville's Country Music Hall of Fame, it's no wonder that the town's traditionalists were suspicious of Olivia Newton-John when she burst on to their music scene, not from the Appalachian mountains but from Melbourne via Wales, Cambridge and a smart house in London. 'Appalachia? I've never heard of it,' Olivia would respond to early interviewers quizzing her about her roots. 'I sing easy listening, middle-of-the-road music . . . I sing new songs, old songs, and country songs. I didn't think I would be considered a country singer. I was just hoping for a hit record, no matter what it was.'

Nashville had been given an early taste of Olivia the country singer when a well-known local DJ called Ralph Emery had given her version of 'If Not For You' an airing on his WSM show. But if the folks in Tennessee were a little surprised to find Olivia now being hailed as a country artiste, no one was more amazed than Olivia herself. 'I didn't realise I was a country singer,' she said, 'until I got a phone call from my publisher in America. He called me up one day and said: "You know you have a country and western hit and you should really come over here." I didn't know what that was. In the UK, the charts were all the same, but I discovered there was a whole new world of country music.'

The first sounds of discontent from Nashville diehards about Olivia's C-and-W credentials were heard when she won a Grammy award for the Best Country Vocal Performance, Female, for 'Let Me Be There' in 1973. The Grammys are music's equivalent of the Oscars. For Olivia to win the 1973 award over Nashville's established female stars, women like Loretta Lynn, Dolly Parton, Tammy Wynette and Lynn Anderson, was an extraordinary and unexpected triumph.

Her success was vindication for MCA, Olivia's US record company, who deliberately marketed 'Let Me Be There' as a country-flavoured record. Advertisements for the single in the trade press featured Olivia, photographed very simply and sporting a sunny smile, in a wood. Above it, the blurb proclaimed: 'Olivia Newton-John lives in the country in England and sings for the country in America and is as pretty as her newest single.'

The purists could hardly disagree with Olivia's being hailed as pretty as John Rostill's melody that had won her the award, but it rankled with them that she had come to prominence in America's country music circles via England by way of Australia and that she had never in her life strummed a guitar in an American honky-tonk bar or set foot in a Nashville recording studio, much less the Grand Ole Opry.

'It's probably the first time an English person won an award over Nashville people,' Olivia innocently acknowledged on receiving her Grammy award, little realising that there was deep consternation in some quarters over what she intended as a light-hearted rather than a loaded observation. The significance of such a truthfully accurate remark was too much to stomach for some country traditionalists. And yet, by pipping Nashville's finest, the reality was that Olivia had nothing to apologise for.

While country music may be regarded in some circles as a distinctly American art form, aficionado of the genre Peter Doggett says, in his introduction to *The Guinness Who's Who Of Country Music*: 'Like the nation which spawned it, country music is deep and wide. It can encompass the hillbilly laments of Hank Williams, the honeyed velvet tones of Jim Reeves, the feminism of k.d. lang, the cowboy ballads of Gene Autrey, the mountain music of Bill Monroe, the energetic showmanship of Garth Brooks, the outlaw imagery of Waylon Jennings, the honky tonk anthems of Lefty Frizzell, the traditional Irish songs of Daniel O'Donnell and the infectious mimicry of The Rolling Stones.'

MCA clearly had no doubts about Olivia's credentials as a country star. And in August 1974, just when she was topping the US charts with 'I Honestly Love You', a special luncheon was held in her honour in Nashville by MCA's vice-president Owen Bradley. It gave Olivia the chance to explain that she had rescheduled a stateside concert tour to make a stopover in Nashville specifically to show her gratitude to the many people there who had fostered her country music success.

'In Tennessee they told me that unless you're born and bred in Nashville, it's usually impossible to be accepted as a country artist and that I should realise how lucky I was,' she said. 'Country fans are much more loyal than pop fans.'

The Nashville visit was a genuine gesture of thanks by Olivia, but it didn't entirely stop the debate as to whether she qualified as a true country singer. Which explains, in its own way, several derogatory stories about Olivia that did the rounds of Music Town thanks to mischief makers: how, upon hearing a record by Hank Williams for the first time, she had allegedly expressed a desire to meet him (Hank died in 1953); and how, when informed she had a country hit on her hands with 'Let Me Be There', she had to ask for an explanation of what country music really was.

She was by no means the first singer to blur the boundaries between country and pop. But the issue came to a head in startling fashion when the Country Music Association (CMA) controversially voted Olivia the 1974 Female Vocalist of the Year. The other nominees included Loretta Lynn, Dolly Parton, Anne Murray and Tanya Tucker, four popular, bona fide, country music queens, and there were howls of protest about Olivia's win from various sections of the Nashville music fraternity and from diehard country fans alike.

As with her Grammy award, it was hardly Olivia's fault she had won. The annual CMA awards were then, as now, decided by their members, who include singers, musicians, record company officials, promoters, agents and broadcasters. And the awards themselves are given not to honour long-term service to the genre but to acknowledge the previous year's most popular country songs and singers.

By this yardstick Olivia was a worthy winner and yet, despite Nashville heavyweight Loretta Lynn, who also won an award that year, declaring she was glad someone new had come along, Olivia's award still caused discontent and uproar. 'Some of them weren't too thrilled about this impostor, this outsider, this Australian person from England,' Olivia said with understatement. 'They couldn't quite figure me out.'

The Tennessean, the state's primary daily newspaper, firmly stuck the knife in by declaring that Olivia couldn't drawl 'with a mouthful of biscuits'. Another critic called

her 'as country as a kangaroo'. The basic objection was
that Olivia lacked the traditional roots of a country singer.
The purists felt she hadn't paid her hillbilly dues and they
were horrified that she had scooped prestigious awards for
records that bore little resemblance to the traditions of
Hank Williams or Bill Monroe. Olivia's pop-flavoured hits
had no place in country music, the traditionalists argued;
they cited country stalwart Waylon Jennings, who
famously said: 'I couldn't go pop with a mouthful of fire-
crackers.'

Olivia wasn't, in fact, at the CMA awards ceremony
when she was named Female Vocalist of the Year. She was
back in England for some television performances and had
pre-taped an acceptance speech in case she won. She was
largely oblivious to all the fuss that ensued and only
learned about the controversy much later on. She therefore
had no chance to speak up for herself when the commotion
was at its height.

The debate over Olivia's country qualifications raged so
heatedly in Nashville's tree-lined streets, known as Music
Row, that it led to a serious split among the members of the
Country Music Association, an organisation that had been
solidly united since its formation in 1957. A few days after
the announcement of Olivia's contentious award, an angry
protest group of singers, musicians, songwriters and studio
officials gathered at the home of traditional country music
greats Jack Jones and Tammy Wynette, then Nashville's
most celebrated married couple, to determine what to do
about Olivia and other pop-influenced songs muscling in
on their country territory.

Among the angry protesters pledging their solidarity
were more than twenty leading country singers, including
Dolly Parton, Johnny Paycheck, Porter Wagoner, Jim Ed

Brown, Dottie West, Bill Anderson, Faron Young, Mel Tillis, Conway Twitty and Barbara Mandrell, established performers all. Johnny Paycheck, born Donald Eugene Lytle, and a man for whom trouble was a close companion for much of his life, summed up the injustices they all felt by saying of Olivia: 'We don't want somebody out of another field coming in here and taking away what we've worked so hard for.'

The outcome of the meeting at George and Tammy's home was the formation of a breakaway country solidarity movement, called the Association of Country Entertainers (ACE), dedicated to 'preserving and recognising the basic and traditional country singers'. ACE's aim was to challenge the establishment's intention to modernise the country music industry, and the new organisation also demanded valid representation of traditional artistes on the CMA's board of directors and on the playlists of country radio stations.

Such an outcry could have done irreparable harm to Olivia's standing in America, but the breakaway group soon found themselves overtaken by changing trends, popular opinion and commercial values. ACE turned out to be short-lived, and eventually the group broke up when founding members such as Dolly Parton went off to Hollywood to become movie stars. 'I'm not gonna leave the country,' Dolly assured her fans. 'I'd just like to take it with me wherever I go.'

Olivia was understandably hurt when she eventually found out about the furore she had unwittingly caused. She always wanted to do the right thing and was upset that she was perceived as a Nashville transgressor. 'I feel like I was a scapegoat in the whole thing for some angry local artistes who weren't winning any awards,' she said. 'I've never claimed to be a country singer. To call yourself that, you'd have to be born into that background. I simply love country music and its straightforwardness. And since the records have also sold well outside the country audience, it seems to me that we're broadening the acceptance for country music.'

Olivia stressed: 'I wasn't out to do anybody out of an award. I didn't put myself up for it.' She also pointed out that popular music in the UK was not categorised as either pop or country in the way it is in America. All she had done was simply set out to make the best records she could.

'It's all music,' she said. 'Country music has a style and I love it for its simplicity. But I also believe you can't put a passport on music. It doesn't belong to one section of the country. Music is international. The notes, the sounds, belong to anyone who can sing them.'

Dolly Parton later reproached herself for initially aligning with the traditionalists against Olivia and was thoughtful enough to reassure her that the whole issue had been blown way out of proportion. She encouraged her to ignore all the fuss, and in 1977 Dolly was only too happy to accept Olivia's eighth American Music Award on behalf of her absent fellow songstress. 'Dolly and Loretta Lynn stood up for me, which I've forever been grateful for,' said Olivia, who recorded a cover version of Dolly's composition 'Jolene' on her 1976 album *Come On Over* as a way of thanking her.

Interestingly, it was Dolly's lesser-known sister Stella, the sixth of the twelve children of the struggling Parton family from Locust Ridge, Tennessee, who mounted the most conspicuous counter-offensive on Olivia's behalf. Stella, a country singer like Dolly but not a big country star, was so incensed at Olivia's castigation by the Nashville protesters that she wrote, recorded and released a special song in Olivia's defence. 'I was embarrassed for all my country cousins and sisters here in town,' explained Stella, 'so I wrote the song "Ode to Olivia".' The lyrics exposed the hypocrisy of other countries welcoming American country singers while America failed to offer a similarly warm welcome for Olivia's country songs.

In hindsight, the fuss was all much ado about nothing by a few. Olivia persevered by opening shows for Charlie Rich, voted the CMA's Entertainer of the Year in 1974, and by playing country fairs where the reception she was given was never less than enthusiastic. The fans showed they didn't care about her lack of bona fide, dues-payin' country roots by buying her records and by snapping up tickets to see her live. They went in such numbers to see Olivia perform at the Dixie National Livestock Show 6 Rodeo in Jackson in early1974 that the all-time attendance record was comfortably broken.

In strict terminology, a steel guitar – an electronic instrument with pedals and strings – is what officially puts the twang into a 'country' song. By that criterion, Olivia's next two singles, 'I Honestly Love You' and 'Have You Never Been Mellow', were not officially 'country'. But by sending both records to number one in the national US singles charts as well as high into the country charts, the fans showed they were none too bothered about categorisation, nor by the slight Aussie accent they could detect when they heard her speak.

Olivia even had the courage to perform live in Nashville, although her concert was staged at the Municipal Auditorium and not the Grand Ole Opry. Any remaining resentment was dispelled when she chose to go to Nashville to record in America for the first time. 'We actually started recording in Los Angeles but it was an uncomfortable scene,' she said at a local press conference. 'My producer and I were only going to do a single at first but somewhere between LA and Nashville, we found three great songs to go with the four we already had. So the session turned into an album.'

The LP *Don't Stop Believin'* was released in 1976 and produced a number-33 single with its title track. It earned Olivia a gold disc, her sixth in succession, and spurred ABC-TV to realise her dream of having her own TV special. Woven into the show's song and dance format on 17 November 1976 were several big guest stars of the day, including the actor Elliott Gould, TV's Six Million Dollar Man Lee Majors, Ron Howard and Tom Bosley from the hit television sit-com *Happy Days*, and Lynda Carter, TV's Wonder Woman.

It's a fine line between pop and country and not too many country singers have managed to become crossover stars with any consistency. Once the CMA row had subsided, it was Olivia, with John Denver hot on her heels, who managed it with ease. 'If You Love Me (Let Me Know)' was a number-two hit in America's country chart as well as reaching number five in the national singles chart. 'I Honestly Love You' was a number-six country hit and a national chart-topper. 'Have You Never Been Mellow' reached number three in the country charts and also became the nation's number-one single. 'A lot of people are listening to country music because of me,' Olivia was able to say, and even the Nashville hardliners had to agree.

Olivia had opened the door for a brand new audience into country music and the likes of John Denver were quick to follow through it. It was Olivia's and MCA's good fortune that both country and pop music lovers continued to buy her records in vast quantities and that her concerts attracted audiences who appreciated her soft country vocals as much as her sugar-coated, slicker-sounding hits.

'When I branched out, I found that country people were extremely loyal and stayed with me when my songs weren't country,' Olivia reflected.

And to country music journalists quizzing her about the fuss she had caused, Olivia countered: 'I think it was understandable in a way. Someone new comes along who isn't even American and steals an award that was theirs and it gets up their noses a bit. But music has to expand. You can't keep it in a bag.

'I felt like I was a scapegoat. I really think now they have to admit it's been beneficial to them. They're getting a pop audience they never had before. A lot of people are listening to country music because of me. You don't have to live in Nashville to sing or like country music.'

Still, not everyone was entirely happy at the country-pop crossover part-pioneered by Olivia. At the 1975 CMA awards, Charlie Rich, 1974's Entertainer of the Year, was entrusted with the task of announcing the name of the new winner of the CMA's top award. Charlie, who had seemingly been enjoying some refreshments backstage prior to his appearance, proceeded to pull out his Zippo lighter and, with a triumphantly mischievous smile playing on his lips, set light to the card bearing the name of 1975's Entertainer of the Year . . . John Denver.

8

Rama-Lama-Ding-Dong

*'There was only one person on this planet who could be
Sandy and I was hell-bent to get her in the movie'*

John Travolta

In the early 1970s, America was awash with nostalgia for the
1950s. On television, 1950s-era shows like *Happy Days* and
Laverne And Shirley had captured the mood of the age, pulling
in huge audiences. In the pop charts, a reissue of 'Heartbreak
Hotel', Elvis Presley's first hit in 1956, made the Top Ten in
1971, and the following year Elvis was even hotter, with
'Burning Love' hitting the top spot. Don McLean also reached
number one in 1971 with 'American Pie', a song about 'the
day the music died' – a reference to 3 February 1959, when
Buddy Holly was killed in a plane crash – and Elton John in
'Crocodile Rock' professed to millions of record buyers what
fun he'd had 'when rock was young'.

Further 'fifties' fever was fanned when Elvis Presley's
birthplace, a two-room house in Tupelo, Mississippi, was
opened for the first time to inquisitive fans, who formed
long queues. And in 1972 even New York City's New
School for Social Research jumped on the bandwagon by
becoming one of the first institutions, if not the first, to
offer a course on rock 'n' roll music.

That same year, 1972, a new stage musical called *Grease*,
written by two semi-pro American actors, Jim Jacobs and

Warren Casey, first found a home for itself at the off-Broadway Eden Theatre in New York. Essentially an amiable 'period' musical, *Grease* turned out to be a vibrant, gritty but fun, rocking 1950s comedy. With a satirical and highly entertaining score, it took an irreverent look at the era's fashions, music and morals, which it gently and affectionately mocked with numbers like 'Look at me, I'm Sandra Dee/ Lousy with virginity'.

Grease the stage show took excited audiences, and not a few approving critics, back to the rock 'n' roll days of the 1950s when bored, sexually frustrated teenagers went around in gangs with names like the Pink Ladies and the Burger Palace Boys. At a reunion of the class of 1959, the assembled group relive the days when Danny Zuko and Sandy Dumbrowski unexpectedly meet up again at Rydell High School after an innocent summer romance. At first they appear an unlikely couple – Danny with his tough, macho image and Sandy so prim, proper and virginal, very different from Betty Rizzo, the hard-bitten member of the Pink Ladies. However, by the end of the piece, Sandy changes her attitude and dons leather jacket and tight pants, adopting the uniform of a greaser's steady girl and landing her man, Danny.

The stage production had obvious appeal to teens as well as a carefully built-in attraction to older age groups rejoicing in the memories of their own college days, and it caught on, in the words of one of its songs, like 'greased lightning'. It was so popular that it went on to become one of the longest-running shows in Broadway history. By the time the final curtain came down on its six-year run on 13 April 1980, *Grease* had notched up an impressive 3,388 performances, a Broadway record that stood until it was overtaken by *A Chorus Line*.

The stage success of *Grease* earned a fortune for its co-writers Jacobs and Casey, who had first met in Chicago through their mutual interest in amateur dramatics. Jim Jacobs played guitar and sang with rock groups in his native Chicago before becoming involved with a local theatre group, The Chicago Stage Guild. It was there, in 1963, he met Warren Casey, who had moved from New York to the windy city armed with a fine arts degree and a similar interest in becoming involved in the local theatre scene.

In 1970 Casey was fired from his job as a lingerie salesman and bought himself a typewriter in preparation for a new job he was taking as an advertising copywriter. It was the best purchase he ever made.

With Jacobs drawing on his experiences as a 'greaser' in 1950s Chicago, the duo tapped out a play with music satirising the dress, manners, morals and the doo-wop music of teenagers in the rock 'n' roll era. Little did the co-writers know they were creating a phenomenon.

Jacobs remembers that the germ of the idea for *Grease* came to him during an after-show cast party for a small production both he and Casey had appeared in. 'Just for a laugh, I pulled out some old 45 records from the 1950s,' he recalled. 'These songs sounded extremely dated compared with the very hip psychedelic funk of 1970. But it was a change of pace among the repetitious favourite dance tunes of the day.

'It was after singing along to several of these old, scratchy 45s by the likes of Little Richard, Dion and The Belmonts, and The Flamingos, that I first suggested to Warren Casey what a funny idea I thought it would be to see a Broadway musical that utilised this type of score: i.e. the basic acapella/falsetto/doo-wops/hic-cupping/ R&B music of the late 1950s instead of the traditional, "legit" show tune type melodies.

'Warren raised the rather obvious question: "Yeah, but what would the show be about?" A few beers later, with daylight rapidly approaching, I hit upon the idea that it should be about the kids I went to high school with, mainly the "greasers" and their girlfriends back in the golden days of rock and roll. Harking back to a lifestyle that seemed centred on hairstyles (oily, gooey quiffs), the food (cheap, fatty hamburgers and soggy fries) and cool custom cars (more gunk and sludge) or any and all things greasy – I suggested we call it *Grease*.'

The Jacobs–Casey musical was staged for the first time as a five-hour amateur production in Chicago on 5 February 1971, at the small experimental Kingston Mines Theatre, a damp and draughty converted tram shed. With a cast of eighteen non-professionals, *Grease* played to full houses of 120 seats for its four scheduled performances. It went down well enough with the audiences to earn an extension, and a pair of alert New York producers caught the show and made an on-the-spot deal to adapt it for New York.

The following year, 1972, on St Valentine's Day, it moved, with slight alterations, to New York to the off-Broadway Eden Theatre, where it gained recognition by receiving four prestigious nominations for a Tony award, Broadway's equivalent of an Oscar. Eventually, with a further reworking of the script, the show moved on to Broadway proper on 7 June 1972, at the Broadhurst and thence to the Royale and from there to the Majestic.

Explaining its runaway success, *Grease*'s Broadway producer Kenneth Waissman said: 'Ours was the first show that spoke to a new generation, and it spoke about that generation.' He conceded, however, that it was the musical's good fortune to hit Broadway at a time when 'the theatre was menopausal'.

'It's not just nostalgia for the 1950s that has made it such a hit,' he observed. 'I think it's because *Grease* deals with the universals of adolescence, with problems we all go through, problems of relating to the opposite sex or to peer groups for the first time.

'There are many uncomfortable teenage moments in the show – like being rejected by someone you have a crush on. But, here, you laugh at these things, you have a good time. It's escapism that minimises the pain of what were once major problems for us all.'

Long before the stage show gained its irresistible momentum, the film rights were purchased by Allan Carr, a chubby, caftan-wearing, larger-than-life camp showbiz entrepreneur, who in time would change Olivia Newton-John's life for ever. Born the son of a Chicago furniture salesman, Carr had been smitten by showbusiness from an early age. Even as a teenager he had taken to investing his weekly allowance in Broadway shows and, inevitably, he eventually headed for Hollywood in the mid-1960s intent on grabbing himself some showbiz action.

With flamboyance and flair, he worked his way into a position where he personally managed an impressive roster of major stars, including the actresses Dyan Cannon, Melina Mercouri and Rosalind Russell, singers Petula Clark and Peggy Lee, and actors Tony Curtis and Peter Sellers.

Now, with the film rights to *Grease* in his pocket, Carr was ready to hawk his hot Broadway property to the major movie studios. Their initial response was far from encouraging. Hollywood experts told him he had made a big mistake. The studio sceptics pointed out he had bought what they considered to be an out-of-date property. Nostalgia for the 1950s had been and gone, they said, and it was such a flimsy story to boot – high school tough boy meets high school goody-goody girl, boy loses girl, girl wins boy back. Furthermore, the major film studios asked: 'How can you cast a song-and-dance romance between a hip greasy rocker and a squeaky clean high school virgin?'

Carr ignored the negative reaction to his purchase. Not for nothing had he acquired the nickname Caftan Courageous. He was not to be deterred. He had absolute faith in the project and he was determined to prove the pessimists wrong. He knew, in any case, that he had time to spend. The producers of the Broadway show would not immediately sanction a movie while their stage production was continuing to do such incredible business. By reaching a mass audience, a *Grease* movie would have jeopardised not just the Broadway box office but the profitability of touring franchises for *Grease* in theatres all over the world. Carr had no option but to accept the terms of the stage producers and postpone his film plans for a year. In the end, a release date of spring 1978 was negotiated for the movie.

Among the number of stars Carr personally managed at the time was the versatile actress-singer-dancer Ann-Margret, and initially he ambitiously envisaged her teamed with Elvis Presley in the lead roles for *Grease*. Elvis and the ultra-glamorous Ann-Margret had already proved an exciting pairing in the movie *Viva Las Vegas*.

Later, more realistically, Carr's choice came down to two TV favourites: Henry Winkler from TV's *Happy Days*, and Susan Dey, a pretty young actress from another TV hit, *The Partridge Family*, who later went on to make her mark in *LA Law*.

Winkler had become a massive star playing the cool but

narcissistic, greasy-haired motorcycling kid Fonzie in the sit-com *Happy Days*, an updated version of teenage life in America in the mid-1950s. He had started out in the series as a supporting actor, but once the programme centred itself round Winkler as the Fonz, *Happy Days* became a bigger and bigger hit until it was America's number-one show. Accordingly, from fifth billing, Winkler rapidly rose to become US TV's most popular actor, and his character's thumbs-up gesture accompanied by a laconic 'aaaayyh' became trademarks.

The prospect of the Winkler–Dey pairing evaporated, however, when Winkler decided his career would be better served if he avoided for a while any more projects set in the 1950s. *Happy Days* had made him an international star and now he feared being typecast. *Grease* would have pinned him still further to the 1950s. 'He just felt the role of Danny Zuko in *Grease* was too much like the Fonzie,' said a disappointed Carr. 'I could understand that.'

Carr eventually found his leading man for *Grease* one uncomfortably hot late summer's night in 1975 when he switched on the TV in his hotel room in New York to see a hitherto largely unknown young actor called John Travolta in a new series called *Welcome Back, Kotter*. Newly launched by ABC, this was a sit-com about a Brooklyn-born teacher, played by Gabriel Kaplan, who returns to the inner-city high school from which he had graduated ten years earlier to take up a post teaching the toughest cases – a remedial academics group.

His 'sweathogs', as they were known, were the dregs of the academic system, streetwise kids unable or unwilling to make it in normal classes. They were also the roughest, and funniest, kids in school, and the coolest and toughest of all the 'sweathogs' was blue-collar punk Vinnie Barbarino, played by Travolta. 'I thought he was terrific,' Carr said of Travolta, 'and he showed up just at a time when Henry Winkler was out of the running.'

After spotting Travolta on his TV screen, Carr immediately telephoned the international impresario Robert Stigwood, who had become his co-producing partner in the *Grease* movie project. He told him to switch on his television and take a look at the young man playing Vinnie. Carr felt he was clearly destined to become the heartthrob of the TV series and had the potential to become a perfect Danny Zuko.

Once he had also tuned in to *Welcome Back, Kotter* and spent five minutes assessing Travolta's onscreen presence for himself, Stigwood agreed with Carr that the young actor was well worth pursuing. On meeting Travolta, they were heartened to find he was thoroughly familiar with *Grease* because he had appeared as Danny Zuko's young sidekick, Doody, in the show's first national touring company before he signed up for *Welcome Back, Kotter*. John professed to loving the show. He said he could identify with the coolness of the greasers, and he had longed to play the lead role of Danny. In no time Carr and Stigwood had secured Travolta's signature for a $1million three-film package deal with the Robert Stigwood Organisation.

Carr never doubted that they could turn Travolta into a big movie star. For many years afterwards, whenever *Saturday Night Fever* or *Grease* cropped up in any conversation within his earshot, the colourful Carr would say of Travolta: 'I was the one who said, "Put him in the movie!"'

Stigwood's input for *Grease* was crucial. He had the showbiz clout to persuade the major Hollywood film studio Paramount to adapt the stage show into a movie. The Australian-born entrepreneur was by now one of the

most successful figures in the entertainment industry,
heading up a group of companies encompassing theatre,
film and TV, records, concert tours, personal management
and music publishing.

As a music mogul, Stigwood had founded RSO Records
and had managed, and brought to lucrative prominence,
the prolific and hugely successful songwriting pop group
The Bee Gees, as well as Eric Clapton's supergroup Cream.
At one point Stigwood had even joined forces with Brian
Epstein, manager of The Beatles, to become co-manager of
Nems Enterprises.

Never averse to backing fresh talent, Stigwood could
also number among his stage shows the musicals *Hair*,
which he produced in 1968 and which ran for five years in
London's West End, and *Jesus Christ Superstar*, by young
co-writing team Andrew Lloyd-Webber and Tim Rice. He
made a first foray into movie musicals as producer of the
film version of *Jesus Christ Superstar*, and followed up
with *Tommy*, a rock opera written by Pete Townshend of
the British pop group The Who.

It was after Carr proved himself so adept and imaginative in promoting and partying *Tommy* for the Stigwood
Organisation that Stigwood joined forces with him in a
creative business partnership. And *Tommy*'s success
prompted Stigwood to use his dominance in the pop field
to develop further movie musical projects, and the first of
his three productions for Travolta would be *Saturday
Night Fever*, a musical to cash in on the new disco dance
craze.

The movie had been inspired by an article by writer Nik
Cohn in the June 1976 issue of *New York Magazine*, head-
lined 'Tribal Rites of the New Saturday Night'. It focused
on kids in Brooklyn who got through their mundane lives

Monday to Friday ready to 'explode' on Saturday nights in the disco clubs. There, they stepped into a different world with its own codes of hierarchy, dress, dance moves and courtship. 'The new generation takes few risks: it graduates, looks for a job, endures. And once a week on a Saturday night it explodes,' wrote Cohn.

The plan was for Travolta to play the king of the disco dancefloor in *Saturday Night Fever* then move swiftly on to star in *Grease*. Both movies would be made by Paramount and *Grease* would be allocated a budget of $6million.

While Travolta was now locked into the movie's lead role of Danny Zuko in *Grease*, the search continued for an actress to play his teenage sweetheart Sandy. Travolta as yet was untried as a box office attraction so Paramount required a bona fide star to play opposite him. Several were considered, fewer still were auditioned and only three came anywhere near to clinching the role. They were Marie Osmond, primarily a singer rather than an actress, and Deborah Raffin and Cheryl Ladd, both primarily actresses rather than singers.

Marie, a strict Mormon, reportedly baulked at having to portray Sandy's makeover from innocent student to schoolyard siren at the end of the movie. It was claimed she was unhappy at the idea that prim and proper Sandy in the end had to resort to exuding come-hither sex appeal in order to get her man.

Deborah Raffin was a slender young blonde actress who had won good notices in a charming film called *The Dove*. In it she had convincingly played a love-struck young girl faithfully following her round-the-world yachtsman boyfriend to various romantic stop-off points across the globe to find true love with him at the end of his voyage. There was an undeniably sweet, virtuous look about

Deborah, and she would have been a better bet than Marie to play Sandy. But by the time *Grease* was ready to roll, Deborah had moved on to other projects.

Cheryl Ladd had made her name in the mega-hit TV show *Charlie's Angels* when she replaced Farrah Fawcett-Majors as one of the three sexy police-trained detectives working for an unseen boss. Cheryl had enough of a voice to warrant making an album, but her *Charlie's Angel* image as a capable undercover cop was hardly conducive to playing a high school student.

Carr was still without his ideal Sandy when he was invited to a dinner party hosted by the singer Helen Reddy and her then husband Jeff Wald. Also at the dinner was Olivia, who had been befriended and loyally championed by the hosts ever since she had chosen to base herself in California. Theirs was a natural friendship since Helen had been the first Australian female popu-lar singer to make it big in America and she'd become something of a social godmother for Aussies in the entertainment business who happened to pitch up in Los Angeles.

In Hollywood circles, it's frequently said that it's the deal not the meal that really counts at dinner parties. And by a stroke of good fortune, Olivia happened to be at the right dinner party with the right person at the right time. Among the other invited guests was California Governor Jerry Brown, but he was late in arriving and the dinner went ahead without him, leaving the colourful Carr free to radiate his customary enthusiasm for all things showbiz.

Carr was, of course, familiar with Olivia's successes as a singer. But gazing across the table at her in the flesh for the first time, Carr was struck by Olivia's natural fresh-faced beauty and her soft, feminine appeal. And then he saw something more. 'At first she was her usual self, almost a waxen figurine,' Carr later recalled of that first meeting. 'But then all of a sudden she started telling a joke, screwing up that perfect face in some cute but hilarious contortions.' Now he was captivated, and his mind was racing. Could Olivia produce the same range of expressions in front of a camera?

When Carr was moved to come out with the tried and tested Hollywood line 'You ought to be in pictures', he meant it, absolutely. Olivia had, of course, heard that line many times before, but Carr seemed deadly serious when he told Olivia about his *Grease* movie project and suggested she would make a good Sandy. She was a proven singer, she looked very young for her age, and she could be made to look younger still, he said. And, despite her inexperience when it came to movies, Carr was confident she could make a good job of it.

Next day Carr arranged for a script to be sent to Olivia. In the original *Grease* stage show Sandy Dumbrowski was an all-American girl, but Carr assured Olivia this was a minor problem. He explained she could either take dialect classes or the script could be adapted to accommodate her Australian accent. Sandy could be an Aussie student on a foreign-exchange placement.

Although she was first and foremost a singer and enjoying huge success, Olivia had been keeping an eye out for a suitable movie vehicle for some time. In all her contracts a clause was included that would allow her to take time out to star in a movie as soon as the right script came her way. She had been offered films before, of course, but she'd never found one that suited her. She had flatly rejected several scripts because of their violent content, and her movie ambitions in general were clouded by the less than happy memories of making *Toomorrow*. Almost ten years had passed since then, but she feared that another film flop might seriously damage her standing as a singer and her recording career.

Olivia had come close to taking the role of Strawberry Fields in *Sgt Pepper's Lonely Hearts Club Band*, a movie presented in rock opera form and starring The Bee Gees, with music from The Beatles' landmark LP woven into a story about a pop band's struggles within the music industry. But in a multiple cast of characters, Strawberry Fields would have given Olivia little scope to shine and she felt it failed to offer enough of an opportunity to broaden her scope.

A major role in *Grease*, however, was a very different proposition, but although Olivia was flattered by Carr's approach, she didn't take it all that seriously. She shrugged off the very idea of playing a teenager on screen, much to Jeff Wald's chagrin. 'Are you out of your mind?' he berated her at one point. He kept urging her not to dismiss it so lightly. He could see it was a golden opportunity that deserved her proper attention.

Olivia had been to see a stage production of *Grease* in London in 1973 with a young and, back then, virtually unknown Richard Gere in the lead role. Bruce Welch had taken her to see the show and they had come away from the theatre having enjoyed a fun night out. That was some years ago, but now, at Wald's urging, she began to give some serious thought to the prospect of starring in a movie version. It did sound promising, she finally acknowledged, but she told Carr she had reservations. Recalling years later the dinner party that was to change her life, Olivia said:

> I guess Allan had seen me and wanted to meet me as he was looking for Sandy. But I was very reluctant because *Toomorrow* was a bit of a disaster, really. So I'd

thought: I'm going to leave the movies out and concentrate on my music. My singing career was going quite well and I didn't want to blow it.

Also, I was concerned because I was twenty-nine and the role in *Grease* was for a seventeen-year-old. I look back now and think, what the heck was I worried about? But at the time I was freaked out about this. So I said: 'I'll consider doing the movie but I'm not sure, so if you can get me a screen test with the leading man and I like it, then I'll do the movie.'

Normal Hollywood procedure would entail the producer and the director demanding a screen test for an artist of Olivia's limited acting experience. But to the surprise of both Carr and Randal Kleiser, a director who would be at the helm of a feature film for the very first time, Olivia was pre-empting their request. Kleiser recalled:

Olivia was now our first choice, but she was nervous about acting, feeling comfortable with us and whether she could pull it off at all. She was concerned about playing a seventeen-year-old. I told her it was a bigger than life musical, that all the actors were going to be about the same age, late twenties into thirties. It would be a style, a kind of surreal high school. She requested a screen test to see how it would all work. Afterwards, she would decide if she would do the movie. It was very unusual because normally the producer requests the test to determine whether they want to hire someone or not.

Carr and Kleiser readily agreed to Olivia's request for a screen test, but in case she wasn't satisfied with the results and turned the role down, producer and director decided they must line up another actress too.

On the Hollywood grapevine there were favourable reports of Carrie Fisher emanating from the *Star Wars* production where the young actress was playing Princess Leia. The movie's director George Lucas had been room-mates with Kleiser at college and obligingly invited him to come and watch him working on the mixing of one of the movie's space battles so he could gauge Carrie's potential. But Kleiser remembers it proved fruitless: 'I watched a fast-cut sequence with lasers and explosions. Every once in a while there was a quick cut of a girl with big hair buns turning to watch a ship whiz by. "That's her," George pointed out. But there was no way to tell if she could carry a musical.' Kleiser left the editing room hoping ever more fervently that Olivia's test would work out.

At this point Olivia had yet to meet John Travolta. She had seen him on TV in *Welcome Back, Kotter* and had occasionally recognised him when she caught sight of him driving around Los Angeles. Now an arrangement was made for the two to be introduced, and John drove out to Olivia's home in Malibu. The actor was then still living in his modest one-bedroom apartment at 100 South Doheny in Beverly Hills above Santa Monica Boulevard, and the splendour and setting of Olivia's home took his breath away. 'I was awestruck because she was an established star and I was working my way up,' he says. Olivia remembers Travolta was wide-eyed at the framed gold records on her walls, her swimming pool and the amount of land she owned. There were even telephones in the bathroom, John noted with amazement.

Olivia found John engaging and easy to talk to from the start. 'John was playing this supposedly tough guy but he has this sweetness which comes through no matter what he plays,' said Olivia. 'The first time I met him was that time he came to my house and he was so cute. That was my first impression, but I wasn't sure about working with him.' She was, however, prepared to go ahead with the screen test.

In a town where every waitress and bellhop wants to be a film star, there was a time in Hollywood when aspiring actors and actresses could walk in off the street and buy a screen test for $25. It was said that a Hollywood career hung upon the result, and now it would be no different for Olivia, except that Allan Carr was not prepared to arrange just a simple straightforward no-frills screen test. He set out to give Olivia every chance to shine.

Carr put the call out for full lighting and full crew, as well as the presence of the co-star. Additionally, he arranged for Olivia to have full make-up and hairstyling and a complete wardrobe. The instruction went out that unlimited retakes would be allowed and, on the appointed day of Olivia's test, John Travolta was briefed about her anxieties and was encouraged to do his utmost to set her at her ease. Gamely he proceeded to make the experience as painless for her as he could. 'I knew my job was to coerce her into doing the movie,' he remembers. Kleiser and Carr watched nervously as their leading man took Olivia under his wing, cracked jokes, encouraged her and made her feel relaxed before the cameras started turning.

* * *

The scene in which Danny takes Sandy to a drive-in movie and offers her his high school ring was selected as the best opportunity for assessment of Olivia's potential, but she emerged not overly impressed with the outcome. She found the test to be something of an ordeal, describing it as 'a very nervous thing, at least for me, and I wasn't thrilled with my own performance. I kept thinking: here I am, a singer wanting to be an actress, working with an actor who sings. I was very mixed up and frightened.'

She later explained: 'Well I had no training, really, and as much as I loved the idea, all I could do on such short notice was hope that some natural ability would come through. I was never sure it would work.'

Kleiser, however, felt her test could hardly have gone better. 'Olivia came across naturally and she was able to handle the comedy beats,' he said. 'She looked great.' Crucially, there was an obvious rapport with Travolta.

Olivia still needed some convincing. 'I didn't want to go into something I couldn't handle or have something to say about,' she later explained. 'I was playing a naive girl but I didn't want her to be sickly.'

After the test, a forty-eight-hour breather was agreed for considered reflection. Allan Carr did not need two days in which to decide whether he wanted Olivia or not. He knew at once that Olivia was right for Sandy. He liked the chemistry with John, who had been pushing for Olivia to get the role as soon as he was told she was up for consideration. 'She was America's sweetheart,' Travolta remembers.

Olivia similarly had forty-eight hours in which to decide whether she liked the look of herself on the big screen. One day later, on 8 May 1977, she was to be found pacing up and down the sitting room of her suite at Central Park's Sherry-Netherland Hotel on Fifth Avenue, with good reason to be nervous. In a few hours she would make her much-heralded New York concert debut at the prestigious Metropolitan Opera House, a venue that had attracted some of the world's greatest singers over its illustrious ninety-five-year history.

Among those whose voices had graced the Met had been

Dame Nellie Melba, Australia's superstar soprano from Olivia's hometown, Melbourne. For Olivia, the prospect of following in Dame Nellie's footsteps to sing pop and country hits in front of a sell-out crowd of 4,000 people at the Met was nerve-wracking enough, but she also now needed to make the decision about *Grease*.

In the corner of Olivia's luxury hotel suite stood a stereo system she'd had installed so she could listen to the Broadway-cast album of the musical and familiarise herself with some of the songs she might be expected to sing. On a nearby table was a well-thumbed copy of a film script for the show's proposed screen adaptation. Olivia had read it and reread it and yet she was still undecided whether the role was suitable for her.

The film called for her to play Sandy as the sweet, ponytailed high school cheerleader who falls for the greasy hood every mother warns her daughter about. Sandy's demure innocence was akin to Olivia's own public image, and she was certainly comfortable enough with that, but she was not sure whether her fans would take to her transformation at the end of the movie into a sexy, gum-chewing, leatherjacketed biker's moll. 'The role appealed to me because I got to play very sweet Sandy One, as I called her, and really bad Sandy Two, but I was really nervous about that because it was something I'd never done before.'

Equally worrying for Olivia was still the question of whether she was too old for the part. She was then twenty-eight; she would be twenty-nine by the time the film was released. Would cinema audiences accept her as a teenager at high school?

The one certainty for Olivia was John Travolta, who, at that point, was filming *Saturday Night Fever*. 'I'm just not sure of this,' Olivia fretted. 'Maybe if I talk to John I'll feel better. I know he's in New York here shooting the movie.'

Arrangements were made for Olivia to speak to John on the telephone in between takes for *Saturday Night Fever* and during their conversation the young actor finally won her round. 'Don't worry,' he assured her with genuine enthusiasm, 'you're absolutely right for it and we'll make a great team.'

After weeks of indecision, Olivia's fears had finally been allayed by Travolta's youthful confidence and optimism, and his sincere belief in her. And for that, Olivia would remain profoundly grateful to him for decades to come.

Travolta later said: 'It was Olivia I wanted from the start. I'd heard her songs, I'd seen one of her TV specials and, bearing in mind I really knew *Grease* from having been in the Broadway show, I thought: there's the definitive Sandy. We had to get her. There was only one person on this planet who could be Sandy and I was hell-bent to get her in the movie.'

In truth, John had fallen a little in love with Olivia long before he met her. 'At that time Olivia had been a star for about five years and every guy's dream was to have Olivia as their girlfriend,' he said. 'And, I tell you, I was the same way.'

John's crush on Olivia stemmed from the moment he had seen her photograph on the sleeve of her album *If You Love Me Let Me Know*. In the cover photo, she was wearing a blue denim shirt and staring straight at the camera with her arms folded. John was so captivated that he even went so far as to wear a similar denim shirt and strike a similar arms-folded pose for the cover of his own album *Let Me Be*, released in 1976.

'I was mesmerised by that LP cover,' he admitted. 'When my record company asked me what image I wanted to portray on the cover, I didn't say I wanted to mimic Olivia's cover but something like it. When I got cast in *Grease* I showed everyone that cover of Olivia and I said: "You see this girl, it's not just because she's had a hundred hits and she's America's sweetheart, this girl belongs in the movie *Grease* as Sandy."'

There were still some contractual hurdles to be overcome concerning the star billing and her fee, but now Olivia's mind was made up: she would sign up to play Sandy in *Grease*. 'But that's when the anxiety really got bad,' Olivia revealed in an interview, 'because then it wasn't so much a matter of whether I liked myself on screen or my manager or agent or accountant or my friends did, it all of a sudden changed to the big question: will the public like me and accept me in a new sphere, in a new career really?'

It was, she knew, a huge gamble. Her seven albums and sixteen singles had sold around 25 million copies and now she was stepping out of her comfort zone as a singer to try to become a film star.

The enormity of her decision coupled with her usual pre-concert nerves weighed heavily upon her as she prepared for the huge challenge of the Met. Olivia was frightened that New York's super-sophisticated critics were getting ready to dip their pens deep in vitriol. 'I'm expecting to get knocked in New York,' she said just before the concert. 'An artist with my image is up for knocking from the so-called heavy critics. Basically, I know that I please other people but you can't always please everybody all the time. The audience in New York will be blasé. They've seen every-thing – they can see everything – so I've got to be really good. It's a hard audience.'

Olivia became so agitated that she broke down in tears just before she was due to walk out on to the stage of the

Metropolitan Opera House. As her tears flowed, John
Farrar seriously wondered whether she had reached the
point where she would not be able to go on. 'But then she
went out and did the best show she had ever done,' he said.

Terrified she might forget the words of a song, Olivia
wrote the first lines on the palm of her hand as a failsafe,
then went out in a strikingly sexy gown and gave a
performance that earned her two standing ovations. Even
before Olivia had uttered a single note, every single
member of the audience had already warmed to her after
being presented with a long-stemmed rose that had
thoughtfully been de-thorned.

The enthusiastic ovation from the packed audience
added to the general feeling of relief Olivia felt inside now
that her mind was made up over *Grease*, and she was in
buoyant mood at the star-studded after-show celebrations.
Olivia's triumph was topped off by celebrity parties held in
her honour, and the New York papers carried pictures of
her on their front pages.

The next day's reviews showed she had won over the
critics with her performance at the Met. Even the *New
York Times* decided that Olivia had a soprano 'not so negli-
gible as some think. There's a nice husky quiver to it, and
only at full volume does it become shrill.' The *Daily News*
declared: 'Olivia, We Love Ya' the following morning, and
the *New York Post* went one better with the headline 'The
Met's Pop Star – A Sensation'.

* * *

Contemplating her new movie venture, Olivia could take
confidence from the fact that Paramount was the studio
preparing to take the risk with her and with *Grease*. The

studio had a long, proud history as well as a recent rep-
utation for turning out hit musicals. Elvis Presley had
made most of his early rock 'n' roll movie hits at
Paramount, including *King Creole*, *GI Blues* and *Blue
Hawaii*, before moving on to MGM. And since 1968,
Paramount could list among their output musicals like
Half A Sixpence with Tommy Steele, *Darling Lili* with
Julie Andrews, *On A Clear Day You Can See Forever* with
Barbra Streisand, and the Billie Holiday bio-pic *Lady
Sings The Blues* with Diana Ross – a shining example of
a singer with virtually no acting experience stretching her-
self to become a credible movie star.

Despite Olivia's suitability for the role of Sandy, John
Travolta was still somewhat surprised when she took on
Grease. 'Musicians generally aren't interested in being on
film,' he commented. 'But she was. I was thrilled and
relieved, because I thought she was so perfect for the role.'

Carr and Kleiser were convinced they now had the right
lead pairing and set about assembling a supporting cast.
They weren't overly worried if the girls who would form
the Pink Ladies college gang and the boys who would form
the T-Birds looked as if their student years were well
behind them. But they introduced a crow's feet test to
ensure it wouldn't be glaringly obvious.

The rest of the supporting cast was cannily designed to
appeal to the baby boomers who had been teenagers in the
1950s. They included Frankie Avalon, a genuine pop star
from the 1950s who had enjoyed seven US Top Ten hits,
including two chart-toppers, before diversifying into an
acting career in films, notably a series of teen beach movies.
Avalon would be given a cameo role appearing in a fantasy
sequence singing a song called 'Beauty School Dropout'.

Another shrewd piece of casting was Eve Arden from
one of the period's most popular TV situation comedies,

Our Miss Brooks. For four years in the mid-1950s, Eve was American television's best-loved schoolteacher playing Connie Brooks, a wisecracking English mistress at Madison High School. Now, in *Grease*, she was given the role of Rydell High's harassed and wearied Principal McGee, a head despairing of her pupils with comedic lines like: 'If you can't be an athlete, be an athletic supporter.'

Also drafted in was Edd Byrnes, who had become a firm TV favourite in the late 1950s playing a gangling, jive-talking young parking attendant nicknamed Kookie who longed to be a private detective in the cop series *77 Sunset Strip*. As Kookie, Edd had a habit of constantly combing his hair. In 1959 he recorded a novelty song called 'Kookie, Kookie (Lend Me Your Comb)' as a duet with Connie Stevens and it became a smash hit. Fondly remembered by 1950s TV audiences, Edd was given the role in *Grease* of a lecherous, narcissistic, smooth-talking TV presenter who visits Rydell High to host the National Bandstand dance competition.

To complement the Broadway score, there would be versions of golden oldies as well as some original songs by the rock 'n' roll revivalist doo-wop comedy group Sha Na Na, who would also be given cameo roles performing on stage at the dance-off.

For Randal Kleiser, *Grease* could hardly have been a more challenging project. Here he was at the age of twenty-nine directing his first major feature movie and it was a musical to boot. Any fears he may have had about his ability to pull it off were heightened even before principal photography began. His former university instructor, Nina Foch, obligingly threw a dinner party to bring him together with Robert Wise, the director whose expertise had made such a resounding success of the musicals *West Side Story* and *The Sound Of Music*. The hostess was trying to be helpful, and Wise for his part was happy to be quizzed for any tips or advice he could pass on from his own experiences.

'How much prep time do you have?' Wise began by asking of Kleiser. 'Five weeks,' came the reply, and Wise's follow-up shocked him. 'He told me to get out of the assignment right away, it was going to be a disaster,' Kleiser recalled. 'That terrorised me, but luckily I decided not to quit.'

Kleiser may have been raw but he had plenty going for him. While studying filmmaking in the late 1960s, he had also simultaneously worked as an extra on several movie musicals. 'By being on the set of *Camelot*, *Hello Dolly*, *Thoroughly Modern Millie* and *Double Trouble* with Elvis Presley, I was able to observe different ways musical numbers can be staged,' he pointed out. 'I learned how songs are broken down into short phrases of lyric and shot in sections. I watched directors yell "Play back!" instead of "Action!" So when I showed up on the set of *Grease*, I didn't feel completely lost.'

Kleiser, who had originally been set to direct *Saturday Night Fever* before being switched to *Grease*, also had the advantage of having already worked both harmoniously and to critical acclaim with John Travolta in a made-for-TV movie drama called *The Boy In The Plastic Bubble*. The director handled with great sensitivity the story of a boy born without a natural immune system who is forced to live in an artificial germ-free environment. From inside a sealed plastic bubble he can only watch the world go by.

By the time *Grease* was ready to go, Kleiser was presented, however, with a very different John Travolta from the one he had worked with before. Previously,

Travolta was simply a fledgling actor. Now he was older, more assured with a real sense of who he was, and he was on the brink of superstardom. John was literally flying high. Instead of buying himself a house with the $1million fee for his three-picture deal, John had preferred to splash out on a twenty-three-seater DC3 aeroplane after using his time away from filming *Welcome Back, Kotter* to gain a solo pilot's licence.

By now John had also become a major TV heartthrob in *Welcome Back, Kotter*, attracting 10,000 fan letters a week – a mailbag that was costing ABC an incredible $30,000 a week to deal with. Travolta was also brimming with confidence as an actor from having set the screen alight while filming his role of the finger-snapping, hip-grinding disco dance king Tony Manero in *Saturday Night Fever*. He recalled:

> I went almost directly from *Saturday Night Fever* to *Grease*, so making *Grease* was a wonderful change of pace. And since no one really recognised me as a big star yet – *Saturday Night Fever* wasn't yet out – I felt good because people obviously thought I had the ability to do the heavier drama stuff and the light comedy singing and dancing too. It was exciting to assert myself in both styles, especially at a time when I was known only as one of the sweathogs on *Welcome Back, Kotter*.

Everyone in the movie industry predicted John would be a sensation in the movie, and so it proved. 'Move over, Elvis. There's a new pelvis in town,' wrote one celebrated showbiz observer, who went on to describe John as the hottest thing in Teenybopper Heaven since peanut butter. The good vibes rubbed off on John. 'The first thing I did when I got to New York to promote *Saturday Night Fever* was walk down Fifth

Avenue,' he said, 'and every fifth person would recognise me and yell, "Hey, there's John Travolta!" It was great. I got off on it.'

By the time filming was under way on *Grease*, word was getting round that *Saturday Night Fever* had created a major new Hollywood star. Wherever the *Grease* filming took him, John was increasingly greeted with female hysteria and, as his co-star and love interest on screen, Olivia received envious looks from jealous teenage girls, notably when it was eventually, and inevitably, rumoured that she and John had become romantically entwined off screen as well as on.

John had come to the *Grease* set toned, fit, reed thin, perfectly attuned to the role ahead and ready to dance his colourful socks off. An early glance at the script had told Olivia she would not have to match him step for step. In fact, there were no plans for the couple to dance together at all. But once choreographer Pat Birch realised Olivia was more than capable of putting one foot in front of the other, the script was altered to include a major dancing sequence for her with John. Pat was impressed with the way Olivia could move and arranged for her and John to team up in a scene where Rydell's students pair off for the televised dance-off competition. Olivia found the prospect daunting. 'Boy, can he dance!' she marvelled after seeing John's electrifying, liquid-limbed moves for the first time in *Saturday Night Fever*.

For the movie that was to make him a superstar, John had gone into training for five months with a strict regime that included dancing for three hours a day and running for a further two. 'I had to lose twenty pounds to get what you see on the screen,' he explained, 'and so I hired the boxer who trained Sylvester Stallone for *Rocky*. When I started I couldn't even do one of the knee bends I do in the film. By the end I had a whole new body.'

Olivia knew she could not hope to match John's dynamism in their dance sequences, but she willingly subjected herself to rigorous training under Pat, who had been hired after choreographing the original Broadway *Grease* stage production, winning herself a Tony award in the process. Olivia was up to speed by the time she had to film her hand-jiving rock 'n' roll dance sequence with John. The scene was not made easy by being shot in sweltering high summer heat in a gymnasium with no air conditioning, and it was made all the more uncomfortable by the malodorous smell of a nearby pork processing plant wafting in through the windows.

* * *

From day one, Randal Kleiser and Allan Carr set out to create a fun element to filming *Grease*. 'Making this movie was like being president of the class at high school,' quipped Allan Carr. 'The first day we started, we didn't have a rehearsal or a read-through, we had a sock-hop. It was magical times for everyone. Everybody was coming up – it was my first really big movie, and John's really big movie and Olivia's first big movie and it was joyous. It was one big party from the very first day till it ended.'

Indeed, *Grease* became known to everyone at Paramount as 'the Allan Carr Party'. Everyone on the Paramount lot, from the highest executives to the lowliest studio workers, was granted automatic entry to the set-side parties. The filming of every big production number became an excuse for the champagne to flow, seen by major stars like Warren Beatty who was making *Heaven Can Wait* next door.

Ever mindful of an opportunity to generate publicity,

Carr announced he would throw a big *Grease* party to celebrate his moving into a new beach house. Word soon got around that an invite to his bash was the hottest ticket in town and the guest list grew to such unmanageable proportions that he was forced to divide the guests into two separate groups. Those with surnames A to K were invited for the Friday night, and L to Z for the Saturday. The two parties added to the feel-good factor surrounding the movie, which rubbed off on the cast. 'There was a high school sensibility about the whole production,' Kleiser noted. 'The cast was always joking around and playing tricks. There was a very upbeat atmosphere about making the film.

'We had a soundstage on the Paramount lot where all the dancers and the actors would meet every day. I'd be working with the actors on the dialogue while Pat would work with the dancers. There was such an energy and enthusiasm among the cast.'

Didi Conn, who played Frenchy, one of the Pink Ladies, remembers that they threw themselves into their roles with such gusto that they chose to remain in character all day. They called each other by their character's name and passed the time during film breaks by singing old songs to each other from the 1950s. 'We took all our high school experiences and put them together in this one fun-filled summer,' she said.

'*Grease* had this really fun feeling,' Olivia agreed, 'right from the beginning, from going to costume fittings and trying on these poodle skirts. I was living the school experience I never had. It was the opposite of the school I'd been to in Australia where we all had uniforms, skirts below the knees, socks and shoes, gloves and hats, and the school had separate entrances for boys and girls, separate stairs even.

Rydell High was just the opposite, the fantasy I never had.

'I particularly remember filming the "Summer Nights" number. It was with all the girls and it was really girlie and then the boys were doing their bits separately and we went over and watched them. It was really like being in high school.'

The noisy exuberance displayed by the cast in rehearsals and during breaks proved infectious. But one particular rehearsal aroused the wrath of Jack Nicholson, who was working just across the way on his movie *Goin' South*. Increasingly irritated by the *Grease* girls and boys singing away in full voice, Jack threw open the window of his editing room and yelled to Carr: 'Either close that door or put me in your goddamn movie!' Quick as a flash, Carr shouted back: 'We'll close the door, Jack – I remember your singing in *Tommy*!'

* * *

Carr and Kleiser were especially anxious to make filming fun for John Travolta's sake as the actor was still emotionally raw from the untimely death of his lover, actress Diana Hyland, just three months before. While filming *The Boy In The Plastic Bubble*, John had fallen in love with Diana, who was playing his mother. Diana was then forty and John rising twenty-three and one month after first meeting they embarked on a passionate affair – once John was convinced Diana appreciated him as a person and not just as a young stud.

But over Christmas 1976, Diana felt increasingly unwell and early in the new year she was diagnosed with cancer. By the end of March she was desperately ill and she died in John's arms. They had been together for just seven months. John was devastated. 'Diana was seventeen years older than I was, but we never knew the difference,' he said. 'We talked all day and all night about everything. I've never been so fulfilled in my life and when she died I felt like I lost my centre.'

Under very different circumstances both Olivia and John thus came to *Grease* newly single – Olivia was on what later proved to be a temporary personal break from Lee, although he had been continuing to manage her career.

Like every couple, Olivia and Lee had had arguments but Lee stated it was his own insecurity that undid him more than anything that was said. The couple tried to split up professionally but, when that didn't work, they tried to split up personally. They discovered that wasn't the answer either and after the filming of *Grease* they got back together again.

Thus Olivia and John came to *Grease* as two very attractive, single stars, and it wasn't long before the press began to hint that theirs was becoming much more than a working relationship while making the movie. Both accepted as almost inevitable that showbiz gossips would link them romantically and they were prepared for the rumours. These were partly sparked by Olivia slipping a sympathetic hand into John's and giving him an empathetic squeeze during a joint press interview in which John became visibly emotional when asked how he was coping following Diana's tragic death.

Friends have said they became lovers, but both Olivia and John insisted otherwise. 'Oh yes, all the girls were in love with John, but we never dated,' said Olivia. '*Grease* was the start of a lifelong friendship.

'I met John when he was going through a lot of pain, and I think that's why I gained a lot of respect for him because even though he was in incredible pain he never missed a day, he was so professional. He was always there on time and on the set he was full of energy and vitality. I can't think of anyone else who would have that strength in that situation.'

With John's encouragement and Kleiser's patient direction, Olivia's confidence in her own ability in front of the camera noticeably grew as filming progressed and she slipped into the routines and disciplines of filmmaking. A chauffeur picked her up from her home in Malibu in early morning darkness, even before the dogs had woken up, ready to take her to the studio by 6am in time for her to change into costume and be made up.

For the first eight weeks of filming Olivia was 'Sandy One', as she called the demure Sandy. To get into character, she thought back to when she was seventeen and found herself in a completely alien environment. She'd left England for Australia when she was a child and by the time she'd come back to England she had an Aussie accent. In Australia she'd been called a Pom and back in England she was regarded as an Aussie. 'I know what it feels like to be an outsider,' she said, 'the only one with a funny accent. So all I had to do really was to think back to when I was suddenly plonked into a strange country not knowing many people and just beginning to really discover boys, falling in love with a guy and being rejected. It's something everyone goes through one way or another, but there was definitely a bit of myself in there, for sure.

'At times I feel like the 1978 equivalent to Doris Day,' she was able to laugh in one interview. 'There are those who think I can't be as straight as I look. That's why there's always someone trying to dig up dirt on me. Yet I can't become something I'm not.'

With no training as an actress, Olivia chose to trust her

instinct totally. Fortunately she really hit it off with John Travolta. 'He was very gentle, sensitive, funny, and very professional.'

Travolta also proved to be supportive and generous in the scenes they shared. At one point John saw Olivia patently struggling to get to grips with the scene where Sandy suddenly meets Danny again at school for the first time after their summer fling. A reaction shot was required from Olivia while John was off-camera. Halfway through the scene John fluffed his own lines and apologetically asked for a retake. Later John told her that he had deliberately made a mistake because he knew that Olivia could do a whole lot better, that she probably knew it, and that he wanted to give her the chance to do so by ensuring they started filming the scene all over again.

The opening scenes in the movie capture Danny and Sandy strolling by the sea and pausing to kiss as they enjoy their romantic beach holiday before parting to go back to school. 'Having to kiss John Travolta wasn't so rough,' Olivia allowed. 'But having to do that in front of the camera was new to me.' John said of their first smooch: 'It was wonderful for me because I got to kiss her and it was all within the rules. You know, if you dated someone like Olivia, God, who knows when you'd get to that first kiss!'

The filming of Sandy One's transformation into Sandy Two was something Olivia looked forward to with relish. This was her chance to show the sexy side not just of Sandy but of Olivia Newton-John, too, and she was going to make the most of it. She spent hours in discussion with the wardrobe and hair and make-up departments trying on various outfits and experimenting with different hairstyles.

Olivia was at that point super-slim and it made sense to find an outfit that showed off her figure. She says:

> We all sat around and played with costumes. We decided on black, and I tried things on and found these trousers with very elastic material, sort of Spandex, in the wardrobe department. I was really skinny, you know. I look at pictures of myself back then and my sister and I were both really slim. Those pants did have a little stretch in them. They were real, already made, from the fifties, and they were made of that sharkskin material. I've still got them, I wouldn't dare try to get them on now!

To gauge the impact of her ensemble of skin-tight pants, red backless high-heeled platform shoes, low-cut off-the-shoulder blouse, whore-red lipstick, black leather jacket and teased blonde hair, Olivia casually strolled unannounced on to the set where Kleiser was setting up the night-time scene for John Travolta's solo number after he has taken Sandy to the drive-in.

Olivia wanted to surprise the director by her transformation as well as to get his approval for the outfit she had chosen. Kleiser recalls: 'When she walked on to the set in those pants, the whole crew began acting like adolescents with catcalls and whistles without even recognising it was Olivia. She was so sexy, the whole camera crew were around her and everyone was reacting so differently to her. Cast member Sean Moran commented that half the dancers fell to their knees in amazement, and the other half wanted the outfit.'

Olivia was tickled pink by the gasps from the girls and the lascivious looks from the boys. She said:

It was one of those moments I'll always remember. For two months as Sandy One everyone was really sweet and very nice to me. Now I walked around the back of the crew as Sandy Two, all dressed up with a cigarette dangling from the side of my mouth and they all turned around and I got this incredible reaction from the men. I got a lot of offers. No one knew it was me, and I thought: 'God, what have I been doing these last two months? This is how I should have been!' It was really freeing, and fun. It's amazing how other people react to you when you change your hair and your clothes. It can determine people's attitude to you.

Sandy's eye-popping morph into a sex kitten remains one of the high points of the movie. Cigarette dangling from her pouting red lips, sunglasses pushed well back on her saucy blonde curls, she licks her lips, stubs out her cigarette with her heel, pauses a moment for effect then gives Danny the come-on with the sultry line: 'Tell me about it ... stud.' With a shove of her foot she sends him sprawling backwards before dancing off through the fairground's Shake Shack to the John Farrar number, 'You're The One That I Want'. Randal Kleiser originally thought the song 'sounded awful' but Olivia knew it would be a massive hit as soon she heard the infectiously vibrant intro for the very first time.

For this pivotal scene at the fairground, Kleiser made use of a travelling carnival that conveniently happened to be in the area. But when he looked at the dailies it was with a critical eye. He wasn't happy with the overall impact of John and Olivia's duet and decided that although it had the required energetic quality, it was 'a little rough around the edges'. He resolved to add a few close-ups to give visual punch to 'You're The One That I Want', and arranged for further filming of the number two days later, only to be dismayed to find that the travelling carnival had moved on. As a compromise, a carnival soundstage with rented fairground machines was hastily mocked up on the football field of Marshall High School in Griffith Park.

Filming this pivotal scene in her figure-hugging pants had its drawbacks for Olivia. 'The zip had gone,' she explained, 'so they had to stitch me into them every day. I wondered what on earth I was going to do if I wanted a pee, so I didn't eat or drink anything from morning till evening. I was forced to drink almost nothing all day. But all the girls wanted the outfit and the boys were all over me, so it was worth it.'

Olivia's contract stipulated she would be allotted one song to sing solo in the movie. But when *Grease* went into production, there was as yet no sign of the song, nor did Kleiser have any idea where he would include it anyway.

It wasn't until halfway through shooting that John Farrar came up with 'Hopelessly Devoted To You' and presented Kleiser with a demo disc of his own rendition of the ballad. Hearing the song for the first time, sung not by a woman but by a man just accompanying himself on guitar, Kleiser confessed he wasn't sure if it was suitable or not, but he was prepared to take Olivia's word for it.

With time running out, the director chose to integrate 'Hopelessly Devoted To You' into the story by having Sandy sing about Danny while wandering around the backyard after the Pink Ladies' slumber party. A set was hastily built and Olivia nailed the song in one take.

* * *

The cast generally felt it was a good omen for their movie

when a stage production of *Grease* returned to the Pantages Theater on Hollywood Boulevard in Los Angeles while they were in the process of making the film. By an eerie coincidence, however, Elvis Presley died on the very day Stockard Channing filmed Betty Rizzo's musical homage to him in the song 'Look At Me, I'm Sandra Dee'. The very last day of filming, 16 of August 1977, found Stockard singing the line: 'Elvis, Elvis, let me be, keep your pelvis far from me.' When the cast learned of the rock 'n' roll king's death at such a poignant moment in the production, they wondered if this too was some kind of portent for *Grease*.

Once the movie was completed, the studio executives at Paramount were none too sure what to make of it, nor of its chances of success. True to form, however, Allan Carr enthusiastically promised them audiences would find John Travolta just as much of a sensation as he had been in *Saturday Night Fever*. As for Olivia, he said: 'She couldn't have been more adorable on screen. She'll be a big star.'

Paramount's nervy in-house reaction resulted, however, in a decision to test-market *Grease* in an out-of-the-way cinema just in case the audience reaction was unfavourable. In that eventuality, a damage-limitation exercise could be mounted and controlled, hopefully curtailing the unflattering word of mouth that could follow.

Honolulu on the island of Oahu in Hawaii was chosen as the location for the first *Grease* trial preview, and it doesn't get much more remote than that. To further preserve secrecy, the cans of film were flown out from Los Angeles to the Hawaiian capital marked not as *Grease* but with a fake title. Despite all the subterfuge, a local Honolulu radio station somehow found out John Travolta's new movie was being given its first screening in town that night, which resulted in lengthy queues outside the cinema.

Top-ranking Paramount executives accompanied Randal Kleiser to the Hawaii screening and they all nervously seated themselves in different areas of the cinema, the better to observe audience reaction.

'When the first number came up,' Kleiser later recalled, 'Travolta began singing and strutting down the football bleachers and the audience burst into laughter. My stomach sank. I thought it was a bad laugh, that they thought it looked ridiculous and we had bombed. But as the laughter continued, I realised that it was a good laugh and they were delighted.'

At the end of this first public screening, Kleiser and Paramount's top brass emerged from the cinema heartened by the audience's response. Further market research revealed that kids lapped up the fun times Kleiser had created at Rydell High of teacher-baiting, backseat snogging at the drive-in, hot-rodding, the girly get-togethers of the Pink Ladies, the camaraderie of the T-Bird boys. The girls enjoyed Danny's awkward veering from cool greaser when among his pals to romantic boyfriend showing his true softer feelings when alone with Sandy.

Additional previews confirmed Paramount's belief that they had a potential hit on their hands and they were prepared to back their hunch with a hefty $5million promotion for the US alone. A similar amount was allocated for the rest of the world.

The marketing campaign proclaimed 'Grease is the word', a line from the movie's theme song sung by Frankie Valli, best known as the lead singer of the Four Seasons harmony group, who had a string of hits in the 1960s. And by mid-June 1978, Valli's recording of 'Grease' was number one in the US singles charts, which gave the movie vital impetus just as it was about to hit US cinemas.

At the Los Angeles premiere, Olivia and John rolled up

in an open-top car to an ecstatic welcome from the large and excited crowd that had gathered outside Mann's Chinese Theatre. Thanks to the hit songs from the movie and the carefully crafted promotional campaign, *Grease* really was proving to be the word. 'We thought it was fun, but we had no idea it would create the hoo-ha it did,' said Olivia. 'Even when we went to the premiere in LA before it had been released, they were storming the car. This was long before the internet. It was bizarre, but there was just a buzz about it and people loved the idea of it.'

Olivia emerged from the car wearing a pretty pink prom dress symbolic of Sandy One. Later she was to change into a skin-tight pink catsuit as Sandy Two for the after-party where she and John happily danced the night away.

Inside the theatre, the warmth of feeling towards the movie was tangible from early on in the screening. Stockard Channing recalled the reaction of the audience when the first big production number came up on screen: 'Whoosh! There was a ripple of excitement and then it was just like a big wave hitting a beach. It was really thrilling.'

Reviews of *Grease* tended towards the word 'slick' and mostly picked up on the film's youthful energy and charm, and Travolta's sex appeal and dancing. *Variety* pronounced the movie 'slick as a ducktail hairdo' and commented: '*Grease* has got it, from the outstanding animated titles of John Wilson all the way through the rousing finale as John Travolta and Olivia Newton-John ride off into pre-Vietnam-era teenage happiness. The Robert Stigwood–Allan Carr production values complement superbly the broad comedy-drama, zesty choreography and very excellent new plus revived music.'

The *New York Times* said: 'Olivia Newton-John, the recording star in her American film debut, is simultaneously very funny and utterly charming as the film's ingénue, a demure, virginal Sandra Dee type. She possesses true screen presence as well as a sweet, sure singing voice . . .'

In general the critical reaction was highly favourable and picked up on the film's pervading sense of fun. Both critics and audiences also seemed prepared to overlook the fact that most of the high school pupils looked too old to answer Rydell's roll call even if they'd had to stay behind to resit their exams five years running.

Olivia and John worked hard to promote *Grease*. It was in their financial interest to do so, of course, as they both had a small stake in the movie, but together they attended world premieres as well as many of the big-city openings in America. At every one they were greeted by hysterical screams from excited teenage girls for John, and the couple were both wildly mobbed, sparking scenes reminiscent of Beatlemania. John was by now the hottest young star in the world.

The excitement surrounding the movie was reflected in record-breaking takings at the box office. In America, *Grease* grossed an incredible $58million in its first month, and the soundtrack album raced to number one in the LP charts where it stayed for twelve weeks. It remained in the Billboard pop album charts for seventy-seven weeks, and it has gone on to become the second bestselling movie sound-track of all time, behind *Saturday Night Fever*, selling 25 million copies.

In years to come Olivia's daughter Chloe would take great comfort from the soundtrack whenever her mother was away from home touring, recording or filming. 'When she'd go away or travel I'd put on *Grease* every night to go to sleep to so I could hear her voice,' says Chloe. 'I'd put it on replay. It's really sad, but I've seen it a few hundred times. It was like having my mum in the room.'

The money-spinning success story of the movie and the album continued in every territory in which *Grease* was released, even though the title didn't translate too easily into a foreign language. The Spanish for 'grease' is *grasa*, which literally means fat or oil, so it was released under the title *Brilliantina* (Brilliantine), and in Venezuela as *Vaselina* (Vaseline).

By the time *Grease* reached London on 13 September 1978, the film had already been given five international premieres and there had been violent incidents at the first nights in Chicago and Japan. John and Olivia were warned that the London crowds might prove the most riotous yet and they could expect trouble getting into the Empire cinema in Leicester Square.

Crowds started arriving several hours beforehand, some in 1950s cars. Many of the girls massed behind the barriers wore 1950s dresses, bobby sox and ponytails and the boys turned up in Teddy Boy outfits of drape jackets, thick crepe shoes and slicked-back ducktail hairstyles. By the time *Grease*'s two stars were expected at the cinema, around 5,000 fans had crammed into Leicester Square.

John, his new girlfriend, actress Marilu Henner, and Olivia were delayed by the chaos and when they did arrive there was a stampede as fans fought and kicked to break through the cordon of two hundred policemen who linked arms in a vain effort to hold them back. Soon hysterical girls were swarming all over their car and two youths clambered on to the roof and started jumping up and down. It was a terrifying moment. 'They were on the roof and all over the outside of the car,' Olivia remembers. 'It was the scariest mob situation I've ever been in. John and I were smiling and acting like everything was fine, but I felt like they were going to come through the roof. It was exciting, but I was worried someone was going to get hurt.'

John was visibly scared. 'I thought the roof of the car was going to cave in under the crush,' he said. 'I genuinely thought my life was about to end. It was panic for me. And yet it was exciting, too. Part of me was loving it. But I'll never go through this again. No one could imagine it would be like this. I was terrified.' Police, bodyguards and film executives eventually managed to escort them safely through the screaming mob to the foyer.

John was so shaken by the experience that he left by a back exit and missed the film as well as the after-party laid on for 1,000 revellers at the Lyceum in the Strand. Olivia took it all more calmly. 'I was shaken but not hurt,' she said. 'It was quite exciting really. They mean well, they're only trying to touch you, but thousands of people trying to touch you can be frightening.'

Pictures of the couple looking like frightened rabbits in the crush made the front pages of all the newspapers the next day. Scary it may have been for the two stars, but it was nevertheless priceless publicity for the movie.

The British reviews of *Grease* were largely favourable, and the first day's takings at the Empire cinema, £6,874, smashed the previous box office record of £4,640 – for *Saturday Night Fever*. Within three days the Empire had £50,000 worth of advance bookings, which was a record in itself, and within a month the soundtrack album was top of the UK LP charts, where it stayed for thirteen weeks.

* * *

Quite simply, *Grease* has become a phenomenon, the most successful movie musical of all time. It was the top money-making movie of 1978 and earned Olivia a Golden Globe nomination for best actress in a musical. Eventually the movie made $340million worldwide, an incredible return on its paltry budget.

The video, released for rental in January 1990, grossed $96million, and when it was released for sale in April 1993, it became one of Paramount's top-selling videos of all time with sales of more than 11 million. Such remarkable figures earned *Grease* an induction into the Video Hall of Fame, which recognises movies that have continued to perform well in both video sales and rental over an extended period of time. The release on DVD has also proved to be a money-spinner for all concerned.

For Olivia, the lasting worldwide financial success of *Grease* has been lucrative. The reported 2.5 per cent she was contractually due will have more than made up for her original bargain-basement fee of $125,000 for taking the role.

The imprint of *Grease* upon Olivia remains with her to this day. '*Grease* was the single biggest event of my life,' she has said. 'It affected everything.' The role of Sandy recently ranked number 89 in the movie magazine *Premiere*'s list of 100 Greatest Movie Characters of all Time.

For years, a day barely went by without someone or other referring to Olivia as Sandy or asking her about John. At her concerts she has found successive generations of audiences turning up with their children or grandchildren dressed in ponytails and Sandy-style outfits. 'To me, it's almost like a cartoon,' is Olivia's explanation of *Grease*'s enduring appeal. 'It's so larger than life, so brilliant and colourful. It's almost animated, and then one breaks into song. I think that's why it has such broad appeal. And I just think it had a lot of magic in it – the movement, the colours, the costumes. The young kids love that, and the older kids love the risqué stuff, which I admit I was clueless about when we were filming. I guess I was pretty naive!'

In the glorious certainty of hindsight, Olivia has often wondered why she hesitated for so long before signing up for *Grease*. And she admits that if she hadn't begun working on the movie before *Saturday Night Fever* had been released, she might not have gone through with it. 'If John had been a big star at the time I'm sure I would have felt intimidated. Especially as I didn't know him first.'

Wisely, as it turned out, neither Olivia nor John Travolta signed up for *Grease 2*. Exploratory talks were held with the two stars about a sequel, but both felt they could not top the original. The sequel went ahead with Maxwell Caulfield cast as an English cousin of Sandy's who joins the senior class of 1961 at Rydell High and has to prove himself a cool rider on a hot motorbike before he can win the heart of the queen of the Pink Ladies, played by Michelle Pfeiffer. Although *Grease 2* went some way to launching Michelle Pfeiffer's career, the movie proved to be a pale shadow of its predecessor when it was released in 1982.

Down the years there have been persistent reports that John Travolta and Olivia would team up for a sequel that would examine what happened to Danny and Sandy and all the other main characters in the original movie after they left Rydell High. Randal Kleiser has been reported as saying he felt fans of *Grease* would welcome such a movie and that he would jump at the chance to direct it if a deal could be struck with the two main stars. But no concrete plans have emerged.

When Allan Carr saw that audiences were willing to shell out $50 for a ticket to the Broadway revival of

Grease, he convinced Paramount executives to re-release the movie. *Star Wars* had shown that a re-release could make a financial killing and Carr reckoned the feel-good factor surrounding *Grease* could also generate similar big business. 'I told them they were sitting on a goldmine,' he said. 'The appeal of the stage show and the movie just never died. It's timeless entertainment.'

Randal Kleiser was all for it. He had seen the potential in a re-release after taking Olivia and Didi Conn to a late-night showing of the movie to see if it still stood up on the big screen.

> We slipped in the back and were surprised to see the audience dressed in fifties outfits. The crowd sang along with the songs and repeated lines back to the screen, very much how I remember midnight screenings of *The Rocky Horror Picture Show* when I was in college.
>
> After the show we lay low waiting for the theatre to clear, not knowing if anyone had spotted Olivia and Didi. When we came outside the audience was waiting gathered under the marquee. They broke into applause and began singing 'We Go Together'. Didi and Olivia were moved to tears. They treated them like cult superstars, taking pictures, asking for autographs.
>
> I never expected *Grease* to become a cult favourite, but sitting in the theatre hearing the audience sing and yell out the dialogue along with the actors was invigorating. It gave me the idea for the rerelease, of putting back-up singers and hand-claps in the surround speakers to encourage audience participation.

The first task was to examine the original 35mm music masters in the vaults. Much to everyone at Paramount's dismay, the adhesive on the film had become, in Kleiser's words, 'a flaking gooey mess'. The music tracks had deteriorated so much that they were unplayable until Cecilia Hall, Paramount's vice-president of post-production sound, gambled on trying a special heating technique to save them.

Kleiser told the *Los Angeles Times*: 'She took these original music masters to her Tujunga home and baked them in her kitchen oven at 150 degrees for six hours. Miraculously it worked and she saved the tracks, allowing the Dolby six-track mix to be done.'

By enriching the colour and digitally enhancing the stereo re-mix for its twentieth anniversary rerelease, Paramount gave the movie a fresh look and atmosphere and relaunched it in 2,000 cinemas across America. Naturally Carr arranged a starry repremiere in Los Angeles, attended by both John and Olivia who had not seen some of the cast for twenty years.

'Just out of interest,' said Olivia, 'I thought I'd try the pants on again. But I put one foot in and the elastic had gone. I couldn't get them past my ankle, so I never had to embarrass myself in them. Not that I was ever really considering wearing them – I think that might not have been appropriate twenty years on. I'd given away the red shoes to a charity auction, but I did wear my jacket to the premiere.'

Even though many millions had seen the original at the cinema first time round or on video or TV, audiences still flocked to see *Grease* all over again, many of them dressed as Danny or Sandy.

When *Grease* was eventually issued on DVD, Olivia turned the launch into a major event by flying in her band and singing with John Travolta for the first time for many years. 'I wouldn't trade *Grease* for any other movie I've ever been in,' said John, 'because it meant so much to so many people. I feel a part of history, so I'm pretty proud of it.'

Twenty-eight years on from the film's original release, John Travolta filmed a brief tribute to Olivia for the Australian TV version of *This Is Your Life* in which he said of her *Grease* role: 'I promised you'd be great in it, and I came through with my promise. At the end of the movie, when you come out in those tight black pants and that hair and that cigarette, I don't think anyone would ever think either of us were wrong.'

Olivia has been equally supportive of her co-star. In March 1996 she took out a big advertisement in the showbiz trade paper *Hollywood Reporter* to mark John's selection as ShoWest Male Star of the Year.

The advert read: 'Dear Danny, I am Hopelessly Devoted To You.' It was signed: 'Love Sandy'.

Olivia is unequivocal about what *Grease* means to her:

> It's the most successful movie I've been in, probably will ever be in. And that's enough. That's great. I've left my mark on celluloid somewhere. And I feel very lucky.
>
> My image had been so white bread, so milk shake, and *Grease* was a chance to do something different. I didn't want to be forty years old and still be the girl next door.
>
> At least when *Grease* hit, I was accepted. *Grease* proved to be so important for me. It meant I could have a hit movie with hit songs and a new image. Suddenly, if I wanted to be outrageous, I could. If I wanted to sing rock 'n' roll, I could.

Olivia's next album, *Totally Hot*, a mixture of soft rock and light disco and released a few months after *Grease*, proved the point. Olivia smouldered in black leather in the cover photos and the album included a cover version of the Spencer Davis Group's international hit 'Gimme Some Lovin' as well as a couple of disco numbers. The album was another big seller for her, reaching number seven in the US charts, while the single taken from it, 'A Little More Love', peaked at number three in the US and at number four in the UK.

9

Hell on Wheels

'Suddenly, there I was with this beautiful star in my arms.
I felt so important dancing with her, it was absolutely
magical and I never wanted it to end'

Matt Lattanzi

Ever since *Grease* had proved to the movie industry and, more importantly, to Olivia Newton-John herself that she could be a success in Hollywood, a search began to find another screen vehicle for her. In the movie echelons that mattered, Olivia was now considered to be 'box office'. Major Hollywood players were knocking at her door and she, in turn, was ready to build on the status she had acquired from co-starring with John Travolta in such a massive international mega-hit as *Grease*. Success gave Olivia the confidence to take her movie career one step up from co-star to fully fledged movie star. And the feeling in Hollywood was that Olivia was now capable of carrying a film commercially on the strength of her name, provided she had a strong supporting cast and some decent song-and-dance numbers to perform.

Olivia had seen what pleasure *Grease* had given to so many people, and fittingly, of all the movie projects inevitably sent her way after *Grease*, the two that came up for serious consideration by Olivia and her management were both new musicals – *Can't Stop The Music* and *Xanadu*.

The former was another Allan Carr enterprise and was

basically designed to be a pseudo-biography of the chart-topping disco group The Village People. They were a colourfully camp, all-male vocal group formed after Frenchman Jacques Morali saw a young man called Felipe Rose dressed in Indian tribal regalia in a New York gay discotheque, and then one week later spotted him in another gay club with other costumed characters. It gave Jacques an idea: 'I say to myself: you know – this is fantastic – to see the cowboy, the Indian, the construction worker with other men around,' he explained. 'And also, I think to myself that the gay people have no group, nobody to personalise the gay people, you know?'

To anyone hip to the New York scene, such flamboyantly garbed clubbers in gay discos was not unusual. But in the eyes of a visiting Frenchman this became a showbiz fantasy: why not put together a pop group comprising young men dressed up as stereotypical American males? Morali then set about recruiting six good-looking young men, mostly models, to front a selection of catchy songs and gave them the name The Village People as a nod to the men of Greenwich Village in New York.

When their first album sold 100,000 copies and their single 'San Francisco (You've Got Me)' even made the British Top Twenty, Morali put together a Village People group, including Felipe, who could actually sing as well as look macho. Soon The Village People had an international smash hit on their hands with 'YMCA', and a camp dance routine to go with it. The concept caught on like wildfire. The single even reached number one in the UK early in January 1979. It had sold 150,000 copies in just one day over the Christmas period. The group's follow-up single 'In The Navy' reached number two in the UK charts and a third single 'Go West' was a Top Twenty hit.

Such was the group's worldwide popularity that Allan Carr was prompted to write a movie around The Village People which would be a thinly disguised version of the group's rise to fame. Carr also wrote in a part for an actress to play Samantha, a retired top model who uses her connections to gain the group the recording contract that launches them to fame.

Naturally, after persuading Olivia to star in *Grease*, Carr was confident he would have little difficulty in securing Olivia for the role of Samantha. But by now she was the one who could call the shots and Carr needed her more than she needed him. 'Don't be fooled by Livvy's doll-like appearance,' Carr remarked. 'Behind that virginal look is a very full-blooded woman. And she is very smart too. Nothing has happened in her career by accident.'

The alternative project Olivia was seriously considering was *Xanadu*, a movie envisaged as a slice of celestial whimsy with music, a light fantasy in which Olivia would play a muse who comes down from her father Zeus's mythological Mount Helacon to inspire two earthlings, an ageing ex-jazz musician and a struggling artist, to fulfil their dreams of creating a roller-skating disco palace. This nightclub would be called *Xanadu* after the nineteenth-century poet Samuel Taylor Coleridge's *Kubla Khan*: 'In Xanadu did Kubla Khan / A stately pleasure-dome decree'.

Of the two projects, *Xanadu* clearly had the more obvious appeal to Olivia. She would be the undisputed star of the movie as its central character, whereas she would be a more peripheral figure in *Can't Stop The Music*, which was essentially all about the six men who comprised The Village People.

The driving force behind the attempt to bring *Xanadu* to the screen was a young movie executive called Joel Silver.

He was working in Hollywood for producer Lawrence Gordon with the job of developing film projects, and *Xanadu* was the one he had set his heart on getting off the ground. Silver was a movie buff and he was determined to produce a disco-flavoured remake of the 1947 film *Down To Earth*, which starred Rita Hayworth as the muse Terpsichore who comes down to Earth to help a Broadway producer fix a stage show in which she is featured.

Silver was so keen on the project that he once claimed that he was 'prepared to stab myself in the back' to bring it to fruition. And the circumstances surrounding Silver's eventual involvement with *Xanadu* were extraordinary in themselves, even by Hollywood standards. Universal's head Ted Nanen had fired Silver, whereupon he promptly went to work for his friend and mentor Lawrence Gordon. Since Gordon was also a producer on *Xanadu*, Joel Silver therefore found himself back on the project as co-producer.

With Gordon, Silver developed the story for Warner Brothers but, to their disappointment, the studio eventually passed on it. 'Maybe they were right to do so,' Gordon later reflected. 'A musical fantasy is chancy, and at that time we didn't have Olivia or Gene Kelly, the eventual stars. But Joel and I still believed in the project. We took it to Universal and they decided to do the film.'

Faced with playing either a heavenly muse in *Xanadu* or a retired model in *Can't Stop The Music*, the choice for Olivia became increasingly obvious, particularly when Universal agreed to Lee Kramer coming on board as *Xanadu*'s executive producer. Besides, *Xanadu* would be an Olivia Newton-John movie, they assured her, whereas in *Can't Stop The Music* she would be playing second fiddle to half a dozen men dressed up respectively as an Indian, a construction worker, a cowboy, a cop, a GI and a leatherman.

When Jeff Lynne, a prolific and talented composer for the pop group Electric Light Orchestra, was hired to write the score for *Xanadu*, and an assurance given that John Farrar would in addition contribute five new songs for Olivia, the key components for a commercially successful movie venture appeared to be falling into place for her.

The icing on the cake was the signing of Gene Kelly, the legendary dancing star from the golden age of Hollywood musicals. It was a shrewd piece of casting. Although well past his prime as a hoofer, Kelly retained an aura as one of the most innovative and respected figures in the history of the screen musical. Already behind him was a body of work that was equalled only by that other master of dance, Fred Astaire. Kelly's *Singin' In The Rain* was arguably still the most popular Hollywood musical of them all and it was thought that his very presence would broaden *Xanadu*'s appeal and draw in a very different generation of cinema-goers from those whom Olivia appealed to.

Olivia was genuinely thrilled when Gene Kelly signed up for *Xanadu*. She was the envy of millions for dancing with John Travolta in *Grease* and now she would get to partner arguably the greatest dance star of them all. Kelly was sixty-eight years old but, given his remarkable track record, it was nonetheless a coup for Olivia when she secured top billing in a musical over such a giant of the genre.

Carr was disappointed and frustrated when Olivia chose *Xanadu* rather than his own project. His negotiations with her over *Can't Stop The Music* had not been as cordial as he might have hoped. When he finally lost her to *Xanadu*, he attempted to save face by indicating it was he who had eliminated her from his plans rather than the other way round. 'I've just thrown her off my next twelve-million-dollar picture because of her excessive demands,' he was quoted as saying. 'Her demands now are what Barbra Streisand's were after *Funny Girl*, and she ain't no Streisand,' he added.

Olivia's demands could hardly have been construed as excessive. All she wanted was a starring vehicle and *Can't Stop The Music* quite clearly offered her a subsidiary role to that of The Village People.

Carr eventually wished her luck through gritted teeth and gave the part of Samantha in *Can't Stop The Music* to Valerine Perrine, a blonde former Las Vegas showgirl-turned-actress, who had made a big impression playing Lenny Bruce's wife opposite Dustin Hoffman in the 1974 movie *Lenny*.

As with *Grease*, there would be a director making his feature-film debut on *Xanadu*. Robert Greenwald was hired on the strength of his work on several TV movies as well as his stage experience. *Xanadu*, he decided, would be fun, bursting with vitality, colourful, full of music and dance. For this he would need to hire a top troupe of liquid-limbed dancers and a casting call went out to find them. One of the hopefuls who answered the call turned out to be a handsome young man by the name of Matt Lattanzi. He was a total unknown at that point – but he would soon come to be known as Mr Olivia Newton-John.

* * *

Matt was a fifteen-year-old schoolboy living in Portland, Oregon, a small town situated some seventy miles from America's west coast, when he was first struck by the radiant golden beauty of a girl gazing back at him from a photograph in the pages of a magazine.

Underneath the picture of the blonde who had caught his eye in *Billboard*, America's music-trade publication, was a one-word caption. It simply said: 'Sam', and Matt presumed Sam must be short for the girl's full name, Samantha – he was unaware that the picture was, in fact, of Olivia Newton-John and that the page was part of a marketing campaign for the singer's new single, 'Sam'.

Matt gazed admiringly at the photo then ripped the page from the magazine. This Sam was his perfect fantasy girl, he decided, and he duly pasted her picture on his bedroom wall. Like thousands of other teenage boys, Matt regularly went to bed dreaming that one day he might just meet his beautiful pin-up and they would fall in love and live happily ever after.

Born the son of an Italian immigrant who worked as a petrol-pump attendant, Matt was one of an unusually large family comprising ten brothers and sisters. When he left school, the obvious local employment option beckoned: working in one of the town's sawmills. But Matt never looked to a future as a lumberjack. Like most of his teenage pals, he was interested in music, the movies and the theatre. But, unlike the rest of his friends, Matt wanted to get into show-business and he was prepared to work hard to gain an entry.

There were no drama classes at Matt's school, so he chose to travel to an all-girls school for lessons every day. 'The first time I went into class must have been the most horrifying experience of my life,' he remembered. 'But it broke my inhibitions with girls completely. When you've done that, you can do anything. I was very happy there because I didn't get on very well with the macho locker-room types at my school.'

From school Matt went on to Portland Community College to learn dance and drama. He worked hard at his dance classes seven days a week, and was so conscientious and single-minded that he ended up not just training to be a dancer but also teaching dance as well. 'It was only when I was using tracks on the album *Totally Hot* for teaching dance classes that I realised my bedroom picture was of Livvy,' he later revealed. 'I'd never bought any of her albums or tapes before – despite the fact she was one of the biggest-selling acts at the time, alongside Elton John.'

Matt proved to be so diligent and dedicated at his dance classes that he managed to cram three years of learning into just twelve months. He was fired with ambition and the drive instilled in him by his father who, from his modest beginnings pumping petrol, worked his way up to become a draughtsman and technical engineer.

Matt worked hard not just to learn to execute dance steps expertly but also to add a touch of flamboyant style to his dancing, a bit of showmanship. It was an astute, calculated approach. 'I always thought I sold my dancing rather better than I actually danced,' he once explained. 'That was the only way to survive.'

Armed with this belief that he had an eye-catching edge over other dancers, Matt headed for Los Angeles in the hope of breaking into television or movies. 'I arrived in Los Angeles on July the second 1979,' he recalled, 'and all I had was my suitcase full of dance costumes, a fishing rod and £3,000, which I had saved up from working as a welder during my holidays. I had nothing planned and I knew no one. I just knew what I wanted to do.'

Matt quickly found a small room to rent then set about trying to find work. 'After going through all the trade papers, I found some film extra work. I wanted to see what films were all about. I wanted to soak up everything – the atmosphere, the jargon directors used, the way the actors moved, everything.' For Matt, it would prove to be time well spent.

Just four weeks after he had first set foot in Los Angeles came the fairytale break that was to change his life. He auditioned for a part in a new movie, a musical fantasy called *Xanadu*, and initially his heart sank when he turned up at the casting call to find that he was facing the most intense competition – he was just one of six hundred dancers all chasing peripheral parts in the movie's chorus line. Some had already appeared in movies and television and Matt reckoned his chances of selection were slim at best.

Six hours later, however, that number had been whittled down to seven girls and seven boys, fourteen couples – and Matt was one of them. To his joy, he was then told he had been hired. He could barely contain his excitement when he was informed that he would be dancing in a movie that would feature one of Hollywood's all-time great dance stars, the legendary Gene Kelly. The other big name in *Xanadu*, he learned, would be none other than Olivia Newton-John, who had been such a smash hit in *Grease*.

Matt could hardly believe it, and allowed himself a quiet smile at the thought that Olivia's picture had once adorned his bedroom wall. He had, of course, long since taken it down, but he was nevertheless thrilled at the prospect of appearing as a background dancer in her movie and he couldn't wait to meet her.

Rehearsals for *Xanadu* were scheduled to begin almost immediately Matt and the other dancers were cast and, on 6 August 1979, as Matt vividly registered in his memory, he was introduced to Olivia for the first time – and in the most unlikely circumstances.

Olivia's leading man in the movie was still to be cast and, in his absence, she needed a man to interact with in rehearsals. Her eyes fell upon Matt, who was busy conscientiously practising his roller-skating, and she liked what she saw. 'He was very striking, you couldn't miss him, that's for sure,' she said after singling Matt out to be her stand-in.

Matt was astonished. 'We had just begun rehearsing when the choreographer called out: "Hey, Matt, I want you to try out a step with Olivia." I couldn't believe my ears. Here was I, Mr Nobody, and they were asking me to dance with Olivia Newton-John.

'Suddenly, there I was with this beautiful star in my arms. I felt so important dancing with her, it was absolutely magical. I never wanted it to end. But at the end of the day we simply said "Cheerio" and Olivia went back to her hotel suite and I went back to the tiny room where I was living.'

As far as Matt was concerned, the day he had spent dancing with his one-time pin-up, and now the star of *Xanadu*, was likely to be a one-off encounter, the sum total of his association with Olivia Newton-John. At least he could tell himself that he had actually danced with the girl he had once worshipped as a teenager.

But the following morning, instead of being ordered back into the ranks of the chorus line, Matt found himself summoned to work on yet more routines with Olivia as her stand-in dance partner while the search continued for her co-star. This state of affairs continued right up until a good-looking young American actor called Michael Beck was finally cast as the male lead.

Olivia had originally suggested a then little known Australian actor by the name of Mel Gibson as her leading man, and also under consideration had been Andy Gibb, youngest of the Gibb brothers Robin, Maurice and Barry who as a trio comprised the phenomenally prolific hit-makers The Bee Gees. But Beck, who curiously bore a startling resemblance to young Andy Gibb, won the role of Sonny by virtue of an impressive performance in a movie called *The Warriors* about gang warfare in New York. Joel Silver had been associate producer on the movie and spoke highly of him. It was also felt that Beck's solid training as an actor at London's highly regarded Central School of Speech and Drama would hold him in good stead as a counterbalance to Olivia's inexperience as an actress.

Beck's late casting meant that he did not join the *Xanadu* production until three days before filming was due to commence in the middle of September. By then, Matt and Olivia had developed a warm personal rapport over six weeks' of rehearsal as Matt eagerly continued to be the absent male lead's stand-in. It did not go unnoticed among the rest of the cast and crew how good Matt and Olivia looked together – Matt with his dark, Italianate, fresh-faced handsome looks and Olivia exuding a contrasting golden muse-like glow.

Prior to Beck's eventual call-up, the obvious bond between Matt and Olivia prompted the producers to wonder whether Matt should be cast in the leading male role. He and Olivia seemed such a natural pairing, but Matt's lack of experience as a professional actor and his youth were against him.

As rehearsals continued, however, the couple spent more and more time in each other's company. 'We sweated together, worked together, cried together, laughed together, built up this tremendous confidence together and gradually began to trust one another,' Matt recalled. 'So the next step was that we started confiding in each other and almost without realising, we built up a very close relationship.'

The shooting of *Xanadu* began on 19 September 1979, a year that marked a milestone in Universal's history. Almost exactly fifty years earlier, the studio had released its first musical, *Show Boat*, following the coming of sound. *Xanadu* was primarily shot in and around the Los Angeles area and, during breaks in rehearsals while the film crew adjusted lights and microphones, Matt and Olivia both found conversation came so easily – and they talked and talked. 'I didn't think two people could talk so much and still have things to say,' Matt remembered.

On-set conversations blossomed into daily luncheons and inwardly Matt could not deny to himself that he found Olivia warm, beautiful, and desirable. He explained: 'After the first couple of weeks, I could feel myself thinking: yes, I like her. But forget it, Matt. She's not going to want to know. She was eleven years older and a star. I was just an unknown kid.'

The romantic impulses, nevertheless, were becoming ever harder to resist. Soon it became a challenge for Matt not to show his true feelings when they were up close in their dance routines. It was all he could do to stop himself from hugging and kissing Olivia as he held her in his arms. He said:

> It was strange, because when we were working, we were so close physically. I remember one day all the film chiefs came to see us do one of the big routines. As we were dancing, I tripped up and went sprawling across the floor pulling Livvy with me and she came down slap bang on top of me. I could feel her pressing against me, and we burst into fits of laughter.
>
> But away from the set, even though I wanted her so much, I couldn't bring myself to make a pass at her. I guess we were becoming such good friends I

didn't want to spoil anything. It would have made
working together so much more difficult.

Olivia, for her part, was secretly enjoying the time she was
spending with Matt. Tall, dark, slim with a toned, athletic
physique, Matt had an open and prettily handsome face
with a dazzling smile and Olivia was most certainly drawn
to him. 'There was instant chemistry between us,' she later
admitted. 'I thought he was such a sweet person.' But, like
Matt, she was careful not to show undue interest in the
young dancer to anyone on the film set.

While recognising there was a definite physical attraction between them, realistically she felt that they were
destined to remain nothing more than working friends.
After all, she reminded herself, he was only twenty years
old, and she was thirty-one. Matt had still been a little lad
running around in short trousers when she was a budding
singer making her first record. She had never been out with
a man so much younger than herself. Besides, she reasoned,
any on-set romance would complicate, jeopardise even,
their working relationship, and so she dismissed the
notion.

Even so, Olivia was intrigued and inwardly not a little
pleased when she discreetly asked around about Matt and
discovered that he appeared not to be a gigolo and there
was no special girl sharing his bed of a night. Matt: 'I didn't
have a girlfriend at the time even though there were lots of
pretty girls around. I made sure I didn't, because I
suspected that Livvy was finding out what my sex life was
like.

'She wouldn't have been interested in me if she'd thought
I was sleeping around. Anyway, from the first day I met
Livvy, I wasn't interested in any other girl.'

As filming continued, Matt was increasingly in a quandary. With every passing day he was becoming more and more enamoured with Olivia, and wrestled endlessly in his mind with how he could possibly ask her out on a date. The more he thought about it, the more daunting it appeared: Olivia was a famous international star; he was totally unknown. She was worldly, hugely successful; he was a twenty-year-old beginner. She was a millionaire many times over; he was earning very little. Her home was a fabulous Malibu ranch house; he barely existed living from hand to mouth in a tiny room in the wrong part of Los Angeles.

They were poles apart, he told himself. And how would she react if he did coax her out on a date and he tried to kiss her, he asked himself. Would she push him away or would she pull him towards her? And if he made a move and was rejected, how could they continue to work harmoniously together for the remainder of the *Xanadu* shoot?

Matt pondered all the uncertainties over and over. One thing was for sure, he found he could not get Olivia out of his mind. He thought about her constantly until twelve weeks into filming he resolved he must at least ask her out, if only to preserve his sanity. Perhaps he had false hopes, he told himself, but he genuinely sensed there was a mutual physical attraction and he had to discover if there really was a spark between them. With his heart in his mouth, he decided to call up Olivia on the telephone and ask her for a date. He admitted:

> I could no longer stand working with her without letting her know how I really felt. On October twenty-fifth, I asked her out. It had taken me three months to pluck up the courage. The following day was free so I

phoned her at the Beverly Wilshire Hotel where the film company were putting her up and asked: 'Would you like to come hiking with me? I know a great place to go.'

I suggested that we went for a hike in Will Rogers State Park, not far from LA. She said yes right away. We knew each other as friends by then, so there was no embarrassment. If you work closely with someone on a film then the barriers come down.

For Matt, asking a girl to join him on a hike in a park was, in his eyes, about as authentic and natural an invitation for a date as you could get. Matt's boyhood had largely been spent in outdoor pursuits in the City of Roses, as Portland was known. The city was just seventy miles from inviting Oregon beaches where Matt had regularly enjoyed sailing and windsurfing. He had also spent happy days hiking and exploring the seventy miles of trails in Portland's Forest Park or simply walking along the banks of the Columbia and Willamette rivers.

The Will Rogers State Historic Park in Los Angeles, named after the most popular and highest-paid Hollywood actor in the 1930s, had long been a favourite with hikers like Matt. Its 186 acres in Santa Monica offered trails through lush clover and eucalyptus trees and had glorious views of both the Pacific Ocean and the Santa Monica mountains. Matt planned a romantic route for himself and Olivia through the park that would entail climbing a small mountain.

For Olivia, well used to men wanting to impress her on dates by lavishly wining and dining her at the most expensive must-be-seen-at restaurants, an invitation to join Matt on a Sunday hike was a most refreshing change.

'Outdoorsy, strong and fun' is how Olivia later described

young Matt. 'I was a career woman, constantly working, with less time for fun things. He was sweet, genuine and open, like a breath of fresh air after some of the men I'd met in LA.'

Matt's impecunious state and his youthful naivety dictated that his hike with Olivia would be no gourmet picnic. 'I bought a large tub of Kentucky fried chicken for us to eat cold,' he revealed. 'Not exactly your Hollywood smart scene. I was so excited I forgot to bring anything to drink so we had to hunt around for a water tap. We didn't eat much in the end. We just talked and talked for six and a half hours.' And finally they kissed.

'It took all the courage I had,' Matt later admitted. 'We were standing at the top of a cliff overlooking the Pacific. It was the first time we had actually been on our own. I put my jacket down on the grass for her to sit on and sat down beside her. There was a long silence – the first one of the day. My heart was pumping so loudly, I was sure she could hear it.

'I knew I had to make the first move so I edged slowly towards her to see what she would do. She moved a little closer. So I moved closer still. It was like being a teenager again. And suddenly we were kissing. It was just like a scene from a film.'

As if to further enhance such a romantic scene, they headed down to the beach hand in hand and then, arm in arm, they strolled along the shore, pausing for more kisses, as the Pacific rollers thundered in towards the shore. Together they watched the sun drop like a penny into the pocket of the far horizon and then the date ended with Olivia getting back into her Mercedes and Matt climbing into his battered old Saab as they headed back to their respective beds on different sides of town – Olivia to the luxurious comfort and grandeur of her suite at the Beverly Wilshire hotel, sited at one of the world's most famous intersections, Rodeo Drive and Wilshire Boulevard, and Matt to his room barely big enough in which to swing a cat.

The following day they greeted each other on the film set with knowing, but discreet, smiles. Inevitably their working relationship had changed. Suddenly they were closer, the chance to dance together more enticing, the touches more exciting. And what had once seemed like straightforward and innocent dance routines now seemed charged with sensuality and excitement. 'Once we went hiking together, well . . . love began to take its course,' said Matt. 'Livvy knew how to make her feelings known all right.'

But, although not yet lovers, neither found it easy to take on board that they had gone beyond the point of being simply friends and working partners. Matt remembered:

> Livvy backed off for a while to see how I would react and what I would do. She was taking a risk and had a lot to lose as she was the star and eleven years older than me. It was easier for me. I didn't really have anything at stake except my vanity.
>
> But, as an old-fashioned girl, Livvy likes her men to be men. She later told me that if I hadn't made the running, asked her out and so on, nothing would have happened – even though she wanted it to.

Hopping into bed with a man she had only just started dating was never Olivia's style of behaviour, however much she might have been attracted to Matt. She also wanted to be sure that this good-looking young dancer working on his first film was not just looking for an on-location fling for the duration of the shoot. Such liaisons are common-place in the world of movie-making, but Olivia wanted a proper courtship while she got to know Matt a great deal better.

As the days went by, it became obvious to them both that they were falling for each other, and the first time they made love was at the Beverly Wilshire. Matt carefully slipped quietly into the hotel a few minutes after Olivia to avoid any suspicion that they might be an item. He made his way to Olivia's suite and they immediately fell passion-ately into each other's arms.

It was a clandestine routine they kept up for months without detection, and on set they acted as if they contin-ued to be nothing more than good friends who were enjoy-ing a fruitful, professional working relationship. Only the director Robert Greenwald was in on the secret that Olivia and Matt were lovers and he loyally maintained the discre-tion they sought. He was naturally happy for them both – there was nothing a director liked better than to make a movie with a leading lady who was happy in her personal life. And there was nothing like a passionate new love affair with a sexy young man to ensure an actress turned up on a film set each morning with a smile on her face and feeling good about herself.

Preserving such secrecy was far from easy for the couple. They were longing to shout their love for each other to the world. But they had a film to complete first and if, for some reason, their affair failed to last until the movie was completed, news of their intimate liaison could have proved a major embarrassment for Olivia – especially as Lee Kramer was executive producer of *Xanadu*.

'I was paranoid about the age difference at first, very self-conscious and embarrassed,' Olivia has conceded. In her circle of friends she knew several women who had happily taken much younger lovers but somehow she could never quite imagine herself in a similar position. 'I used to tease my older sister about her younger boyfriends,' said Olivia, 'and now I was dating a much younger man.'

Olivia dreaded what the tabloids would make of her affair if they found out. Given her prim and proper public image, the newspapers would have had a field day. 'Younger men with older women weren't so common then,' she has pointed out, 'and, of course, I always wanted to do the right thing.'

Matt understood the need to keep their relationship under wraps but lamented: 'It was very hard not being able to go out and have fun, or go out to dinner together.'

Quite apart from the problem of trying to keep the lid on her affair with Matt, the making of *Xanadu* proved to be a far from smooth experience for Olivia. She had the misfortune to fall and fracture her coccyx during a roller-skating sequence for the song 'Suddenly'. Gamely she put up with the severe pain and in true showbiz fashion, she resolved that the show must go on.

Another major obstacle, according to Olivia, was that the script was unfinished when filming began and confusingly it was being rewritten as production went along. This, in itself, is not uncommon – *Gladiator*, for example, consisted of just thirty-five pages of script when filming began on what turned out to be a multi-Oscar-winning epic. Director Robert Greenwald clarified Olivia's complaint about the problems of *Xanadu*'s script being rewritten on the hoof when he gave an interview to *Entertainment Weekly* twenty-seven years later. He said: 'I wish it *was* being rewritten on the hoof. It was being written on the hoof! In my enthusiasm for the idea of doing a musical, I signed on before there was really any kind of script.' Olivia had done exactly the same. She had taken on the project on the strength of a twenty-page treatment.

Kenny Ortega, one of the film's choreographers, explained just what difficulties this presented: 'You were not quite sure why you were doing what you were doing.' Ortega, who went on to mastermind the dance scenes in the smash-hit movie *Dirty Dancing* before directing Disney's hugely successful TV movie *High School Musical*, added ruefully: 'You know, it's kinda nice knowing what takes you into a musical number and why you're coming out of it.'

The script was not the only thing undergoing a major change as filming progressed. *Xanadu* was originally conceived as a straight-on roller-disco movie, but the imminent release of two quickie roller-disco rival films, *Skatetown USA* and *Roller Boogie*, prompted a major rethink and the introduction of a blending of 1940s and 1980s styles for *Xanadu*. For Matt, at least, this was a bonus, as there would now be an additional glimpse of him on screen playing the clarinet in the old-time swing orchestra in a flashback scene as young Danny Maguire.

Along with the changes, the original $4million budget rose accordingly. The vast two-storey set of the *Xanadu* club alone cost $1million and took almost three months to build in Studio 4 of the Hollywood General Studios. The final *Xanadu* budget ended up at around $13million as Joel Silver developed the project.

Throughout all the shenanigans, Gene Kelly looked on with some bemusement. It was hardly the way they went about making musicals in the golden age of Hollywood, the sixty-eight-year-old actor wearily confided to friends.

The legendary dancer had taken his role in the movie partly because filming was just a short drive from his home in Beverly Hills, which meant he could remain close to his family throughout. He had originally served notice that he would not 'touch a toe', as he put it, for *Xanadu* but he was persuaded to change his mind and feature in dance sequences. The legions of devoted Gene Kelly fans were not slow to note that his *Xanadu* character Danny Maguire bore the same name as the character he played in the movie *Cover Girl* opposite Rita Hayworth in 1944 – about the same time as the Danny Maguire of *Xanadu* was supposedly at his peak.

Xanadu's story opens in southern California where Sonny Malone, played by Michael Beck, is a struggling young artist who works for a record company painting large versions of album covers to be used as promotional placards and posters outside record stores. Frustrated by what he sees as a waste of his creative talents and unappreciated by his overbearing boss, Sonny's life changes when he is handed an album by a band called The Nine Sisters, which has on its cover a beautiful blonde passing in front of an art deco auditorium. Sonny at once realises that the girl on the cover is the same as the one who had collided with him on roller-skates earlier that day, planted a kiss on his lips then skated away.

Obsessed with finding her, Sonny bumps into her twice more the same day, once while she roller-skates along the pathway at Venice beach, and once at the auditorium. But all he discovers from her is that her name is Kira. Unbeknown to him, Kira is one of nine beautiful muses who literally spring to life from a local mural in town near the beach.

Sonny's coincidental meetings convince him that he and

Kira are being set up, and shortly afterwards, while
strolling along a California beach, he gets talking to an
ageing former band leader and jazz musician-turned-
construction-magnate named Danny McGuire, played by
Gene Kelly. While nostalgically recalling a club he opened
back in 1945, it transpires Danny had a relationship many
years before with a girl who eerily resembled Kira.

During their conversation, the two men find they both
share a love of the arts and strike up a friendship. Kira then
encourages them to team up to fulfil their respective
dreams by opening a nightclub at the old auditorium
featured on the album cover by The Nine Sisters.

At the venue, Sonny once again meets up with the mysterious Kira and romance is in the air. But there is a problem
when they begin to fall for each other because Kira is no
mortal beauty – she is Terpsichore, the Muse of Dance, one
of the nine daughters of Zeus. Any romantic feelings she
might have for Sonny transgress immortal law. But once
the club is a spectacular success, love triumphs when Kira
talks her father Zeus into making her a human being, free
of all of her muse responsibilities.

The trailers for *Xanadu* seemed enticing enough, promising audiences it would be 'the most dazzling romantic
musical comedy in years'. It purported to be a movie with
something for everyone: it had a love story, a strong
musical score, a cartoon sequence when Kira and Sonny
turn into fish to pronounce their love, 1940s-style music
for the mums and dads, rock music for the teens, some
energetic dances on wheels and some Busby Berkeley-style
special effects.

'This musical fantasy appealed to me,' Olivia explained
to one interviewer. 'I'm concerned and saddened by conditions in the world now, and I hope that seeing *Xanadu* will

provide pleasure and a chance for people to get away from their problems. If only for a little while.'

* * *

Xanadu was released in August 1980 backed by a lavish marketing campaign that included specially themed *Xanadu* boutiques created in department stores where customers could buy copies of the film's costumes. Encouragingly for everyone connected with *Xanadu*, prior to the film's release Olivia had already taken John Farrar's song 'Magic' from the movie to the top of the US charts, beating off stiff competition from Billy Joel's 'It's Still Rock And Roll To Me' and Elton John's 'Little Jeannie'. That was no mean feat.

'Magic' debuted on Billboard's Hot 100 on 24 May 1980 and went to number one in the singles chart ten weeks later, staying there for four weeks. The hit record contributed an important three months of promotion for the movie.

For Olivia, her muse-like face prominently displayed on the promotional posters and her name taking pride of billing in front of Gene Kelly's, one of Hollywood's true greats, it was generally an anxious time. 'Open your eyes and hear the magic' was *Xanadu*'s promotional catchline. 'A Fantasy, A Musical, A Place Where Dreams Come True.' But by the time the marketing campaign was in full swing, Olivia must have had an early inkling that *Xanadu* was not going to make her dreams of fully fledged movie stardom come true.

When asked about the prospects of success for the movie, she wisely focused on the music and added: 'We hope the songs will be the songs of the eighties. They're kind of an ethereal music, written for the character I play.

It's a new style for me, which I like. I try to grow each year.' But she could not hide her fears for the film's success. 'My stomach is in my mouth,' she added. As it turned out, Olivia had every reason to be apprehensive.

On 25 July, two weeks before its release, *Xanadu* was given an important promotional showcase on TV when Olivia hosted *The Midnight Special* show and much of the airtime was devoted to the movie. But no amount of promotion was able to prevent the critics from slaughtering the film when it was released. While no one connected with *Xanadu* was promising it was a movie to rival *Singin' In The Rain*, they were not prepared for the savagery of the reviews.

Variety, the Bible of the entertainment industry, called it 'Truly stupendously bad', and likened Olivia, outlined on screen in special-effect ethereal fluorescent glow, to a 'roller-skating light bulb'. *Esquire* magazine said: 'In a word, Xana-don't.' *Time* magazine presented its review of the film under the headline, 'Oh, shut up, Muse!'

When *Xanadu* reached England, the verdict from the critics was much the same. They too panned it and Felix Barker, veteran critic of the *London Evening News*, went so far as to describe it as: 'The most dreadful, tasteless movie of the decade. Indeed, probably of all time.'

Even Michael Cotton of The Tubes, a pop group who had been given an early break by their inclusion in the movie as an up-and-coming rock band, looked back and described the film like this: 'It was just a train wreck.' Cotton, who featured with The Tubes in a sequence where Danny and Sonny are envisaging what kind of music their club should present, did, however, qualify his verdict by adding that it was 'a big, giant, colourful train wreck'.

One of the problems facing *Xanadu* was that by the time

it hit cinema screens, roller discos were passé. Youth culture and its taste in music had moved on. Punk bands, not disco, were in. In the week when *Xanadu* was premiered in Los Angeles, the city's Santa Monica Civic Auditorium was hosting the first Urgh! two-day festival of local national and international punk and new wave rock bands, featuring The Dead Boys and The Dead Kennedys. Anything further from the roller-skating romp on screen at the cinema round the corner was hard to imagine.

In retrospect, the omens for a disco-themed movie like *Xanadu* had not been entirely favourable from the start. By the time the film went into production, the disco-dancing craze generated by *Saturday Night Fever* had cooled considerably. A sign of the times and of changing moods and musical tastes came on 12 July 1979, just a matter of weeks before the *Xanadu* cameras started rolling, when a Disco Demolition Derby was held at Chicago's Comiskey Park. More than 10,000 dance-floor-flavoured records were blown up with explosives, accompanied by rousing cheers from a watching crowd including a large percentage of teenagers. Now *Xanadu*, released in 1980 as a roller-skating disco extravaganza, looked instantly dated. Word of mouth coupled with the terrible reviews condemned the movie to failure.

For the most part Olivia herself escaped direct savaging from the critics. It was the film as a whole that took a critical hammering. But she was nevertheless devastated at the reaction. She hated being linked with failure.

Olivia's dialogue in the special effects-laden movie was minimal, but at times Kira the Muse noticeably spoke with an Aussie accent. Olivia was not helped by cringeworthy exchanges with Michael Beck. 'I'm a Muse,' she tells him at one point, which prompts his reply: 'I'm glad somebody's having a good time.' Then, to explain to the dumbest in the audience what a muse is, the couple hamfistedly look up the word in a dictionary together. Another corny line had Gene Kelly exclaiming on opening his club: 'I'm back in showbusiness!' All that was missing was a wink to the camera.

'The film did fall a little short in the dialogue stakes,' Olivia finally conceded two years after *Xanadu*'s release. 'The script used to change daily and I was really embarrassed with some of the lines I had to say. We even came back from a Christmas break to find the whole story had changed.'

Apart from a few awkward wobbles, Olivia coped competently enough with her roller-skating sequences and never appeared to be anything less than enjoying herself. She looked alternatively heavenly, alluring, stylish, raunchy or beautifully groomed in 1940s fashion, as the scenes and clothes demanded.

The Xanadu club's opening-night extravaganza, which formed the film's spectacular finale, took three weeks to shoot and involved no less than 237 roller-skaters, dancers, jugglers, gymnasts, tightrope walkers, acrobats and other speciality acts. It also offered the extraordinary sight of the great Gene Kelly getting his skates on and leading a veritable army of dancers in a wild spin on wheels around the club's outer circle.

This fast-moving vibrant sequence also gave Olivia the chance to shine in a variety of eye-catching costumes. She tap-danced in a 1940's halterneck sun-suit with her hair teased into a Betty Grable-style, and rocked up a storm in a tiny tiger-print mini-skirt with matching waistcoat and knee-high black leather boots. For a country-tinged number Olivia switched to a white-tasselled buckskin cowgirl outfit, then later she glided up a ramp in an exquisitely elegant Erté-style gown.

As the enchanting Kira, Olivia was mostly dressed in simple, off-the-shoulder dresses slashed to the thigh and teamed with . . . leg-warmers! Asked in 2007 to comment on this wardrobe oddity, director Robert Greenwald said with his tongue tucked very firmly in his cheek: 'One of the points I think it's important to make is the hidden political meaning in the film. I want people to look carefully for the politics in the leg-warmers.'

* * *

Nearly three decades after its original release, *Xanadu* still divides opinion. It's easy to spot its failings and yet it has acquired a passionate cult following who revel in its gloriously camp approach.

Xanadu the movie may have been a commercial and critical dud, but the soundtrack LP was a huge hit for both Olivia and Jeff Lynne's Electric Light Orchestra. Issued as a single, the movie's title song reached number eight in the US charts and was number one for two weeks in the UK. Jeff Lynne has said that he was asked to include the word *Xanadu* in the song as many times as possible. He managed a total of twenty-one.

In all, five tracks from the movie became hits in both Britain and the United States. Olivia's solo 'Magic' topped the US charts to notch up her third number one in America. 'Suddenly', a lovely John Farrar romantic ballad on which Olivia duetted with Cliff Richard vocally but not on screen, peaked at number twenty.

The appalling reviews may have enveloped the movie with an atmosphere of calamitous failure, but the fact remains that the gloriously awful *Xanadu* made $22million at the US box office alone, almost double its outlay. The soundtrack album sold two million copies, and some tracks still feature on radio playlists around the world to this day. Olivia took one of its songs to the top of the US charts for a month and another to the top of the UK charts. The film also yielded one of Olivia's own personal favourites, 'Suspended In Time', another beautiful ballad written by John Farrar.

The DVD of *Xanadu* has sold surprisingly well for a film given such a panning and the highly dubious honour of being largely responsible for the creation of Hollywood's Golden Raspberry Awards. This is an annual awards event held pre-Oscars night to celebrate the year's worst dross to reach the cinema screen. The Razzies, as they have become known, were created in 1981 by a certain John Wilson after he had paid the sum of 99 cents to see a double bill of *Xanadu* and *Can't Stop The Music*. He was so appalled at what he had seen that he demanded a refund for his ticket but was flatly refused. At the inaugural Golden Raspberry Awards, held among friends in Wilson's sitting room, *Xanadu* picked up seven nominations – Olivia was nominated as Worst Actress – and 'won' one award for worst director. *Can't Stop The Music*, the film Olivia had almost taken as her follow-up to *Grease*, was named Worst Picture.

Like *Xanadu*, *Can't Stop The Music* was released some time after the disco craze had peaked and Allan Carr's let's-form-a-group-right-now movie with The Village People received much the same butchering from the critics. *Newsweek* said: '*Can't Stop the Music* ushers in a whole new concept in entertainment – it's the first all-singing, all-dancing horror film; *The Dawn Of The Dead* of the disco era.' *Film Review* called it: 'The most conspicuous box office calamity of the summer.'

Some twenty-seven years on, John Wilson's opinion of *Xanadu* had not changed. '*Xanadu* is a touchstone of movie wretchedness,' he seethed. 'Seeing Gene Kelly, who did *Singin' In The Rain*, doing those clunky roller-disco moves with people throwing bowling pins over his head – it's almost like he had gone to hell before he died.'

Three years on from the release of *Xanadu*, Olivia experienced one totally unexpected, unwanted and alarming side effect from the movie which so terrified her that she felt compelled to leave the country temporarily for her own safety. She found herself named as a potential victim on the hit list of a violent killer by the name of Michael Owen Perry, a dangerously disturbed young man who had escaped from a mental institution. Perry was living in the summer of 1983 in a trailer behind his parents' house in Port Arthur and, after watching *Xanadu*, he became convinced that Olivia really was a Greek goddess and that she was responsible for the corpses Perry hallucinated were coming up through his floorboards. He also came to believe that she communicated with him by changing the colour of her eyes.

Perry went so far as to write a letter to Olivia in which he explained: 'I heard voices and the voices said to me that you are a muse and trapped under Lake Arthur.'

Strange letters from oddballs are an occupational hazard for the famous. Most are harmless but there was something sinister about this one and so it proved. On 17 July 1983, Perry armed himself with guns, including a 357 magnum and a Beretta pistol, and embarked on an horrific orgy of killing which left two of his cousins, a two-year-old nephew and his parents all dead. He shot both of his parents through the eyes. Then Perry vanished, leaving behind in his parents' house a number of names on a death list. One of them was 'Olivia'.

While a massive police manhunt got under way, the threat was enough for Olivia to leave the country for a while. 'She was so worried she packed her bags and stayed in a hotel before getting a plane to fly out here,' Olivia's father told reporters from his Manly home in Sydney.

But on 31 July, two weeks after his sickening shooting spree, Perry was tracked down to the Annex Hotel in Washington DC and apprehended. There in his room police discovered nine television sets all switched to static. On some of the screens there were eyes drawn with a felt-tip pen. Perry was convicted of the murders in 1985 and remains on death row to this day.

'I guess because I was playing this ethereal character, he got reality and showbusiness confused,' commented Olivia. 'I left the country for a while. That was a very scary time.'

* * *

Xanadu achieved and has held on to cult movie status, particularly among women and the gay community. It refuses to fade away. In 2001, a stage parody *Xanadu Live!* ran in Los Angeles – its director Annie Dorsen described the film as 'the queerest movie that's not actually about being gay'. And the following year, a '*Xanadu* singalong' took place at Hollywood's John Anson Ford Amphitheatre as part of Outfest, LA's annual gay and lesbian film festival. The 1,200-capacity venue was a sell-out.

In 2007 a new $4million stage production of *Xanadu* opened on Broadway to favourable reviews, which surprised many. The *New York Times* called it 'outlandishly enjoyable'. Broadway was used to staging productions adapted from big-screen hits but rarely from a screen flop. According to its writer, Douglas Carter Beane, however, he was given carte blanche with his pen and retained only a handful of lines from the movie. Beane says when he saw the film, he could not believe how bad the dialogue was and how the plotting was abandoned. 'The first time I saw it I thought they had misplaced a reel,' he commented.

Bravely, Olivia has described *Xanadu* as a 'character-building' bomb, and is honest enough to admit: 'When I was really close to it, when we made it, I thought: why did I do that?'

She was later able to joke: 'I certainly wouldn't die of over-exposure. Not enough people saw it. I don't regret it or anything I've done. I learned a lot and the music was successful. I would have been upset if the music had flopped.'

It's to Olivia's credit that these days she can look back fondly at the cinematic calamity. For a long time after the film was initially released, mention of *Xanadu* was quietly avoided in connection with Olivia's career. But on 10 July 2007, she joined the New York cast of the Broadway production for the opening-night curtain call and was given an enthusiastic reception.

Gene Kelly was professional enough not to say in public at the time precisely what he thought of the last movie in which he danced. After such an illustrious career, he must have been disheartened to be associated with such a bomb. Much later he did go on record as saying he thought *Xanadu* was a bad film but chivalrously noted that working with Olivia had been a joy. Suffice to say that after *Xanadu*, Kelly never took on another acting role in a feature film. It was a sad finale to a glittering career. He died on 2 February 1996.

After *Xanadu*, producer Larry Gordon went on to make the Bruce Willis hit *Die Hard*, co-produced by Joel Silver. Robert Greenwald in recent years has been directing documentaries, but Michael Beck lamented: '*The Warriors* opened a lot of doors in film for me, which *Xanadu* then closed.'

For Olivia's ambitions as an actress, *Xanadu* was a body blow. It severely damaged her standing as a bankable box office movie star. But there were consolations: two chart-topping hits and a dream achieved of partnering a true legend on the dance floor. 'I never thought I'd ever get the chance to dance with Gene Kelly,' she said. 'I had great fear and trepidation at the thought of dancing with him. But on the first day of rehearsals he put me at my ease completely.'

* * *

On a personal level, the greatest benefit for Olivia from her *Xanadu* experience was her blossoming love affair with Matt. She had found the man she would eventually marry. She had always been drawn to confident men with a touch of arrogance about them, but in Matt she had found for the first time a lover she felt was not competing with her.

Olivia and her young lover kept their affair secret right to the very end of the production. Even at the party after the Los Angeles premiere of *Xanadu*, the couple took care to distance themselves from each other. 'It was very tough,' said Matt. 'I wanted to dance with Livvy and couldn't, which was silly really because she danced with lots of other guys from the set. But it was something we had agreed before going.'

Inevitably, when Olivia gave interviews to promote the

film in various countries, one question continually cropped up: 'When are you going to settle down?' She successfully continued to conceal from journalists, and therefore the public, her romantic involvement with Matt. But anyone reading very carefully between the lines might have realised there was now someone special in her life. 'Lately I've found myself doodling little pictures of cottages with whitewashed walls and picket fences,' she told Australia's *Women's Weekly* on the eve of the Aussie premiere of *Xanadu*. 'Very old-fashioned, isn't that?' she asked. 'Inside the cottage I see a happy family, children.'

One reason why it took the press so long to cotton on to Olivia's love affair was that she deliberately altered her appearance. 'After I'd finished filming *Xanadu* I just decided to cut all my hair off,' she revealed. 'It had been ruined by filming anyway and I decided not to dye it any more either.

'It was wonderful. I felt like a whole new person. Nobody recognised me on the streets of LA for months. I was just a girl with short dark hair who looked a little like Olivia Newton-John.'

A year after Matt and Olivia shared their first kiss on their hike in Will Rogers State Park, Matt went out to Olivia's ranch house in Malibu with its own swimming pool, riding stables, floodlit tennis court and jacuzzi. For a boy used to sharing a small house with eleven others back in Portland, Oregon, it took his breath away. This was the sort of luxury celebrity home he had only read about in glossy magazines. The contrast with his own humble rented apartment in Los Angeles and the frugal way his large family lived back in Portland could hardly have been more marked. 'It was such a weird experience,' he said. 'I couldn't believe it. My family wasn't poor. We always had plenty of good food, but when you're one of ten kids, there's not much left for luxuries. There was one small black and white TV for all twelve of us.'

By February of 1981, Matt and Olivia were a solidly entwined couple who were in love and planning a future together. When they began living together, they resolved the time had come to be perfectly open about their relationship. 'That's when we started hitting the town together, the cameras started clicking and the press started talking about us,' said Matt.

The press of course made much of the fact that Olivia was a millionaire and Matt was a hard-up actor ten years her junior who still had to sign on the dole in between film parts. Matt told the world that they intended to marry at some point in the future. 'I want to wait until I am financially able to contribute,' he said. 'We are very much in love. We do everything together. But I refuse to take anything from Olivia. I insist that I must earn my own money.'

As for the ten years between them, Matt said:

> There never has seemed any age difference. I think it's partly because I always liked older people. I'd play with kids my own age but I preferred the conversation of older people.
>
> I dated girls my own age too, but I never felt any commitment to anyone until I met Olivia. The only confession I can make on fantasising about older women is that I was terribly in love with Doris Day. I used to stay home on Sundays to watch all her movies.

While relieved that he and Olivia no longer had to preserve their secrecy, Matt had to face up to a new reality. *Xanadu* had given him a foothold in movies, but as far as his career was concerned, essentially he was just another dancer in Hollywood. The fact that he was the lover of a very famous singer was what set him apart from his peers. 'The trouble was, I was becoming better known as Livvy's guy than as an actor,' he lamented. 'That was very worrying, but I couldn't do much about it.'

Grease had done wonders for Olivia's image, and the emergence into the public eye of Matt on Olivia's arm added further spice to it. 'People had to revise their view of her,' said a member of the *Xanadu* crew. 'She looked as though butter wouldn't melt in her mouth. And then suddenly it turns out she's secretly been making out with this much younger guy who looks like a sexy hot young stud. And what's more, you could tell she was really into him, and once the secret was out she wasn't afraid to show it. It made you wonder which was the real Olivia Newton-John – white bread or a white-hot cookie?'

Matt fanned the flames of debate by giving an interview to an American magazine in which he was quoted as saying of Olivia: 'She's not just white bread any more, and she's showing it. I think I've brought out the female animal in her.'

Ironically, Olivia's passionate affair with Matt coincided with her emergence as a gay icon thanks to the camp appeal of *Xanadu*. The movie gave her an unexpected following among the gay community and, thanks to a totally inno-cent remark Olivia had made on Johnny Carson's *Tonight Show* many years before, whispers resurfaced about her being a lesbian.

Olivia had been a guest on Carson's chat show at a time when she was first enjoying success in America with her smash hit 'I Honestly Love You'. After performing the song on his programme, she was asked by Carson about the friends she kept and Olivia had replied that she had lots of girl friends. She meant that she had a supportive network of friends who were female, but Carson's raised eyebrows and quizzical expression at the singer's answer gave entirely the wrong impression about Olivia's sexual preferences to the millions of viewers who watched his top-rated TV show.

Del Shores, the gay writer-director with whom Olivia became a long-standing friend and whom she would eventually work for on his 1999 movie *Sordid Lives*, liked to joke that he stayed straight for two decades because whenever he questioned his sexuality, he felt he must be straight because he was attracted to Olivia Newton-John. 'Then I found a lot of gay men are attracted to Olivia Newton-John,' he said. Matt was most certainly not one of them.

Getting Physical

Grease may have hinted that there was a great deal more to Olivia Newton-John than met the eye. And her perceived image as the eternal ingénue certainly required a radical rethink after she moved a hot young lover in the virile shape of Matt Lattanzi into her Malibu home.

To those who knew Olivia well, she had never seemed happier. She and Matt were madly in love and Matt clearly adored her. 'I love her because she's a woman, a very mature woman who, apart from being beautiful, I find tremendously inspiring,' he said. 'She lives life instinctively, she seems to do everything right.'

Matt maintained the age difference between them was meaningless, but he nevertheless had to put up with critics predicting their relationship wouldn't last. 'People said "It will never work out" so many times I gave up giving them a reply,' he said, and added: 'I was never really aware of being known as her toy boy. We were so happy I didn't think of anything else. In fact, I was blind with happiness.'

Once Matt had moved into Olivia's ranch and the couple were living openly together, they spent happy days walking the dogs by the sea, going out riding together, hiking and making love. Neither of them was interested in the Hollywood party scene, and they preferred to live privately and quietly enjoying each other's company.

Matt's unspoiled youthful exuberance, his sense of fun, his love of the outdoors and his boyish spirit of adventure rubbed off on Olivia. She found Matt's easygoing sense of freedom to be infectious and it was something she had to some extent missed out on when she was younger. From the age of fifteen she had pursued her career as a singer, and there was always the next song, the next record, the next TV show and the next concert to consider and plan. Olivia was a career woman who had become accustomed to signing autographs from the age of fourteen, and by the time she fell for Matt, she had been working pretty much solidly for nigh on fifteen years, almost half her life. Matt loved nothing better than going off on a long hike to explore some new remote area with a backpack and a fishing rod and a willingness to pitch a tent by a river or sleep out under the stars. He was, he said, a man for the wilderness and every year he'd cheerfully take off for a week on his own in Death Valley.

Matt also liked to go running regularly, up to seven miles a day, by the sea, or hit the beach to go surfing, scuba diving and sailing, and he showed Olivia that there was more to sport than playing a couple of sets of tennis, which seemed to be the obligatory game of the Hollywood elite.

Olivia was pleased to follow her young lover's energetic lead. 'She has such a youthful manner, she runs around with me all the time,' Matt said approvingly. Some of Olivia's happiest days off were spent on camping trips with Matt in California or in Matt's home state of Oregon. Other times they'd simply drive out in a van together to destinations unknown and sleep in the back of the van or pitch a tent by a lake and get up in the morning and catch fish for breakfast.

Some cynics unkindly hinted that Matt's hitching himself to a superstar was no bad career move for a budding young actor like him. But he showed he was serious in his ambitions by conscientiously attending acting school and asking Olivia for advice rather than favours. With her considerable experience of the showbiz scene and knowledge of the Hollywood rat race, Olivia was determined to help her boyfriend avoid the pitfalls of Tinseltown. 'Hollywood is terribly rough on kids who come here all by themselves with no friends and nobody to talk to,' she said.

'I tell Matt that if you have good people working for you and friends to encourage you, and if you have talent, you'll be fine. I give him advice and encouragement, but that's about all. I advise him to be picky, and not believe the flattery or his own publicity, and to keep his feet on the ground.'

In 1981, the year after *Xanadu*'s release, Matt secured a role in what turned out to be legendary Hollywood director George Cukor's last film, *Rich And Famous*, starring Jacqueline Bisset and Candice Bergen as two women whose long-standing friendship is tested when one rises from obscurity to success as a novelist.

Matt played a hustler who has a one-afternoon stand with Jackie Bisset, a role that included some rear-view nudity for the young actor. Outwardly Olivia appeared unconcerned about her lover filming his romp in the buff with an actress as alluring as Jackie Bisset. Olivia was professional enough to know that Matt and Jackie had a job to do when the script called for it but inwardly she was not best pleased, as Matt found out – but not until two years later. He recalled:

Showing my buns on camera was a big decision for me, but I decided to do it for the sake of art. I was never going to be nude for that film. But George Cukor, the director, took me to one side and said: 'You don't want to wear any clothes for this scene, do you? You're a bad boy, and bad boys don't wear clothes.' I asked Jacqueline if she minded. She took one look and said: 'Yeah, go for it.' So I took the lot off. I was bare-ass naked, nothing.

And you know what Livvy said when she saw the film? Absolutely nothing. Then two whole years later the subject of the film comes up and she suddenly said: 'You little creep!'

The truth is that she's so sexy I never even think of another woman. She once had an album called *Totally Hot*, and that's exactly how she is in real life.

Rich And Famous, with its starry cast and illustrious director, should have presented Matt with a terrific opportunity to show what he could do but, looking back, he felt he failed to capitalise on it. 'I used to wonder at all the talk about how tough it was to get started. But I was living in the comfort zone. No one pushed me to make something of my part. The result was that I wasn't great. It didn't do my career any good.'

In 1983, Matt starred in a new movie called *My Tutor*, a coming-of-age comedy in which he played a teenager who learns a lot more than French when his father hires an older but beautiful blonde as his son's private tutor for the summer. Caren Kaye starred as the teacher who preferred to take her pupil out of the classroom and give him lessons in the more worldly setting of the bedroom.

Matt was required to film a tasteful love scene with Caren, as well as a much more risqué scene with a lissom young brunette called Jewel Shepard. Olivia chose to be on set for the latter, but Jewel is on record as saying that the singer kept her cool when the cameras rolled as she watched Jewel get to grips with her beau.

'I played a fantasy girl,' Jewel reported. 'I was in a phone booth when lead actor Matt Lattanzi sees me and dreams of having sex with me. In the fantasy sequence, he pulls me out of the phone booth, throws me into a limousine, rips off my top and starts to have sex with me. Come to think of it, that was the first limo I was ever in. Olivia Newton-John, who was Matt's girlfriend, was on the set to make sure that everything was kosher. She was a nice woman who didn't seem to be jealous or anything.'

'She isn't unhappy about me doing those sorts of films as long as I don't flash myself around,' Matt said of Olivia when promoting the movie. 'And I'm not seen nude in *My Tutor*. One of the good things about our relationship is that neither of us are jealous people. Livvy wasn't upset or jealous that I was in bed with another woman, that was part of the job. It was just a stepping stone.'

Years later he reflected ruefully: 'I got caught up in a treadmill of work I didn't want to do. I had no control over my career and the roles were superficial.'

But as he pursued his own career, Matt was able to say: 'There were never any ego problems between Livvy and me. It was no use me looking at her success and thinking: "When's it going to happen for me?" I don't understand that sort of attitude. I was glad every time Livvy had something good coming along and supported her in it.' And one of Olivia's projects he gave his backing to was a single and an album, which showed Olivia in a very new and controversial light.

* * *

Given Matt's heartthrob good looks, it was perhaps only to be expected that casting directors saw him as a prime candidate for sexy screen roles. What was totally unexpected one year on from *Xanadu* was that it would be Olivia who would find herself embroiled in a controversy about sex. It was all because she made a record containing such blatantly sexual connotations that she landed herself in hot water with broadcasting authorities and caused ructions that were felt as far away as South Africa.

The record was called 'Physical', and no matter from what angle the lyrics were analysed there was only one conclusion. 'Of course the song was about sex,' said Aussie Steve Kipner, who co-wrote 'Physical' with Terry Shaddick.

With Olivia delivering a vocal invitation to get physical horizontally, it could hardly be about anything else. And just before the single was due for release to record stores right across America in November 1981, she worked herself up into a terrible lather about the damage it could do to her image and career.

'I knew it was a great song and a hit for somebody,' she said after she had recorded 'Physical'. 'But then I had a panic attack. I thought: this song is way too out there, it's too sexual, it's way too bold and too cheeky.'

The more she thought about the implications such controversy would have upon her career, the more worried she became. Several months earlier, on 5 August, America's entertainment industry had accorded Olivia one of its most visible accolades – a star bearing her name on Hollywood's Walk of Fame outside Mann's Chinese Theatre on Hollywood Boulevard in Los Angeles. America had indelibly honoured the singer they all saw as an absolute sweetheart through and through.

Now, with the imminent arrival in the shops of 'Physical', Olivia's nerves were in shreds and she phoned up her new manager Roger Davies with a desperate plea for him to pull the record's release. 'I freaked,' Olivia recalled. 'I was terrified. I never wanted to offend anybody. I phoned my manager and said: "Roger, this has gone way too far, it's way too sexy. I think we should pull this. And he said: "It's way too late, it's gone to radio."'

Olivia kept imploring him to put a stop on the record. She saw herself alienating many of her loyal fans. They might be so offended they could desert her for ever. Even Tina Turner, never the most reticent of songstresses when it came to singing it like it is, or frightened of strutting her stuff and exuding sexuality on stage, had passed on the song before it was offered to Olivia. Tina ventured the opinion it was too sexy, too obvious, when Lee Kramer offered 'Physical' to her as a carrot in a bid to take over Tina's management.

The story goes that the song came Olivia's way after Roger Davies, then Kramer's assistant, had happened to overhear Steve Kipner and Lee Chadwick playing a demo disc of 'Physical' for Kramer in another room in Kramer's office. For once the two songwriters had collaborated on a song about physical rather than emotional love and when Roger heard it he thought it was worth offering to Olivia.

Roger, who went on to become Olivia's manager after her personal and professional split from Lee Kramer in 1980, came from a rock and roll background and he was therefore more adventurous and willing to take risks. He felt 'Physical' provided an ideal chance for Olivia to change musical direction, and Roger's view was endorsed by Matt, who encouraged Olivia to regard the project as a bit of fun and showed his support by being present during the recording.

But as the release drew near, Olivia was getting cold feet. Roger did his best to soothe her nerves over the lyrical content and Olivia found her pleas for the record's recall were in vain. It was pointed out to her that this was the song the record company had identified as the obvious single from the album, also to be called *Physical*, and they weren't about to revise their whole marketing strategy at the eleventh hour. Olivia remembers: 'I was told: "You're too late. It's gone to radio," and before I knew it, it was being played everywhere.' All she could do was sit back, keep her fingers crossed and wait for the anticipated flak.

The first mutterings about *Physical*'s questionable taste were already beginning to be heard just as Olivia was due to film a video to promote the single and the album. Her management team racked their brains as to how best to go about it without possibly causing further offence. 'We needed to tone it down in the video, to do something to counteract the sexuality of the song,' said Olivia. 'And the answer was exercising.'

The aerobics craze was just starting to take a firm hold in America at around this time, and the video was deliberately set in a gymnasium to latch on to it. The idea was to divert the ear away from the dubious lyrics and concentrate the eye on Olivia, alluringly kitted out in trendy gym kit and singing along during a workout.

Wearing a headband over her hair cropped short and clad in a clinging leotard, a playful Olivia starts off by ogling several hunks working out in just-decent briefs but they then morph into a grossly overweight bunch of fatties sweating away on the exercise machines. After taking a shower still in her workout gear, Olivia returns to the gym wearing badminton kit, and finds the fatties have vanished. Just a few hunks remain, and, in a clever twist at the end, the beautiful hunks of beefcake leave the gym hand in hand and wander off together into the steam room while Olivia walks off with one of the fatties.

'I thought it was a brilliant idea that they switched it round and came up with a gym idea,' said Pat Farrar when she saw the end result. 'I remember Olivia being really, really scared about releasing "Physical" because of the lyric. It was a bit raunchy for her and she was really worried about it.'

During the heat of the controversy Olivia attempted to explain away the furore when she spoke to *People* magazine: 'I just wasn't in the mood for tender ballads. I wanted peppy stuff because that's how I'm feeling. We thought it was a great title because of the keep-fit craze that's going on.'

'Physical' did, in fact, become an aerobics anthem and a favourite workout number at keep-fit classes, health clubs and gyms, but its sexual innuendo was what captured most attention. 'I think the song has a double entendre,' its singer finally allowed with remarkable understatement. 'You can take it how you want to. But it's meant to be fun ... it's not meant to be taken seriously.'

The problem for Olivia was that some radio-programming executives, especially in Utah, took the innuendo very seriously indeed and banned the record for its 'suggestive lyrics'. One music director explained to the influential *Billboard* magazine: 'Once the words sank in, it caused an uncomfortableness among listeners.' The South African Broadcasting Corporation also censored the record as offensive. They insisted that the line 'There's nothing left to talk about unless it's horizontally' be omitted.

In the record business all publicity is good publicity, and the fuss surrounding 'Physical' propelled it swiftly into

America's pop charts. It debuted as the highest new entry on Billboard's Hot 100 at number sixty-six early in October 1981 but took its time to hit number one fully eight weeks later. Once at the top, 'Physical' stayed there for an incredible ten weeks, boosted by the coast-to-coast screening of Olivia's fourth US television special called *Olivia Newton-John: Let's Get Physical*, which featured songs from the album.

The single's longevity at the top placed it in a three-way tie for the second longest-running number one of the rock era. Olivia shared the distinction with Guy Mitchell's 'Singing The Blues' and Debby Boone's 'You Light Up My Life'. Only Elvis Presley, back in 1956, had enjoyed longer at number one – with 'Don't Be Cruel / Hound Dog' which topped the singles charts for eleven weeks. *Billboard* named 'Physical' their record of 1981.

In England 'Physical' wasn't quite the sensation it had been in the less liberal United States, but the record nevertheless reached number seven and enjoyed a run in the UK Top Thirty of sixteen weeks.

The LP was also a winner, peaking at number six in the US and at number eleven in the UK. The international success of both the single and the album went a long way towards moving Olivia on from the panning by the critics of *Xanadu* the year before. In time, post-Madonna, Olivia could look back and ask herself why she had been so worried about 'Physical'. 'It was so tame compared with what happens now,' she laughed. 'But before the song came out it was really white-knuckle time.'

* * *

The television special, *Olivia Newton-John: Let's Get*

The lady is a vamp: *Grease*'s prim student cheerleader Sandy turns school siren with the famous come-on to Danny: 'Tell me about it . . . stud.'

John Travolta, as Danny, jives with Olivia in Rydell High's dance-off contest in *Grease*, the biggest movie musical of all time.

The drive-in movie scene was the one chosen for Olivia to enact during her successful Hollywood audition for the role of Sandy.

Roller-skating with
Michael Beck towards
a savaging from the
critics in the movie
musical *Xanadu*.

Xanadu at least gave
Olivia the chance to
dance with legendary
Hollywood hoofer
Gene Kelly.

With former husband Matt Lattanzi and daughter Chloe, the child Olivia had longed for.

Like mother, like daughter. Chloe has inherited her mother's good looks and is following in her musical footsteps.

© Corbis

(*Above*) Filming the gym workout video in a bid to counter the controversy over her suggestive smash hit *Physical*.

(*Below left*) Back in the arms of John Travolta in the romantic comedy *Two Of A Kind*.

(*Below right*) Striking a very different chord as tattooed lesbian ex-con Bitsy-Mae Harling in the movie *Sordid Lives*.

Photos12.com

© Wenn

A lifelong love, and campaigner, for all creatures great and small: swimming with dolphins in Hawaii.

Strolling the sands of Malibu with her dog.

Happiness is a horse and a hug.

(*Above*) Lost love: One-time boyfriend Patrick McDermott's baffling disappearance at sea remains an unsolved mystery.

(*Below left*) Sibling love: Olivia with older sister Rona who acted as her chaperone during the singer's early singing career.

(*Below right*) Motherly love: Against Olivia's wishes, Irene took her teenage daughter to London from Melbourne. The move set her on the way to stardom. And Olivia remains ever grateful that mother knew best.

Olivia's fifteen-year friendship with Aussie health guru John Easterling blossomed into romance and they married in secret in Peru in June 2008.

Stepping out with John on the first of 228 miles to Beijing along the Great Wall of China to raise funds for a new cancer and wellness centre to be opened in Olivia's name in Melbourne.

Physical, was in many ways ahead of its time. Right from when he took over from Lee Kramer as Olivia's manager, Roger Davies had viewed her as a singer who could become a hugely popular video artist. At that point there was no MTV or cable TV channels showing music videos. But he persuaded Olivia to put up the then large sum of $600,000 to make her own video of the album and gave her his word he would get it shown on television.

A sizeable crew was assembled for the project under London-born director Brian Grant, who won the contract from a field of contenders that included several Hollywood feature-film directors. Olivia viewed the composite reels sent in by each of the contenders and chose Grant, who had worked on pop videos with the likes of Kim Wilde. Olivia appreciated the way Grant captured women on camera and liked him instantly when they met up to discuss ideas. 'He had no preconceived ideas about me, which was terrific,' she said.

Grant was under considerable pressure to make a good fist of the project to ensure television companies considered it entertaining enough to broadcast. The end product was inventive, imaginative, stylish and classy and presented Olivia in a variety of roles from raunchy space cowboy to aggressive business executive ensnaring a younger male colleague, fittingly played by Matt.

Roger was fully aware the venture was a huge risk, and initially he was unable to raise any firm interest from a single major TV company. 'I was terrified,' he said. 'All this money Olivia had put up and it looked like I'd bombed. But finally I somehow convinced America's ABC network to take it as an hour special. They'd never done anything like it before, but they took a chance and it went through the roof. It was the highest rating special of all time, gave a new image to Olivia and took the album to number one worldwide.'

Without a hint of blushing Olivia opened the TV special by telling viewers: 'If you have any preconceived idea about the 1980s or me, you'd better hang on to your hats.' One reviewer suggested the audience should have also been asked to hang on to their libidos as Olivia cavorted through an hour's worth of mini-musicals. 'The costumes were slinky, and the body language was calculated to raise living room temperatures even during the century's coldest winter,' the review concluded.

Prior to the hour-long screening of the programme on the BBC in the UK, Olivia explained: 'At thirty-four I'm too old to be innocent. It's time that I told my public that I have in fact lived up and down the spectrum. I've had lovers and I've been hurt and I've done all sorts of things that Doris Day wouldn't have condoned. And I don't regret a thing.'

Olivia's song of lust may have been the one to catch the ear on the LP *Physical*, but the two tracks that meant most to her personally were 'The Promise (The Dolphin Song)' and an anti-pesticide number called 'Silvery Rain'.

The former was an emotional ode to dolphins and her concern for their future, which she wrote herself. Olivia struggled for some time with the lyrics and the song remained unfinished until she flew to Hawaii for a working holiday where she spent a day frolicking with dolphins at Sea Life Park. Next morning she woke up with the melody and the lyrics fully formed in her head – a gift she believes from the dolphins themselves. 'As soon as I saw the dolphins, it all came to me in a great rush.'

To complete the desired sound effect in the production, the noises of the ocean were recorded at Santa Monica and real dolphin sounds were added. For the video, Olivia swam with two dolphins who pulled her through the water while a third led the way.

'Silvery Rain' was an ecology-conscious song by Hank Marvin of The Shadows, which highlighted the damage suffered by birds and other wildlife from aerial crop-spraying. Olivia cleverly worked the anti-pesticide song into her live concert act by singing it in a shower of confetti. Typically, Olivia was happiest that the album sold millions because the real beneficiaries, so she hoped, were the dolphins she was championing and the environment.

The success of the ABC special, and of the videos in general, was a pointer to the direction Olivia's career would take. As she increasingly cut back on tours and concert appearances in years to come, she was still able to remain a very visible artiste on expensively and imaginatively produced videos filmed to accompany her records and with the MTV generation in mind.

11

Soul Kiss

'Matt has helped me lose my inhibitions'

Olivia

Ever since the phenomenal success of *Grease*, Hollywood power brokers had been desperate to pair Olivia with John Travolta in another major movie. The duo had made history as the stars of the most successful movie musical of all time and it was only logical that one day they would be persuaded to team up again.

In the four years since *Grease*, some thirty different projects had come up for serious consideration by the two stars, but all had been rejected. None had ever proved entirely suitable. Each project always seemed to throw up something that either John or Olivia felt was not quite to their liking, and the couple had begun to despair of ever finding the perfect vehicle.

Finally, in 1982, Twentieth Century Fox came up with an original romantic comedy laced with fantasy called *Second Chance* which, although not a musical, Travolta felt could work well for both himself and Olivia. In essence the story involved a robber who meets an aspiring, devious actress, they fall in love and save the world.

John had always stayed in touch with his *Grease* co-star and, after reading the script for *Second Chance*, he called her up to say he had a great role lined up for her. He was so convinced the movie was tailor-made for them both that he intimated that if they failed to agree on this one, then they might never find another.

John impressed upon Olivia that he felt the part was so good that even Goldie Hawn would be happy to take it on. His own role in the movie, John assured her, would be a plum one, too, provided he could instigate a few changes. 'But I really chose it more for Olivia than for myself,' John revealed. 'I felt it would be very good for her. And the best thing was that we were both playing against type – for half of the movie we're quite obnoxious.' They were both to play good guys gone bad and candidates for redemption.

For Olivia, *Second Chance* represented a considerable gamble. Without a selection of songs to fall back on to carry her through the movie, she knew she would be judged purely on her acting ability, but that didn't faze her. She felt she had coped well in the promotional videos for her records and she was ready for the challenge. John Travolta promised her he would be as supportive as he had been throughout the filming of *Grease*.

Despite John's enthusiasm for the project, the portents were ominous from the start. There had been no fewer than five previous films bearing the title *Second Chance* and, when the realisation dawned that not one of them had been a success, the superstitious movie moguls decided not to tempt the fates and changed the title to *Two Of A Kind*.

As with *Grease*, there was to be a first-time director, John Herzfeld. He found himself in charge of a $14million movie with a plot that was far from straightforward: the story originates in heaven with God all set to destroy the world until a band of angels involve him in a wager. If they can arrange for two selfish earthlings to give up their bad ways and fall in love, then the world will be saved.

Zack and Debbie, the two mortals upon whom the planet's salvation depends, are played by John and Olivia. Zack is a bumbling, unsuccessful inventor of edible sunglasses and barking doorbells who has ended up heavily in debt to a loan shark. Desperate to solve his financial plight and threatened with having his ears sliced off by thugs if he doesn't pay up, he turns bank robber and confronts a flirty teller and aspiring actress called Debbie at a bank. Despite being held up at gunpoint, she cleverly sends Zack away with a bag full of worthless paper and runs off with the real loot herself. Zack sets out to track her down and, when he finds her, the two villains have the chance to redeem themselves and an opportunity to save the world by embarking on a romance.

John Travolta was given plenty of licence by Herzfeld to introduce the changes he required in the script, Olivia took a crash course of acting lessons to prepare for her role and, with a promising background soundtrack in the offing, all seemed set fair when the cameras started rolling. But while shooting a scene on location in New York on the first day, Olivia was bitten on the hand by a dog called Pascha who had been lined up as an extra with his master. She had approached to give the collie a pat, ignoring the warning of Pascha's master that the dog was frightened of large crowds. After sinking his teeth into Olivia's hand, Pascha's film debut was promptly cancelled, much to the chagrin of Olivia who knew she was the only one to blame.

Despite an advertising budget of $6million and considerable promotion by the two stars themselves, *Two Of A Kind* turned out to be a stinker. Just prior to the film's release, Olivia had given the movie a major boost by taking one of the background songs from the film high into the US singles chart. The number, called 'Twist Of Fate', was co-written again by her Australian friend Steve Kipner. But as with *Xanadu*, the public decided they liked the music but didn't like the film. And nothing could stop the film critics.

'Can it really have been that difficult to find a passable screen vehicle for John Travolta and Olivia Newton-John?' the *New York Times* despaired. 'Any old romantic fluff should have sufficed, and yet something as horrible as *Two Of A Kind* has been tailor-made for its stars. The results are so disastrous that absolutely no one is shown off to good advantage, with the possible exception of the hairdressers involved. The coiffeurs don't always upstage the material, but when they do, it's a blessing.'

The *New York Times* critic wasn't the only one to pick up on the magnificently blow-dried hair of the two protagonists. The fact that Olivia firmly kept her clothes on during the obligatory love scene with John also caused some amusement, as did the irony of Olivia playing an aspiring actress in such a mediocre movie.

The generally critical reaction and sluggish returns at the box office were a huge disappointment for John and Olivia. Both badly needed a hit. Travolta's star had fallen dramatically since the dizzy days of *Saturday Night Fever* and *Grease*, and Olivia was desperate to erase the memories of *Xanadu*. John says that *Two Of A Kind* is one of two movies he's made which he cannot now bear to watch. The other is *Moment By Moment*. 'I don't like to look at either of them,' he says. 'They don't have good memories attached. I didn't enjoy the shooting experience on either of them and I didn't enjoy the product of either of them.'

For Twentieth Century Fox's bosses, *Two Of A Kind*'s failure was a thoroughly unpleasant shock. They expected the re-teaming of John and Olivia to excite teenage audiences and to set the box office alight. *Two Of A Kind* did neither.

Just as the soundtrack had proved the saving grace for *Xanadu*, so it proved now for *Two Of A Kind*, albeit without achieving *Xanadu*'s multi-million sales. Olivia contributed three numbers, including 'Livin' In Desperate Times', which reached number thirty-one in the charts. She also co-wrote 'Take A Chance' on which she duetted with John. But it was never going to be another blockbusting hit in the manner of 'You're The One That I Want' from *Grease*.

In promotional interviews leading up to the movie's release, John and Olivia talked of teaming up every few years if *Two Of A Kind* turned out to be a hit. It wasn't. Instead, the movie effectively killed off any realistic hopes Olivia may have had of enjoying a major Hollywood movie career purely as an actress.

She waited another seven years before venturing into films again in *A Mom For Christmas*, a made-for-TV Disney family movie in which she played a shop mannequin who becomes the mother of a little girl who has no mother of her own and a workaholic father who neglects her. Australian director George Miller, who described Olivia's as 'one of the great smiles of the twentieth century', was hugely impressed by her ability to cry on cue in one emotional scene.

After *Two Of A Kind*'s poor returns, a lot was riding on her next studio album, *Soul Kiss*, which was released the following year. The surprise was that, while 'Physical' may have been suggestive, the *Soul Kiss* album sought to portray the singer as a sex siren. And that was even before the LP hit the turntable.

Across the centre spread of the double-fold LP sleeve

stretched Olivia in sheer red tights and matching silk top, her lips plumped and pouting and her hair tousled, in a colour photo by top celebrity photographer Herb Ritts. The front cover had Olivia lounging seductively, while the back cover had her in the most daring of poses in a photograph by Helmut Newton. The late German photographer was dubbed the King of Kink for his series of risqué photographic studies of nude women, and his portrait of Olivia for the *Soul Kiss* LP was startling and no less controversial. On the back cover he had Olivia pose as a semi-nude dominatrix in impossibly tight white riding breeches and black knee-high boots and holding a whip in both hands behind her back while she admired herself in a mirror with just a white silk scarf covering her breasts.

The *New York Times* reported incredulously: 'A topless blond dominatrix stares invitingly into a mirror, her nipples obscured by a strategically placed scarf. She's a study in the complex theatre of the female persona, the softness of her wet perm offset by the strictness of her white jodhpurs and the riding whip she holds behind her back . . . It's testament to the power of Newton's unique libidinal vision that he could make even Newton-John look carnal and knowing.'

Olivia was never entirely at ease with Helmut Newton's photographic take on her for *Soul Kiss*. She wasn't being true to herself. 'It was kind of contrived and I wasn't comfortable with that,' she said many years later. But at the time of the album's release she was happy to try and justify the racier image.

'Matt has helped me lose my inhibitions,' she said. 'He encourages me, supports me and is happy for me to do anything I feel comfortable with. He's not a jealous kind of husband, he's not one of those possessive husbands who says: "How dare you look like that for other men."

'The new look is tongue-in-cheek raunchy, not meant to be taken seriously.'

If the sleeve photos were provocative, the music, or to be exact, the lyrics on *Soul Kiss* were no less surprising. The title track was a thinly veiled ode to oral sex, and the accompanying video had one magazine reviewer blinking in amazement at its sexually charged images: 'How about Olivia lying on a bed-like altar, all but pleasuring herself while huge phallic cannons on either side of her shoot out loads of white feathers? Whereas before she was sexy but not overt, now sister girl was letting you know in no uncertain terms that she was hungry and wanted to eat!'

The *Soul Kiss* album also included a track called 'Culture Shock' in which Olivia sang daringly to her imaginary beau of how she'd like her man on the side to move in so they could all live together. Olivia Newton-John advocating a ménage à trois was hardly what her fans were used to hearing her sing about and it came as a jolt to many.

For all its shock value, *Soul Kiss* still didn't have either the impact of the *Physical* album or the same sort of mega-sales. But at least the hugely influential *Rolling Stone* magazine was impressed and gave her a boost by saying: 'She proves once again that she is the best pure pop singer working today. Check her out live sometime, mark her for range, pitch, phrasing, energy, ballsiness and, yes, commitment to the songs, and see if you don't agree.'

Elton John obviously did agree, as he and his lyric writer Bernie Taupin came up with a jaunty number called 'The Rumour', which became the title track of Olivia's next LP in 1988. The Rocket Man also took it upon himself to co-produce the album, but disappointingly it only reached number sixty-seven in the US charts. It was her least successful album. Olivia, however, was not overly worried at the downward commercial trend that now seemed to be affecting her recording career. By now she was immersing herself in a different world, as a wife and mother.

12

Marriage and Motherhood

'My daughter opened up a world that went beyond me:
her world'

Olivia, on the birth of Chloe

From the moment they first fell in love, Matt Lattanzi always envisaged and hoped that he would make Olivia his wife. He listened patiently to Olivia's reasons for fighting shy of marriage, but that didn't prevent him from asking her from time to time as their relationship blossomed. Matt believed they were absolutely right for each other and never swayed from his belief that they should be married.

Olivia was happy to wear a gold ring Matt had given her on a finger of her right hand as a symbol of their love for each other, but she was still terrified to take the final step. 'If you've never seen a relationship that lasts for ever, then you tend not to believe it's possible,' was one of her choicer remarks on the subject.

After *Two Of A Kind* was a critical and commercial failure, she went to Australia for a while to distance herself from the Hollywood razzamatazz and have some peace and quiet in which to think about how she saw her future. Another movie now seemed the wrong option, and she was becoming less inclined to embark on long, tiring, arduous and repetitive concert tours. In the winter of 1982 she had performed sixty-four concerts in forty different cities and Olivia had indicated that would be the end of road shows for her. After twenty years of largely being controlled by her career, she decided it was time she paid more attention to her personal life.

Importantly, she was also acutely aware that time was moving on. She was now in her mid-thirties and if she wanted to become a mother then marriage was beckoning. By her own personal choice, she was keen to take the traditional path and become a wife first before starting a family. She realised, too, that the reasons not to marry were diminishing: she and Matt had enjoyed five happy years together, they loved each other very much, and they were having good times and good fun together.

One day back in the US, when Olivia indicated her attitude against marriage was now indeed softening, Matt finally won Olivia round. For the first time in her life, it seemed unnatural to her not to get married. There was no grand proposal from Matt, just an acceptance that they would tie the knot, and the couple started making plans for a Christmas wedding in 1984. Given Olivia's hitherto entrenched views, relatives and friends were somewhat surprised but nonetheless delighted for them both.

Although it rained on the actual day, 15 December, Olivia took that as a sign of good luck and the wedding itself was still a blend of pure romance and typical Olivia. The seventy guests comprising family and closest friends arrived at her home via the driveway decorated with tiny fairy lights and even Olivia's animals were suitably dressed for the occasion. The cats wore white lace ribbons round their necks and Jackson the red setter sported white bows in his hair.

Australian designer Nanette Davies, a close friend of Olivia's, had spent six weeks creating Olivia's white silk taffeta bridal gown covered with chantilly lace, crystal beads and ribbons. In keeping with tradition, Olivia also wore something old, tiny diamond earrings, and something blue, a garter under her dress.

There was many a misty eye among the guests as they caught a glimpse of Olivia in her beautiful dress and hip-length veil for the first time. Matt's parents shed tears of joy as they watched Olivia, escorted by her father Brin, take the short walk to meet Matt and stand alongside him to the accompaniment of 'Here Comes The Bride' played by a string quartet.

Jackson caused some amusement by doing his best to join in the ceremony. The dog chose to stand close to his mistress when Olivia and Matt, dressed in a black Armani tuxedo, exchanged their vows and wedding rings before Judge Jerry Pacht of the Santa Monica Superior Court pronounced them man and wife.

The ink barely had time to dry on the marriage register before Olivia's new in-laws, Charles and Jeanette, were talking excitedly of the prospect of the newlyweds producing grandchildren for them. 'It was beautiful, fun and exciting,' Jeanette said of the ceremony. 'Livvy was just like any other bride would be, giggly and happy. We're just hoping she gets pregnant very soon. She does want a family. They didn't really say when they were going to start trying, but I'm sure it will be soon.'

After the couple cut the three-tiered chocolate wedding cake covered with fresh flowers, Charles Lattanzi expressed confidence for their lasting happiness. 'They both have a lot in common,' he said. 'They are both very caring and very considerate of everyone around them. That's something I think will keep them together. They both have very sound qualities which will enable the marriage to prevail through the hectic conditions they both have to work in.'

Olivia and Matt flew to Paris for their honeymoon, where Matt belatedly bought his new wife a pearl and diamond engagement ring, and they carried on by train to the fashionable Swiss skiing resort of Gstaad. Adventurous as ever, Matt booked a hot-air balloon flight over the Alps, which might have been the romantic highlight of their honeymoon but for Olivia's fear of heights.

'It was all fantastic,' she later recalled, 'but my most enduring memory is of being absolutely freezing and utterly terrified. My fear wasn't helped by the fact that the balloonist had the most dreadful hangover and didn't seem to know what he was doing.'

Aside from her jitters, Olivia's abiding memory of the flight was a magical moment when the balloon swooped low over a forest and she was able to lean out of the basket and pluck a snow-covered pine cone from a tree. 'Apart from that, I just remember wishing the whole thing would be over!' she recalls.

Having waited for so long before taking the plunge, Olivia wasted little time in starting a family. She suspected she might be pregnant one day in the spring of 1985 when she developed a craving for avocados, and a pregnancy test bought from a chemist confirmed it. Matt was away visiting his family in Oregon at the time and she broke the happy news to him over the telephone. His very large family were overjoyed – especially his mother and father. They had ten children, but Olivia's as yet unborn child would be their first grandchild to bear the Lattanzi name.

On 17 January 1986, without knowing the sex of her baby in advance, Olivia gave birth to a baby girl with Matt filming for posterity on a video camera the arrival into the world of Chloe Rose Lattanzi.

Olivia had always looked forward to becoming a mother one day, but the experience was much more rewarding for her than she had ever imagined and, after recording *The Rumour* while she was pregnant, she was determined that her career would take a back seat for the foreseeable future so she could devote her time to raising her little girl. She even considered retiring, but instead she was so enamoured with the joys of motherhood that she forsook mainstream pop to record an album in 1989 called *Warm And Tender*, which was essentially a selection of classic lullabies and children's songs.

Olivia persuaded the record company to package the record with recycled paper, and the album also included 120 tips on how to improve the environment – something she felt more keenly was necessary now she had a child of her own. 'When Chloe was born, she totally changed my life,' she said. 'I knew then that I owed her a safe environment to be brought up in, with clean air, clean water and clean food. Having a baby changed my life completely. Suddenly there was someone more important than me. I was transformed. My daughter opened up a world that went beyond me: her world.'

* * *

For the first few years of her life, Chloe's world invariably included another little girl, Colette Chuda, daughter of Jim and Nancy Chuda who lived close by. Nancy, a broadcaster, was one of Olivia's dearest friends, and the two women had planned their pregnancies together, become pregnant at the same time and then both gave birth to daughters. The bond between Olivia and Nancy could have hardly have been closer after Colette and Chloe were born just six weeks apart. Olivia became Colette's godmother, and inevitably the two little girls saw plenty of each other and became the very best of friends, sharing so many of their fun times together.

But when Colette was four, tragedy struck. She was diagnosed with Wilm's Tumour, a rare form of childhood cancer and, after a courageous battle for life, she died in April 1991, when she was just five years old. It was a devastating blow for the Chuda family, and Olivia felt Colette's tragic loss very deeply having regarded her almost as one of her own. The cover of her *Warm And Tender* album featured a picture of Colette kissing Olivia while Chloe looked on.

For Chloe, the death of her best friend was especially traumatic. At the age of five, it was so difficult for her to comprehend what had happened and why, and it was just as hard for Olivia to try to begin to explain: 'I said Colette had gone to heaven to be with God.'

When Colette's cancer was later proven to be non-hereditary, the Chudas sought to discover any contributory factors. Their research eventually pointed towards environmental toxics, such as pesticides, as the probable cause of the illness that had cost Colette her life. Nothing was going to bring back Colette, but now the Chudas selflessly set out to try and raise awareness and prevent other families from suffering the same heartbreak.

With Olivia's help, the couple launched the Colette Chuda Environmental Fund to support scientific research on the risks to children from environmental toxics. This later evolved into the Children's Health Environmental Coalition to inform parents about preventable childhood health problems caused by exposure to toxic substances. Olivia became CHEC's spokesperson.

Not long after Colette's untimely death came another bitter blow for Olivia – the collapse of Koala Blue, the chain of stores specialising in merchandise with an Aussie theme that Olivia had launched with Pat Farrar.

The idea for Koala Blue had come to Olivia during conversations with her manager Roger Davies while they were out on the road on a concert tour. They frequently talked about things they missed from Australia and Olivia thought it would be fun to open a bar and a shop where California's Aussie community could wander in and buy all things Australian, from newspapers to Vegemite, to books, clothing, jewellery and artwork.

The Santa Monica area of Los Angeles, in particular, at that time had a sizeable number of Aussie ex-pats and Olivia envisaged an Aussie-flavoured store where the down under brigade could watch videos of Aussie Rules footie games while eating Aussie sandwiches and cakes and drinking Aussie beers as well as buy typical Aussie gear. The quaint Tudor House on 2nd Street in Santa Monica successfully offered British ex-pats all things British, so why not a similar operation for Aussies?

Pat Farrar was eager to team up with Olivia. She had been thinking of opening a boutique anyway and they decided to go into business together. The two long-standing friends were advised at the start to have separate lawyers because they were warned they were likely to fall out. But they declined, and their friendship never wavered even when their business venture ultimately suffered a catastrophic slide.

All sorts of names were considered for the new business but one day, while she was out driving on her own, Olivia spotted a licence plate that spelled out KOALA and she turned it in her mind into Korner Of Australia Los Angeles. It was, she decided, the perfect name for the company, particularly as the Koala bear is unique to Australia and such a recognisable symbol.

The first shop opened amid much fanfare in 1983 on trendy Melrose Avenue in Los Angeles, and the business grew within a few years at an impressive rate to include nearly sixty stores, either company owned or franchised, around the world. By 1989, Koala Blue claimed revenues of $25million and Olivia was named celebrity business-woman of the year by the US National Association of Women Business Owners. But a combination of too fast an expansion, an economic slowdown and recession, and management decisions that turned out to be wrong, led to Koala Blue's collapse. In 1991 with huge debts and amid lawsuits and recriminations, the company filed for bank-ruptcy.

Koala Blue had started out as a fun idea, and Olivia had worked hard to promote it. But now what had appeared to be a thriving business empire was in ruins. It was a bitter blow and a thoroughly stressful time for Olivia. She hated failure. But, as a disaster, it was as nothing compared with what fate had in store for her around the corner.

13

From a Curse to a Blessing

'She suddenly realised what her priorities were'

Dr Deepak Chopra

The San Juan archipelago off the north-west corner of the United States has long been a favourite holiday destination for Olivia Newton-John. A couple of hundred miles north of Seattle, these pine-scented islands are noted for their outstanding natural beauty, and Olivia has always felt there is something almost magical about the glorious views across the ocean to snow-capped mountains in the distance, and in the foreground the occasional sight of orca whales rising majestically out of the water.

The islands therefore beckoned as the ideal spot for a relaxing, peaceful, back-to-nature few days of holiday over the Fourth of July weekend in 1992 prior to Olivia embarking on her first major American tour in a decade. She had admitted that her financial troubles with Koala Blue had persuaded her to 'go back to focusing on what I do best'. And the tour would help promote her latest album *Back To Basics: The Essential Collection*, which was a retrospective plus four new tracks.

The start of the tour was now but a month away, and Olivia was grateful to be able to get away to the charming San Juan islands because she had been rehearsing hard. She was anxious to be both physically and mentally attuned for the upcoming tour because ahead of her stretched an eagerly awaited opening night in front of a sell-out crowd at Caesar's Palace, Las Vegas, on 6 August, followed by sixteen regional concert dates at major venues. Olivia was both excited and nervous at the prospect, and she knew a holiday with friends would do her the world of good.

But just as Olivia, Matt and her great friends John and Pat Farrar were about to board a seaplane to Seattle, Matt took a telephone call. There were two important messages: one telling Olivia that her father had died, and the second from her doctor telling her he needed to see her urgently. The first message was bad enough, but the second rang alarm bells for Matt because he was aware that Olivia had been undergoing a series of medical tests.

Matt was in a quandary. He knew Brin's death would be devastating news for Olivia, and he wondered how his wife would cope with the additional worry of the call from her doctor and all the implications that went with it. He feared it would be too much for her to bear all at once, so he decided he would pass on the sad news about Brin but withhold the doctor's message until after their holiday weekend was over. 'I've always been grateful to Matt for that,' she says. 'I was in such pain over my father, and Matt knew it was enough for me to deal with.'

That evening, Olivia sat with her friends overlooking the sea at sunset and, as their group were all well acquainted with Brin, they drank a toast to her father, shared their memories of him and recounted affectionate stories about him.

Olivia had known her father was very ill, and she had recently flown back to Australia to be with him as he fought liver cancer. After her visit, she had then flown back to America to continue her rehearsals for the tour. But she had told her father she had every intention of returning to Australia to spend more time with him as soon as her schedule permitted. The news of his unexpected death therefore hit her exceptionally hard. 'It was an incredible shock because I thought I was going to go back and see him. So it was very sudden.'

On the Monday, Olivia was given the grim news by her doctor that she had been diagnosed with breast cancer. A surgical biopsy carried out shortly before she had flown out to Australia to see her father had confirmed it. 'I'd always had regular check-ups and had lumps checked out before and they were benign.' she said. 'But with this particular one, I didn't feel right in myself. This time something felt different. I don't say this to alarm women, but my mammogram was clear and my needle biopsy was clear, but my intuition said I wasn't right. So I insisted on a surgical biopsy and we found the cancer.

'The following week was a bit of a blur. I can remember being in denial and laughing a lot. What else could go wrong? I never had a thought "Why me?" because "Why not me?" I had such a feeling that I'd never felt before nor since. What if the cancer was throughout my body? What if I was going to die? It was that night I made the decision that I would be well, that I would not give in to it.'

Still reeling from hearing of the death of her father, Olivia was now only too glad that he had not been aware of her worries for her own health when she had seen him for the last few times. 'I'm very glad my father didn't know as he was suffering enough on his own,' she said.

Olivia now experienced a mixture of emotions – grief, fear, denial and shock. For just about the first time in her life she knew she had to put herself first.

It was a very, very difficult time. I didn't have a real chance to grieve for my father because I had to cope with my own survival. I couldn't go back for the funeral because I had to get surgery and chemotherapy and see doctors, and I knew that I had to stay strong in order to survive what I was going through.

The first night was the most frightening. I had a night of dread. I shall never forget it. I woke in the early hours with an overwhelming fear. I walked down to the kitchen and my body felt so leaden I could hardly move. Then I just felt terror down to my boots. My knees and legs went weak and I thought the cancer must have spread right throughout my body. I said to myself: 'You're going to be okay,' and from that moment I really believed I could recover.

Olivia was admitted to Cedars Sinai hospital in Los Angeles where she signed a consent form for a double mastectomy, in case it was found to be necessary, and she remembers making light of it all as she was prepared for surgery. 'I didn't want to upset the people around me.' Typically, as ever, she wanted to do the right thing.

Eleven days after her diagnosis, Olivia underwent a radical modified mastectomy and had her breast reconstructed at the same time. Her shocked family were kept informed from the outset, although the whole truth was kept from Chloe. As Chloe had lost her best friend Colette Chuda to cancer, it was felt best not to alarm her unduly. When Olivia began her chemotherapy treatment and had to go to bed for a day, she'd simply say she wasn't feeling well and arrange for Chloe to spend the day with a friend or have a sleepover. She managed to get through a whole year without saying the word 'cancer' to Chloe.

For Olivia, informing friends of her illness proved more

difficult than she could ever have imagined. 'I remember in the beginning, when I was calling people to tell them I had breast cancer, some of my friends took it badly. The second person I called fell apart. I felt: "I don't need to hear this, I need to hear I'm going to be OK." So I stopped calling. I had Pat Farrar and my sister Rona call to tell them. That way I could focus on positive thoughts rather than on the illness.'

But bad news, of course, travels fast, and she was anxious those closest to her should know of her illness before the story was leaked out. It wasn't long before the press got hold of the news, and when Olivia got wind that a report was about to come out saying erroneously that she was dying of cancer, she decided to pre-empt it and spell out the truth.

On 14 July she announced in an official statement that she had breast cancer, and she added: 'I draw strength from the millions of women who have faced this challenge successfully. This has been detected early because I've had regular examinations, so I encourage other women to do the same.' Olivia's concert tour was immediately cancelled and she apologised to ticket-holders saying: 'I look forward to rescheduling soon.'

Privately, Olivia confided to friends that she had had a kind of feeling that somehow she wouldn't get to go on this particular tour. 'I had no reason to know why,' she said. 'But your higher self knows. Something was telling me and so I pursued it and it was so.'

Once Olivia had gone public about her illness, get-well cards, letters, flowers and messages of love and support poured into the hospital from friends and fans all over the world. Among those who wrote to Olivia wishing her strength at this time was her good friend Didi Conn, who had played Frenchy in *Grease*. Didi reminded Olivia how many people loved her and went on to express her own good wishes for Olivia to come safely through whatever she needed to go through.

After surgery, Olivia had eight months of chemotherapy and at first she considered forgoing it and using various alternative treatments instead. 'Common sense prevailed. One of my girlfriends said: "Why would you want to risk even that one cancer cell? You have a child.' In the event, the chemo was not as bad as she feared and she didn't lose her hair, which, she says, was a psychological bonus. 'I wore an ice cap, a sort of tea cosy filled with ice cubes which is supposed to help.'

There were many times, she says, when she thought she would die if she fell asleep. 'I felt constantly nauseous, headachy, sleepy. I was in a fog and my short-term memory, which can be affected by chemotherapy, became terrible.'

To aid her healing, Olivia also used a wide range of alternative treatments including homeopathic medicine, herbs and acupuncture to balance out her chemotherapy treatment. She also practised yoga and meditation and read up on anything she felt might help her.

At the time of Olivia's illness, Matt was building an environmentally correct house, having largely set aside his stuttering acting career and set up a construction business. He said:

> I was obsessed with my work with the house even when Olivia was going through this. I felt the house did rob me of being with Olivia some of the time, so the guilt hit me. Did I do enough? You can never do enough, but you've got to love yourself too.
>
> I was always strong, and when she needed to cry on my shoulder I was always there, and I would just hold her. The lowest moment was when we'd be sitting

together and Olivia would be feeling so bad from the chemotherapy. She'd be in my arms, and you feel so weak and helpless you just want to give up. I'd look at Olivia and ask myself: could I handle this? I don't think I could.

It wasn't so bad most of the time because she had the lightest type of chemo. She was so strong, too strong, I think, but she did have her times. The worst were right after chemotherapy and that would last three days. That's when I'd tuck her up in bed and take care of her.

The thought would come up that I might be left on my own bringing up a young child. I kept pushing it down. Oddly enough, Livvy and I never once talked about it. There may have been a passing moment during conversation when Livvy joked about it, because she joked about her illness often. But there was never a serious discussion.

Olivia's oncologist put her in touch with another woman who had had the same treatment so that she would know what to expect. She believes this was a great help. 'Women at this time feel very alone very often, and it's wonderful if you can get together with a peer group who have gone through it. Because I had this fear, and I know a lot of women have this, but I was too embarrassed to tell anyone, I thought that they'd put the needle in and I would die. I thought that I'd be allergic to the chemotherapy and that was a huge fear.'

Olivia was heartened to learn that this particular woman she'd been put in touch with was six months on from finishing her course of treatment. Just knowing she had got through it and survived was, she says, a great comfort.

Nancy Chuda, who had lost her little daughter Colette

so cruelly to cancer, was also a tower of strength. She pointed out to Olivia that it would be down to her to set the tone as to how others would perceive her illness and how they would react. If she was positive in her outlook, then those around her would also be positive rather than regard her as a victim. 'She was an incredible support to me at the time,' Olivia said of Nancy. 'She took me to a movie and shopping and girlie things like that, and she said we were just going to do normal things.'

Nancy's husband Jim also played a vital part, with the most dramatic and far-reaching results, by telling Olivia when she was diagnosed: 'Congratulations. Now you will grow.' Olivia recalled:

> I was a little puzzled when he said it. I now totally understand what he means. It was one of those moments you never forget. I thought: 'He's a very wise man and he must have reason to say this and I know I will see this eventually.' And I did. It's true that when you go through something life-threatening or really painful, from that you grow. I've grown in so many ways I maybe wouldn't have.
>
> I think he's totally right. Whatever you go through, even though it seems incredibly difficult at the time, when you look back you realise it was an experience you would not give up – if you survive it, which I was lucky enough to do.

Olivia came to firmly believe that illness can be brought on by stress. She also came to believe, after talking to other women, that she was in some probability a typical victim. 'Most of us are a certain type who don't know how to express ourselves,' she said in a revealing interview. 'We try to be everything to everybody, we give, we don't take care of ourselves emotionally. We do things for everybody else and repress our own desires and feelings.'

She said an inability to express her feelings was a trait she had noticed in her father, particularly when she had flown to his bedside shortly before he had died. Olivia said the closest he came then was reading some poems to her and Rona and trying to say something through the poetry that he couldn't express himself.

Olivia credits Dr Deepak Chopra with helping her to take important strides towards recovery. Dr Chopra is an MD and wellness guru, who has been at the forefront of a major trend in holistic healing, and Olivia got in touch with him to her lasting advantage. 'She was very familiar with some of my work,' he says. 'We met and discussed meditation, lifestyle, diet, stress management and she was the most extraordinary student. She took immediately to everything.

'She suddenly realised what her most important priorities were, and her most important was her wellbeing, fulfilment, her happiness and the happiness of her daughter and nurturing relationships.'

Dr Chopra taught Olivia some meditation techniques to aid her recovery. Through him she first learned of the mind–body connection and its part in health and wellbeing, and he also introduced her to the concept of the seven chakras, the energy centres of the body.

Olivia later recounted her own inspiring personal spiritual journey towards healing for *The Seven Spiritual Laws of Success*, a DVD based on Deepak Chopra's best-selling book about living a purposeful and satisfying life. She opened her home to the film to say: 'Very often the things that come out of pain end up being your biggest blessing.'

Cancer changed everything about Olivia and she came to

reassess herself through regular sessions with a psychiatrist.

> I started being able to express feelings I thought I shouldn't have. I learned to express anger, to shout and bang doors, which I always found very hard before. I learned not to feel guilty all the time about being so successful. I used to feel undeserving about having things handed to me on a platter when people around me didn't.
>
> I know I used to be a kind of victim in that I allowed things to happen rather than taking control. I'd give in when I didn't really want to do something. It would often be little things like wanting to be alone but not saying so, or going somewhere when I was really tired.

On reflection, Olivia conceded that all too often she tried to do the right thing lest people felt she was too selfish. She said she was a 'very fearful person' and probably too scared to think deeply about herself. 'I didn't have time to reflect until I got sick,' she said. 'But having cancer freed me and helped me grow up. It has, in retrospect, been a very positive experience.'

Indirectly, Olivia's cancer led her to take a role in 1995 in the low-budget movie *It's My Party* directed by Randal Kleiser who, of course, had directed her in *Grease*. Eric Roberts starred as a gay man who gathers all his friends and family together to say goodbye to them before a friend in the medical profession helps him die a dignified death. Olivia played one of the friends, a married woman in the throes of divorce and with a son who is coming out.

With homosexuality, AIDS and euthanasia as the film's themes, it represented Olivia's first serious screen role.

Major names who agreed to appear in the $3million movie for minimal pay included George Segal, Marlee Matlin, Lee Grant and Roddy McDowall, and Olivia took the opportunity to join them because she felt she could draw parallels with her own battle against breast cancer. 'I've lost friends to AIDS,' she revealed. 'I've been in the room when my best friend's brother died, so it struck a chord with me. I knew I could relate – and I could relate to the humour very much. Some people find that strange, but I remember when I first had cancer, I used to ring my friends and make jokes, because they were so freaked out that was the only way to break the ice.'

14

A Touch of Paradise

'I was alone a lot of the time and I was under immense pressure to do well, and I had a breakdown'

Matt Lattanzi

In the history of television soaps, *Paradise Beach* is unlikely to warrant much more than a mention. It was a short-lived series, and yet it was one that was to signal a turning point with far-reaching effects in the marriage of Olivia Newton-John and Matt Lattanzi.

Olivia's cancer, her continuing brave battle to beat it, and Matt's anxious devotion to supporting her, were inevitably placing a strain on the couple's relationship. So when an opportunity for them to totally change their lifestyle presented itself, they seized it with little hesitation. They put their Malibu home up for sale for £5million and headed off to Australia. The house was expensive to run and they resolved to down-scale and live more modestly and more simply for six months – in Australia.

'I heard there was a job available in a new TV series to be made in Australia,' Matt explained, 'and we agreed that if I got it, then we'd go. Livvy was done with her treatment and this job came up and I said great, let's go. I can get you away from this. Two weeks after I'd sent in a tape of my work to the producers, I was packed up and gone.'

Matt was signed to play Cooper Hart, an American

photographer on assignment, in *Paradise Beach*, a light drama series aimed at the youth market and set in Surfers Paradise, a stunning stretch of coastline around fifty miles from Brisbane on Australia's Gold Coast in Queensland. The series intended to follow the fortunes of a group of good-looking suburban youngsters who find romance and adventure by the sea in an endless summer.

The prospects for the series looked exceptionally good. Beach shows on television tended to succeed, *Baywatch* being an obvious example, and even before *Paradise Beach* went fully into production, it was snapped up by 220 stations in the US on the strength of a glossy pilot alone.

With its staple mix of gorgeous girls flaunting their curves in skimpy, fluorescent bikinis, hunky guys doing press-ups on the beach in their Speedos, big waves rolling in as a challenge to surfers and sun-drenched beaches, it was never going to be Shakespeare. 'It's boards, bodies, boobs and babes,' one of the production team unashamedly remarked. But Matt was prepared to put up with attaching his name to such undemanding material because it meant that together with Chloe, he and Olivia could temporarily relocate to the 200-acre custard apple and avocado farm she owned near Byron Bay.

Olivia had purchased the farm some twelve years before after flying into nearby Lismore with Matt with the specific idea of looking for a rural retreat to buy. She fell in love with the farm on the spot, and after buying it she came back every year to enjoy the view and the energy of the land, and she always planned that one day she would build a little house on the property. But around six years later the adjoining farm, which had a little house on it, came up for sale and Olivia was able to buy it and do it up.

'Basically this was a retreat for Olivia,' Matt said of the

added agenda of his new acting project. 'I wanted to get Livvy to relax. It was just luck and fate that I would be able to work while she relaxed.'

The arrangement suited Olivia perfectly. Their house in California was invariably a hive of activity, but the tranquillity of the farm offered her a much quieter existence and the chance to paint, write music and read, all of which she felt she never really found the time for in Malibu.

The uprooting from California signalled not just a change of scenery for the family but, very significantly, a complete change of lifestyle. Chloe was enrolled at a one-room school for sixty children near to the farm, Matt took an apartment to be on the spot for work on *Paradise Beach* while returning to the farm at weekends, and Olivia embraced a back-to-nature, simple, healthy, recuperative lifestyle in the countryside surrounding her farm.

There were ugly rumours that she had come back to Australia for the last few months of her life. But they simply were not true. She had finished her treatment in February 1993 and she wanted everyone to know that she was fine. The setting of the cosy little farm dwelling was so peaceful, and she delighted in seeing wallabies and kookaburras hopping about on the lawn. The farmhouse was surrounded by rainforest, lush red soil and palm trees, and offered glorious views of green rolling countryside dotted with old Moreton Bay fig trees and stretching many acres into the distance. Matt said:

We had a wonderful home in Malibu, but it was easy to leave it. Our home, and all the things we had acquired over the past ten years, had grown to be a barrier between family life. Our private life had been sacrificed by things. When you walk into a place like ours, you see expense – there's a tennis court, a swimming pool and a horse-riding ring, and then you go inside and there's the theatre and the stereo and the cars and the trucks and the things we've acquired. Things have distracted us.

When I came to Australia this time, I had nothing, just a Land Rover to get me around. We reduced our lifestyle and we live in a very small house the size of our living–dining area in the States. I always know where Chloe is, we can talk to each other and I can go to a little corner of the house to study my lines.

Here we have a chance to go out on picnics, we collect rainwater and experience real life and sit on the lawn. And although I am working five days a week and at weekends I have to study, the time we do have together is so precious and valuable and I'm like a different person. I've changed over the last six months. I've lost a lot of my attachments. The Tibetans call it *samsara*, and it's our ability as the human race to invent all of these things that distract us from what we are used to being – hunters and gatherers. Man was always inventing ways to distract oneself from oneself – computers and telephones and the like.

How many fathers spend much time with their children? It's not that much. I've changed that, and now spend a goodly amount of time with my daughter and my wife. You only get this realisation when you leave your comfort zone.

Livvy and I were both living in our comfort zone and going about our daily routines. It was time to spend the time with family and get away from the things, or involve family in things that we do. We can't take all of our things with us, so we've been letting go of everything.

For Olivia, Matt and Chloe, the transfer to Australia was therefore as much an enlightening spiritual journey for them as a geographical one. 'It was an incredibly emotional time for us,' said Matt.

> Olivia's illness, moving house, leaving the US – all three things happening to us was stressful.
>
> Olivia and I have been meditating. We've been studying a lot of different philosophies. We take from the best of every one – Tibetan, Christianity, Seventh Day Adventists, Jehovah's Witnesses, American Indians, Aborigines. We've been reading extracts from books of masters throughout the world.
>
> Meditation is prayer, and we do it before we eat, before we sleep. I have a couple of prayers and we do the Lord's prayer, too. Chloe is very interested in the Bible and she reads it and we read to her. I was raised as a Catholic but my truth doesn't lie there. I've found the greatest truth within the whole spectrum of Middle Eastern religions and beliefs, all of them. I find great fulfilment in educating myself.

The change of scenery clearly did Olivia the world of good. After the first few months in Australia, Matt was able to say:

> She's unbelievable. She could run a marathon. She's out in the garden digging the earth, carrying in the wood for the fireplace. It took her three months to find her sea legs again and now she's blossomed. We have 200 acres and we go hiking and climbing across rolling grassy hills, dense thick wood, waterfalls and creeks, and she keeps right up with me. I told her: 'My God, Livvy, where do you get such energy from?' She was getting it from the land. We both know she's fine. But she'll probably never tour again, maybe smaller venues.

Olivia's breathtaking surroundings and the feeling of

recovery from her illness produced a burst of creative activity. She had seriously thought about retiring but, while revelling in the peaceful solitude of the farm, she found new songs were flowing quite naturally into her brain. Often in the middle of winter at the dead of night she'd wake up with a new idea in her head and feel compelled to get out of bed and go into the living room where she'd light a fire in the little pot-belly stove and softly sing her ideas into a tape recorder, taking care not to wake either Matt or Chloe.

'She's inspired,' said Matt in admiration. 'She wrote ten songs in a week. She'd wake up at three in the morning and write. On our walks she'd pull out a pad and pencil – she never goes anywhere without them – and write. Her lyrics were coming out, it was that other higher self coming out of her. I told her in amazement: "Olivia, how many songs can you get on one album?" It's fantastic, it was awe-inspiring to see her blossom.'

While Olivia gained renewed strength and her health improved, Matt, however, was plunged into a totally unexpected crisis. He had resolutely remained strong while helping his wife cope with her illness and with the grief she felt over the death of her father. But now that Olivia was patently so much better, the feelings of stressful anxiety he had suppressed for so long got the better of him.

All the strain of the problems he and Olivia had faced over the past few years, and which they had struggled to overcome, now overwhelmed Olivia's husband. In essence, he suffered a terrible bout of delayed shock. He said:

> The 1980s were wonderful. We were in a kind of Shangri-La. Then around 1989 we had to face the music. Chloe's best friend, Colette Chuda, died of

cancer at the age of five. They had grown up together and her death tore us apart.

Then everything crumbled. Everything that I held dear, everything that I considered my reason for being, started falling apart. Financial difficulties arose and there was a need to rearrange and reorganise. There were lawsuits, Koala Blue failing, incredible over-heads, this huge machine and no income coming in, Livvy's father dying, Livvy getting cancer – it was just boom, boom, boom from all directions.

The hammer blow was, of course, Olivia's breast cancer.

Can you imagine the feelings Livvy and I went through when she got ill? I said to myself: 'I must have no feel-ings. I have to be strong and take care of Olivia while she's going through her chemotherapy, while she's going through this illness.' I was blocking my feelings down throughout her whole therapy.

While Olivia blossomed on the farm, I, on the other hand, had no familiar surroundings, no comfort zone and I started working seven days a week. It was an emotional wilderness for me because I didn't have my family, my friends, my support group with me or the familiarity of my house or my dogs, I was alone a lot of the time and I was under immense pressure to do well – and I had a breakdown.

Not for one moment had Matt seen his emotional collapse coming. 'I would never wish what we endured on my worst enemy. It's not even something you step out of the moment your partner starts to get better. My problems didn't really begin until after Livvy recovered.'

Matt had remained positive and strong during Olivia's dark days and now she was coming through he had expected he would feel relieved and optimistic. But the feelings he had blocked out now flooded to the surface. 'It was something I'd never experienced before,' he said. 'All that shit that I'd suppressed for so long came up and hit me, and it was like a left hook from Mike Tyson. It knocked me down. I had thought I was indestructible, Mr Strong who could deal with everything.'

Matt believed it was the death of his beloved dog Digger that finally tipped him over the edge. 'He represented more than just a dog,' he explained. 'I'd had him since a puppy, and he represented the beginning of my relationship with Olivia, when she and I had just met. When I heard the news I suppressed my feelings. A few hours after that, I was listening to some music and I broke down in tears for my dog.'

Digger's death, Matt said, was the end of an era and he couldn't help but wonder whether symbolically it might mean the end of him and Olivia too. Matt's downward spiral was now rapid.

> Then I started wondering what was happening to me. I was getting dizzy, depressed, having anxiety attacks. I would never wish it on anyone as it was so traumatic and Livvy had to watch me go through it helpless, completely helpless.
>
> Olivia understood what I was going through and was in pain for me. But I told her: 'Don't take this on yourself.' I had to believe I was going to get through it even though sometimes I believed I wasn't going to.
>
> I told Livvy: 'Don't worry, you have come through, but I'm going to have to blubber away on the bed and go to work and do my job then come home and fall apart.'
>
> Livvy was fine and I was miserable. It was frightening and I wondered whether I was going to make it out

the other side. 'Is this happening to me?' I asked myself. Chloe, who's sharp as a tack, would come up to me and say: 'Daddy, you just don't seem to be quite yourself. I hope you make it through this. Don't worry about it, Dad. We all feel bad sometimes.'

My grovelling, lowest point came at a time when I realised I was on my own. Livvy wasn't there, she was out of town, and I was at home alone trying to study my lines and I was literally shaking, like I was convulsive, and there were tears, confusion, and I was screaming into a pillow. But I realised I could survive it. I had a couple of those moments, but there was one where I went below sea level. I felt like I was as low as I could get.

If you come up against a traumatic experience, something's going to happen. But I wasn't prepared for it. I didn't know what to expect. I knew the meaning of anxiety, depression, uncontrollable crying and wanting to run away but not being able to. But I didn't understand it.

I thought I was dying. I went to the doctor and had every single test but there was nothing. I asked: 'How could I be feeling like this?' The answer is your brain is a very powerful thing. It had been eating away at me for months and there was the fact that I'd been away from my home comforts. If you have a mental problem it affects you physically – you have dizzy spells, you feel weak, fatigued. The mind is so powerful.

It was a big lesson and it lasted for a solid three months. I was working and trying to pull myself together, and I came out the other end of it a more compassionate human being for people who have gone through this type of thing. I'd lived too much of an insulated life, insulated from all these things, and I learned a lot from this. It's the best thing that could have happened to me.

We are conditioned to ignore feelings or hide from them or preoccupy ourselves with things. But if you're lucky enough to grasp hold of what feelings are, then let them come up, bad, good or indifferent, and experience them, not shove them away or try to hide it.

Matt concluded that the down-scaling of his lifestyle with Olivia, the letting go of possessions and even his mental breakdown had ultimately been good for him.

'I had everything I wanted. You name it, I had it. I could travel, have a new car if I wanted it. A boat? I could have a new one of those too. I had that power. But by having it all, I realised that having everything isn't happiness. It was like a ball and chain around our neck – all this stuff that we couldn't get rid of.'

Referring to his breakdown, Matt said:

I think it was meant to be that I got kicked in the ass with a big boot. And I needed it. There is only one way to be a compassionate soul and that is to experience something like this. It's not being born again, just awareness.

It was a necessary obstacle and it needed to be big to take me off the big mountain. I could have kept going but I certainly wouldn't have wanted to pass on to the next realm, whatever that is, in that state. That would have been a big mistake. I could never understand how some people in their seventies felt ready to die. They didn't want to, but they accepted it because they had a certain knowledge. I'm not saying I have that knowledge but I'm on the right track.

* * *

It was while Olivia was in recovery at the farm that Chloe

discovered the seriousness of her mother's illness. She knew, of course, that Olivia had been unwell but it came as a shock to her when a pupil at her school remarked to Chloe that she'd read in the paper that her famous mother had cancer. That was the first Chloe had heard of it, and she came running home to confront Olivia on the subject.

Olivia and Matt had deliberately chosen not to tell Chloe that her mother's illness was cancer. As Chloe's best friend Colette Chuda had succumbed to the disease, Matt and Olivia were worried that the word 'cancer' would lead Chloe to assume it meant that her mother was going to die too.

Olivia was never totally convinced she had made the right choice in not telling Chloe, but once her daughter demanded to know the truth Olivia didn't duck the issue. 'We sat her down and told her the truth,' said Matt, 'and she took it very well. She said: "Why did you lie to me?" We'd told her Mummy was sick but we never went into details. It was too difficult, and we knew kids would get on to her. She took what we said for what it was worth, but now we had to explain it all to her – and we had to explain it very intelligently as well.'

Chloe was now seven years old and Olivia remembers her daughter's touching reaction to her decision not to tell the whole truth. 'It's hard to explain to a little girl why you did that. She said: "But I could have taken care of you." She was so sweet. But I did what was right at the time.'

* * *

While Matt was fighting his own demons and managing to continue with his role in the short-lived *Paradise Beach*, Olivia's spurt of therapeutic creative activity resulted in the release in 1994 of a new album called *Gaia: One Woman's Journey*. It emerged as an intensely personal but upbeat collection of Olivia's own songs on an album that she also co-produced.

Olivia laid bare her soul in her lyrics and, for anyone still unclear of each song's message, she included clarification on the sleeve notes. 'Gaia', she explained, is the spirit of Mother Earth, the giver of dreams and the nourisher of plants and young children. 'This song came to me at 3am on a cold winter's morning in Byron Bay and I was compelled to write and finish it. I feel the spirit of Mother Earth spoke to me.'

'Not Going To Give In To It' was a song she wrote after chemotherapy. And just as self-evident was 'Why Me', which she composed the night after her surgery. On the album, Olivia dedicated 'Why Me' to her father who, she said, died of cancer with dignity 'and he never complained for a moment'.

'Don't Cut Me Down' was a number which, Olivia explained, she had started to write in the late 1980s and later found in a drawer full of tapes. She went on to complete it to reflect her feelings about forests threatened with being cut down. 'No Other Love', Olivia told her fans, was: 'For the loves of my life, Matt and Chloe.'

It was a declaration from the heart and no one doubted the sincerity, but one year on Olivia and Matt agreed to separate, and the following year they were divorced.

Even before they had uprooted for Australia, there were rumours that their marriage was in trouble. Olivia's illness and the domino effect of all the other setbacks of the past few years had taken their toll on the relationship. While Matt pursued work in documentaries, he and Olivia agreed on what Matt described as a 'tentative separation'. 'It was a separation just in the geographical sense,' he said. But towards the end of 1995 they decided to separate emotionally as well.

By then Matt, through his love of mountain biking, had met a beautiful young New Zealand girl by the name of Cindy Jessup, who was a member of the local cycle club at Lismore, close to Olivia's farm.

They met in October 1993, and Matt struck up a friendship with the blonde sports science student, who had a steady boyfriend at the time. Matt didn't really expect to see Cindy again, but in 1994 their paths crossed once more through a mutual love of biking. And when Cindy told Matt of her plan to go on a bicycle ride across Australia for charity, Olivia agreed to give her support. Cindy was duly invited to the farm and was photographed with Olivia to add impetus to her charity ride.

The gossips, of course, had a field day about Matt and the cute Kiwi, but he and Cindy have insisted their friendship didn't develop into something more until Matt and Olivia had finally agreed to part. By then, Cindy was also single, having broken up with her boyfriend, and she and Matt were both free to embark on a new romance, which they chose to keep low key.

Olivia and Matt announced they were to separate in 1995, and they were divorced in December 1996, after eleven years of marriage. As divorces go, it was an amicable split. 'I think I was about nine, and both were very civil with each other and kind,' is Chloe's recollection. 'There was no malicious childlike behaviour.'

Olivia had delayed marrying until the age of thirty-six because she was desperate to get it right after being scarred since the age of ten by her own parents' divorce. She had married Matt full of hope for a lasting union, but after a golden few years where they seemed to live in a perfect world, their marriage had been buffeted by events and circumstances often beyond their control. Inevitably, they had both changed.

At the age of forty-eight, Olivia was alone again but, as she was quick to acknowledge, the greatest gift from the marriage was her daughter. 'Having Chloe was the greatest pleasure and achievement of my life.'

Chloe was especially precious to Olivia because she had hoped for more children but suffered three miscarriages, one at nearly five months. 'I grieved for them all,' she said simply.

Matt and Cindy eventually set up home together in Malibu so that he could continue to be an attentive father to Chloe and see as much of his daughter as possible. And in June 1999, Cindy became Matt's second wife. They were quietly wed in Malibu in the simplest of civil ceremonies, without either friends or family in attendance, and with only Olivia and Chloe in on the secret. After tying the knot, the couple went off to celebrate by themselves with a meal at a Mexican restaurant.

While Matt had found new happiness, the good news for Olivia was that she had continued to make a strong recovery from her illness. With an attitude as positive as ever, she refused to use the phrase 'in remission' because it sounded as though the cancer was waiting to come back. Instead, she preferred to say it had gone. And she received an unexpected and welcome shot of optimism during a birthday lunch with her mother one year after her treatment had finished when she went to the ladies' room and a woman approached her to say: 'I read all about you in the paper, and I want you to know that I had cancer twenty years ago and I'm fine.'

'That was amazing,' said Olivia, 'a living beacon, and it

was a wonderful moment for me and gave me encouragement.'

As a breast cancer survivor, Olivia knew how fortunate she was. 'I was lucky it wasn't the most aggressive cancer,' she pointed out, and her good fortune spurred her on to set about raising funds for cancer research and to speak openly about what she had been through in a bid to help others.

At the 1995 Fire and Ice Ball, to raise awareness and encourage more research, Olivia happily admitted in a moving speech: 'If you had told me a few years ago that I would talk about something so intimate, I would have cringed. I really felt when I discovered that I had breast cancer that I owed it to myself and to other women to be open about it, and to talk about it and show that if it can happen to me it can happen to anybody.'

Olivia stressed the importance for women of listening to their own bodies because neither her own mammogram nor a needle biopsy showed anything to worry about. She also emphasised that the right mental approach was vital. She said of her cancer: 'I began to think of it not as a poison but a healing white light.'

She added: 'It's vitally important that we do this research to find out what we can about genetics and the environmental effect on our bodies so that when my daughter Chloe asks me, as she has many times: "Mummy, will I get breast cancer?" I can look her in the eye and say no.'

Olivia willingly volunteered to give a number of TV interviews on the subject and she was keen to talk about the importance to women of self-examination. She explained: 'Rather than be frightened of finding it early, you're going to be lucky finding it early and not be scared in getting it seen to. Cancer's not necessarily a death sentence. They have a very high cure rate right now. You think you can't cope, but you do, and you come out stronger at the other end.'

One of Olivia's first public appearances since winning her own battle with breast cancer was hosting a two-hour TV special taped at a theatre in Los Angeles to raise awareness and funds. She was given a standing ovation and went on to sing 'Why Me' and 'I'm Not Going To Give In To It', before inviting breast cancer survivors in the audience to join her on stage. 'There were probably seventy women on the stage of all different ages, sizes and races,' she remembers. 'It was amazing. It was tragic that all of us had had it, but the fact we were survivors was tremendously uplifting.'

During the evening Olivia spoke candidly about her own experiences with breast cancer and recounted how the esteemed American talk-show host Larry King had asked her whether she felt any less of a woman after losing a breast. 'Pretty tactful, huh?' she asked of her audience, and added: 'To anyone thinking of asking that question, losing a breast doesn't make us any less of a woman. It's our spirit and soul that define us as women.'

Olivia's determination to help others didn't stop with speeches and appearances. In a bid to encourage self-examination, she devised the Liv Kit, a simple appliance which looks like a plastic bag with a special gel inside which acts like a magnifying glass and makes any changes in a breast show up more clearly. The Liv Kit was designed not as a replacement for a mammogram nor for a doctor's examination but as an additional aid to early detection and Olivia worked tirelessly to promote it.

She also followed up with a remarkable new CD entitled *Grace And Gratitude*, a spiritual collection of comforting, healing songs which combined Tibetan chanting, Japanese Buddhism, some Islam and some Hebrew. The last song,

'The Poem', is attributed to St Francis of Assisi. Olivia wrote the songs on the album with Amy Sky and freely admitted:

> I really made this for myself as a journey of healing. And I feel that in doing so, maybe I can help other people who have gone through something difficult as well.
>
> It was kind of a wonderful, wild notion to write an album based on the different levels of healing and belief systems. Amy came to my house and I have this beautiful white room that has a lot of light coming through it. In five days we wrote seven songs. If you asked me where they came from, we can't even imagine how we did it, but it just flowed through us. Then we decided to make the album seamless, with no breaks between the tracks so that you can listen to it as one piece. So if you're in meditation or having a massage, you're not jolted between tracks.
>
> The title came from the idea that no matter what you've gone through, if you have gratitude for something, it creates a feeling of wellbeing. It always makes you feel good to thank whatever it is that you want to thank: the universe, the planet, the god you believe in. It's true, no matter what I've gone through, I still have incredible gratitude.

In America, *Grace And Gratitude* was a CD exclusive to Walgreen's where Olivia's Liv Kit and other wellness products of hers were available. 'I had the idea that we should put them together with the CD,' she explained to *Billboard*. 'I went to the Walgreen offices at nine in the morning with my computer under fluorescent lights and sang with a track to the head of the company. And he went: "Yes, I like this."

He got together the head of the music department and the women's health department and said: "I don't know how you're going to make this happen, but do." He got what I was trying to do. It was amazing.'

A Candle of Light

'If someone had said to me all those years ago when I made Grease that one day I'd open a retreat and spa I'd have said they must be crazy'

Olivia

In mid-August 2003, Olivia was in Las Vegas when word reached her that that her mother's health was fast failing. Irene had not been well for some time and Olivia immediately cancelled a concert she was due to give in Albuquerque and another scheduled for the same week at the Greek Theatre in Los Angeles in order to fly to Irene's bedside in Melbourne.

Olivia flew out that same night and arrived in time to be with Irene in the last few days of her life. She had brought with her a candle, which she placed in the sitting room and lit when loved ones came to visit Irene in her final days.

And, as Olivia recounted to Andrew Denton in the most revealing TV interview she's ever given, the candle proved to be of comfort to her in the most extraordinary way just after Irene passed away. Olivia explained: 'I had always said to her: "Please give me a sign after you've gone that you're OK," because my mother had always told me that when her mother died, a photograph of her fell off the wall and she had always felt this was a sign from her mother. I said: "Please give me a sign."

'My mother was not particularly religious – in fact I

would say she was probably agnostic – but she said she would try, with a slight smile on her face. I'm not quite sure if she really believed it but I always hoped she would.'

Olivia says that about an hour after Irene had died, she went in to sit with her and felt an incredible presence in the room, an energy she had never felt before. 'So I said to her: "Mum, please let me know you're OK." I looked around the room and thought: what can we ask her to do? There was nothing in there except some candles going under the window.

'I said: "Can you make the candles move, make them flicker, something." The candles moved. That was enough for me – great, she's OK.'

But just then, there was a shout from the sitting room where Rona and other relatives and close friends were gathered.

> They screamed: 'Olivia, come here!' I thought: can't they just leave me alone to have quiet time with Mum? I got up. I opened the door. I said: 'What?' They said: 'You'll never believe what happened, a second ago the candle in here exploded.' The whole candle went Tcch! right under her picture. So I told them just what had happened. We all kind of hugged, laughed and cried and felt that everything was OK. So that was my sign. It was a pretty powerful one. She was a pretty powerful lady.

Some ten days after Irene's death, Olivia had further reason to believe her mother's spirit lived on. Together with a friend, Gregg Cave, Olivia had gone over to Irene's house in Melbourne to fetch some of Irene's belongings which she wanted to keep as treasured reminders of her mother.

Gregg was a former actor whom Olivia had first met

when he moved to Melbourne to work on the TV series *Carson's Law* in the 1980s, and he had subsequently become a long-standing friend of the Newton-John family. At twenty-seven Gregg had completely changed his life and become an art dealer and hotel designer and now, as they set off together to drive to Olivia's farm near Lismore, the topic of conversation during the journey came around to lifestyle, and Gregg declared that he was looking to buy a small house in New South Wales far away from the hustle and bustle of life in the city to which he was accustomed.

They were just half an hour's drive from completing their journey to Olivia's farm when a For Sale sign caught their eye outside a small house in Brooklet, in the subtropical Byron Bay hinterland near the town of Bangalow. They decided to stop to investigate, and it turned out that they had stumbled across a semi-derelict former health retreat called the Sanctuary, which had originally opened as the Bangalow Palms Health Farm twenty years before, the first of its kind in the area.

The minute Olivia stepped out of the car to inspect the property she was struck by the energy of the place, and her initial curiosity began to take on a new relevance when they started to explore its twenty acres of natural surroundings. She remembers that when she and Gregg reached the highest point on the plot and gazed out over rolling green hills, orchards and vineyards all around them and took in the glorious views to the mountains on one side and the ocean to the other, they both fell in love with it instantly.

That night Olivia couldn't stop thinking about the property and its glorious setting, so much so that she even dreamed that she had bought it and called it Gaia, the title of the spiritual album she had recorded nine years before. When she recounted her dream to Gregg next morning, he was stunned because he said that he, too, had dreamed they had bought it – but named it Bella Vista because of its breathtaking views. The coincidence of their dreams persuaded them that there was nothing they could do except buy it. They knew that the property, a fifteen-minute drive inland from the popular seaside resort of Byron Bay, would need a lot of work to turn it from a run-down and neglected retreat into the kind of haven of health, peace and tranquillity that Olivia envisaged.

To their disappointment they discovered another prospective purchaser was already in negotiations, but when that sale fell through Gregg and Olivia were able to buy the retreat with the help of some financial partners. And they called it Gaia.

Olivia, who dedicated 2, her 2002 album of duets, to Irene, firmly believes it was all meant to be and that her mother led her there. 'You might think I'm nuts – but she was part of it,' she said. 'My mum gave me my love of nature and beauty and it was almost as if she had guided us to this breathtaking tran-quil place in the middle of the countryside.

'If someone had said to me all those years ago when I made *Grease* that one day I'd open a retreat and spa I'd have said they must be crazy.'

Olivia and her partners took ownership in 2004 and Gregg gave up his job as an art dealer to oversee the nine-month transformation of the building into a beautiful retreat.

As a tribute to Irene, who was a fine photographer, and as a thank-you to her mother for leading her to the oasis of calm that is Gaia, the retreat has many of Irene's nature photos processed on to canvas with copies for sale and the profits going to the funding of the Olivia Newton-John Cancer Centre in Melbourne.

16

Missing

'I have worked here for forty-five years and not had a single man go overboard'

Frank Liversedge, landing manager for San Pedro's 22nd Street Marina

On 30 June 2005, a chartered boat by the name of *Freedom* cast off from its moorings at 22nd Street marina in San Pedro, a seaside suburb south of Los Angeles, and nosed its way out of the picturesque port to sea on an overnight fishing trip off the coast of California. On board the 27-metre-long vessel equipped with state-of-the-art electronics were a full crew and a group of twenty-three enthusiastic anglers, all eagerly looking forward to a few hours of sport-fishing. They had each paid $105 for the trip and were hoping for an abundance of sea bass and yellowtail in the waters around San Clemente Island, a hundred kilometres to the south.

It should have been a routine trip, one of dozens regularly taken by the *Freedom* from the San Pedro landing area, which is home to the largest privately owned diving and fishing fleets on America's west coast.

Instead, the *Freedom*'s voyage evolved into the most baffling and, for Olivia, most agonising of missing-persons mysteries. For on board the *Freedom* that night was Patrick McDermott, Olivia's on-off boyfriend of the past nine years. And on the ship's return to port, there was no sign of him. He had vanished.

Olivia had first met Patrick, an American cameraman eight years her junior, on the set of a commercial and there was an instant spark between them. 'I hadn't met her before, I never had a crush on her or enjoyed her music,' said Patrick, even confessing that he had never seen *Grease*. 'But when I got to speak with her and make true eye contact for the first time, we were locked as if we had known each other for years in past lives.'

Both had recently been through divorces, and Olivia found Patrick to be amusing, thoughtful and considerate, handsome, and the most romantic person she said she had ever met. One Valentine's Day, in the most quixotic of gestures, Patrick designed a 'magical mystery tour' for Olivia to follow which led her via a trail of loving notes, cards and signs around Malibu to a tent where he was waiting for her with outstretched arms and a bottle of champagne.

Patrick was never the most visible of Olivia's boyfriends. He was not often photographed by her side over the next few years, but there was no doubt that he felt tremendous love and affection for Olivia, and she for him. Olivia notably referred to him as her special man when she was inducted into the Australian Recording Industry Association's Hall of Fame in 2002.

But now, on a fateful June night, Patrick had inexplicably gone missing, and his disappearance, and the investigations and revelations that followed, proved to be so distressing for Olivia it led her to state: 'I've been through cancer and divorce. Nothing compares to this.'

Fellow anglers and crew confirmed Patrick had definitely been aboard the vessel on the night of 30 June and yet, when the *Freedom* returned to San Pedro, there was apparently no trace of him. Patrick seemed to have completely disappeared and the only solid evidence that he had been on board was a small bag found in his bunk and his fishing tackle. The bag was later found to contain his passport, wallet, an organiser, his car keys, credit cards and some loose coins.

Patrick's car was later discovered in the car park where he was presumed to have left it before boarding the *Freedom*.

Patrick's was an utterly perplexing disappearance which, in time, as investigations got under way, gave rise to theories that he had fallen overboard into the Pacific and drowned, that he had committed suicide, that he had faked his own death and even that he had been murdered.

Olivia was in Australia when she received the terrible news that Patrick was missing and she was shocked to the core. She had been enjoying a break at her Gaia retreat while firming up plans for an Australian tour for the following year. On 7 July she put in an appearance at a Planet Ark tree-planting ceremony and, like everyone else at that point, she was unaware that Patrick had disappeared. Particularly heartbreaking for Olivia on hearing the shocking news was that she and Patrick had been going through a brief separation at the time. They had previously parted more than once but got back together again each time and they were always a couple who gave each other space.

The unknown fate of a man Olivia described as 'the most romantic person I've ever known' was worrying enough for the singer. But her anxiety for his safety was compounded by wild press speculation, fuelled by supposed sightings of Patrick in Mexico. The strain was to take a heavy toll on

Olivia and plunge her into a deep depression.

Patrick had originally booked himself a ticket on the *Freedom* as a relaxing treat to himself while Olivia was away on a working holiday in Australia, where she was preparing to promote her new album *Stronger Than Before*, a part-charity CD she had recorded with several friends in the music business in her continuing campaign to raise funds for the fight against breast cancer.

What is beyond dispute is that Patrick was on the *Freedom* that night. Fisherman Tony Mayo, who befriended Patrick on the trip before he vanished, reported: 'He was a cool cat. I remember he made a couple of good jokes during the safety speech and just seemed a nice guy.'

Mayo went on to say that at 1.45am on 1 July, he was on deck fixing a new line on his fishing reel and there was no sign of Patrick. He added that when he looked for him later that morning he was nowhere to be seen. 'I kept an eye out for him all day long but never saw him again,' Mayo said. 'I just figured he was sick or something.'

Several crew members said they remembered Patrick as being amiably chatty as the anglers spent a pleasant few hours enjoying a beer or two and some good fishing. Patrick was also said to have eaten a light meal on his own in the galley as the *Freedom* headed back to port.

Early on the evening of Friday, 1 July, the boat came to a routine stop at a marker buoy five kilometres from San Pedro harbour as it neared the end of its twenty-four-hour round trip. At this point the twenty-three passengers assembled in the boat's galley to settle up for the incidental costs they had accrued on their trip. This included food, drinks, and the services of the two deckhands, who cleaned and gutted the catch of the day, which mostly comprised yellowtail. Patrick's tab for hot dogs and Cokes was settled up, and the payment of $10 recorded by the crew.

The *Freedom* then began to dock and the passengers disembarked. But no one seemed to remember Patrick actually getting off the boat when it returned to San Pedro. His fishing-tackle box and bag were found in the galley by crew members after the passengers had all disembarked. They were duly handed in as lost property to Frank Liversedge, San Pedro's 22nd Street marina's landing manager, who later said he did not open the bag.

What made the mystery all the more puzzling was that the alarm wasn't raised for fully eleven days. The authorities weren't alerted until 11 July when Patrick's ex-wife, actress Yvette Nipar, called the police after he had failed to turn up for a family get-together for their teenage son, Chance, on 6 July.

Yvette had called Frank Liversedge to ask if any lost property had been handed in. She then gave the marina manager permission to open the bag that Patrick had left behind and to examine its contents. Soon afterwards Patrick's silver Hyundai saloon car was discovered parked in the lot near the San Pedro marina. It was only then that police and coastguard investigations began to get under way.

All the members of the crew and the other anglers were interviewed but none could shed any light on the mystery. No one could actually recall Patrick disembarking from the *Freedom*, thus sparking initial fears that he had fallen overboard. The case began to attract headlines as soon as it became known that the missing man was Olivia's long-standing boyfriend. And the theory that he had possibly faked his own death took wing when it emerged that Patrick was facing a series of problems in a messy personal life.

He had married Yvette on 1 March 1992 and she had

given birth to a boy in August of that year. But they separated on 30 June 1993, and were divorced a year later. A judge granted Patrick and Yvette joint custody of Chance but court papers showed that the pair were in dispute over Patrick's visiting rights.

Legal papers also disclosed that Patrick had filed for bankruptcy in a Los Angeles court in 2000, and that he was also paying $800 a month to Yvette in child support, according to a 1994 divorce filing. It was also revealed that he had recently been chased by Yvette in court for failing to pay maintenance for their son.

The actress, who has appeared in a number of films and TV shows and had regular roles in the soap operas *General Hospital* and *Days Of Our Lives* and the TV series *Robocop* and *21 Jump Street*, had filed court papers in April of that year, two months before Patrick's disappearance, over child support payments, ordering Patrick to pay up. If he did not subsequently meet those payments, he risked a possible jail sentence.

After Patrick's money worries came to light, newspapers began speculating that Patrick might not have been the victim of a tragic accident after all, but that he may have faked his own death and gone into hiding to escape his debts and a bitter ex-wife pursuing him through the courts for child support. The theory that he had arranged to disappear gained further credence when it was revealed that a life-insurance policy of $132,000 would be paid out to his son upon Patrick's death or presumed death.

One line of enquiry was whether Patrick himself had settled up for the food and drink tab he had run up while on board. Or had someone else paid the bill for him?

Particularly puzzling for the investigators was why Patrick had taken his passport with him on an overnight fishing trip.

Frank Liversedge considered it a possibility that Patrick could have staged his own disappearance. 'My opinion is that he wanted to disappear,' he said. 'I believe that he got off the boat at the harbour and just wanted to vanish.

'I have worked here for forty-five years and not had a single man go overboard. There is a one in a trillion chance that he fell into the water – because somebody would have seen him.'

Liversedge thought it inconceivable that Patrick had fallen into the water during the boat's final journey from the marker buoy to the harbour. 'I've seen thousands of trips on that boat,' he said. 'I know the procedure. If somebody had fallen overboard from that buoy to the dock, at least fifteen people would have seen him.

'He used to come here with his son in the daytime. But for some reason he chose to come here alone and go night fishing on the day he went missing.

'What sort of fisherman would have a tackle box so meticulous, a passport on a boat and all his credit cards and leave them behind? It looks like he was trying to set something up.'

US Coast Guard spokesman Scott Epperson also voiced some suspicions: 'Everyone who booked a ticket for that boat has been interviewed and no one can remember seeing Mr McDermott get off,' he said. 'There is also no physical evidence to suggest he was pushed or fell in the water. Is it possible he might have run away? I'd have to say yes, very possible.'

Patrick's neighbours in the Los Angeles suburb of Van Nuys were just as mystified as the investigators. 'I don't believe he's disappeared,' said an incredulous Kathleen Paddon. 'He'd never do anything to be away from Chance. That boy is his sunshine, his moon and his stars.' Privately, that's precisely what Olivia felt too.

The case took on a disturbing new twist for Olivia when a number of eyewitnesses all independently claimed to have seen Patrick alive and well in Mexico.

If they were to be believed, Patrick had been seen in the company of a mystery blonde on Mexico's Baja California peninsula. The couple were said to have stayed in a cheap beachside shack before driving off in the green camper van in which they had arrived. A worker at the Pescadero Surf Camp in Todos Santos told the Australian newspaper the *Advertiser*, 'The lady was here for three days by herself and he came here for a night.' The owner of the camp also claimed he had seen Patrick, and a bar owner ventured he had seen him three months before.

Olivia was quizzed as part of the official investigations, but despite the press clamouring for her to make some sort of comment, she chose to remain silent for nearly two months after Patrick's disappearance was discovered. She cancelled several TV appearances to promote her new CD, but her silence appeared to some as callous. By keeping mum, she suffered unfair criticism about the depth of her feelings for Patrick. But, as she later explained, she decided to say nothing simply out of respect for Patrick's family.

Finally, on 22 August, fully fifty-two days after Patrick went missing, Olivia issued a desperate public appeal for information: 'I am hopeful that my treasured friend is safe and well and I am grateful to the officials who are working so hard to find Patrick, whom I love very much,' she said. 'I ask anybody with information that could help to please, please come forward.'

In an emotional statement for *Entertainment Tonight* Olivia not only expressed her sadness and anxiety but explained why she had decided to remain silent on the subject. Her statement read: 'As you are all now aware, my dear friend Patrick McDermott, who I love very much, is missing. He was last seen on a charter fishing boat on June thirtieth. Out of respect for his family I have chosen not to make any public statements until now. For those of us who know and love him, it has been a truly heartbreaking experience and we have chosen to deal with it privately. I have offered my full cooperation to the authorities who are continuing to investigate the circumstances of his disappearance and we are hopeful that eventually we will find some answers. I am grateful for all of those who have expressed their concern. I would simply ask for your continued support and prayers for his safety and wellbeing and for that of his family.'

Olivia's appeal yielded no new significant leads and, frustrated by the investigations seemingly going nowhere, Olivia eventually turned to Gavin de Becker, the trusted private detective whose firm she had called in during her ordeal over stalker Michael Perry in 1983. But to this day, Patrick's fate remains unknown.

After more than a year spent investigating Patrick's disappearance, the US Attorney's office was unable to find any evidence that the owners of the fishing boat were responsible. A detailed forensic investigation had unearthed no evidence to suggest Patrick was pushed overboard and the Attorney's office closed the investigation in August 2006. They have said they would be prepared to reopen the investigation at any time if they should receive any pertinent information relevant to the case. Meanwhile, the US Coast Guard investigation remains open as an unsolved missing person's case.

* * *

Olivia has always maintained that Patrick was most unlikely to have faked his own death to start a new life. She knew how much his son Chance meant to him and she felt he would never put him through such anguish.

'We had a wonderful relationship,' she said. 'He was so special, and bright and loving and thoughtful and incredibly reliable as a father and boyfriend.'

Intriguingly, however, Emerson Newton-John, her sister Rona's son, later claimed that Olivia's relationship with Patrick had come to a natural end and that she had no knowledge of his financial problems. Her nephew also claimed that Patrick, who had been sober for many years, had started drinking again and was depressed about his money problems and access to his son Chance.

For Olivia, and Patrick's family, the continuing mystery has been hard to bear. Hardest of all has been the lack of closure, as they still have no idea of what precisely happened. In the immediate aftermath of Patrick's disappearance, Olivia was plunged into deep gloom and she built a winding stone path in her garden as a personal, private memorial to her lover, where she could quietly linger and reflect on the good times they had shared. It was somewhere she could feel close to him.

A year earlier, millions of television viewers had seen just how much Olivia meant to Patrick when she was the subject of the Australian version of the TV programme *This Is Your Life*. Olivia was misty-eyed when Patrick declared: 'I love you. The whole world loves you . . . You are the epitome of the word "woman".' In a videotaped message he continued: 'If we could all just be a little bit like you, we'd all be a little better off. I love you with all my heart.'

Olivia admitted that when she was at her lowest ebb

after Patrick's disappearance she resorted to taking antide-pressants. 'I think if you are in a dark place where you can't pull yourself out, you may need to ask for help,' she explained.

After six months she managed to wean herself off the medication. She realised one morning that she didn't need it any more. 'There were a few days when I thought, I don't know if I can do this, and then I had this little voice in my head – that is my guide – and it said you can do it . . . it is an inner strength that I found.'

Olivia believes the healing process really began only when she ceased taking the antidepressants. 'Once you go off them, you can deal with it better,' she said. 'It's impor-tant to go deeply into your emotions. You have to cry.'

The sad irony for Olivia was that Patrick's disappear-ance occurred a matter of weeks before the release of her new studio album *Stronger Than Before*. As Olivia herself stated on the CD's sleeve, the album was comprised of 'songs of inspiration, encouragement and understanding to all those facing breast cancer or any other challenging journey'.

Olivia's own journey had been more challenging than most, but she was at pains to point out that *Stronger Than Before* was made prior to her heartache over Patrick and that she was so devastated by what had happened that she had considered giving up singing altogether. 'Now it's almost like I've made it for myself,' she said. 'I didn't feel like singing and I didn't think I'd ever sing again. The thought of it was terrifying to me. But singing is a part of me and it's my soul. It's how I can express myself and move through it. It's healing for me as well as the audience and I need that. Singing has helped me to deal with the grief.'

Stronger Than Before was recorded specifically as the

cornerstone of Hallmark Gold Crown stores' programme in support of National Breast Cancer Awareness Month. Two dollars of every purchase went to the Susan G. Komen Breast Cancer Foundation.

Among the ten soft-rock tracks was 'Can I Trust Your Arms', a song with music by Olivia and lyrics by Chloe, which the latter had written for her mother as a Christmas present. Olivia had asked Chloe to write a song for the album but her request had failed to elicit an immediate response. Olivia figured that perhaps her daughter wasn't interested in contributing to the album, until Chloe handed her a CD box on Christmas morning with lyrics she had penned on a piece of paper tucked inside. Olivia promptly sat down at the piano and wrote a melody which came to her in ten minutes flat. Olivia was so touched by Chloe's contribution that for the *Stronger Than Before* album she also recorded a song she'd written especially for Chloe called 'That's All I Know For Sure'.

By far the most ambitious, and poignant, track on the album was 'Phenomenal Woman', based on a poem by Maya Angelou. This tribute to womanhood featured a vocal collaboration by several singers who had survived cancer, including fellow Aussie songstress Delta Goodrem, Amy Sky, Mindy Smith, Olivia herself, Beth Nielsen Chapman, Amy Holland, Diahann Carroll and Patti LaBelle.

Olivia was desperate to promote the CD to help raise funds, and she put on a brave front to give interviews although she was aching with sadness inside. In the main, the subject of Patrick's disappearance was a subject she avoided while the investigations continued and she grieved for Patrick in private. But in one interview she broke down in tears and conceded: 'The worst part is not knowing what happened.' And she admitted: 'It's very shocking. In the beginning I was kind of frozen. We miss him. We love him. I loved Patrick very much, I always will.'

Tellingly she added: 'Patrick would want me to go on with my life, I know that.'

17

Mother and Daughter

'My mum has a lot of men after her. She's a gorgeous woman'

Chloe Lattanzi, 2007

Not many people were generally aware of, or even understood the meaning of, anorexia nervosa until the untimely death of singer Karen Carpenter in 1983. Karen was one half of the brother-and-sister act The Carpenters, whose dreamy intimate harmonies on densely layered records produced sales of ten million singles in the early 1970s.

But in 1974, Karen, suffering from eating disorders and worryingly thin, collapsed. Her anorexia nervosa necessitated a slow-down in the duo's frantic recording and concert activity.

As with Olivia's records, the lush melodies of The Carpenters' hits struck a chord with millions of lovers of middle-of-the-road music, and Olivia's path often crossed with Karen's as they simultaneously soared to success. The two singers became firm friends. They were such close pals that in 1983 Karen asked Olivia to accompany her for moral support when she went to sign her divorce papers, ending her marriage to a businessman. But almost immediately after, Karen died of heart failure due to complications related to her illness. She was just thirty-two.

Instead of finding herself playing the supportive

companion for Karen on what clearly was going to be a very emotional day, Olivia found herself attending her funeral.

Karen's death hit Olivia very hard. She knew that Karen had not been well and that she had been receiving treatment in New York. But, like most other people, Olivia knew very little about anorexia nervosa. It was a subject neither spoken about nor written about in the way it is today. And little did Olivia know at the time of Karen's death that her own daughter Chloe would be fighting her own battle with anorexia some twenty years later.

In 2007, Chloe bravely went on TV's *Entertainment Tonight* to speak about her problem and to say: 'I felt like I hit rock bottom.'

In the face of speculation about her health, Chloe told *ET*'s Mary Hart about her struggle with an eating disorder and said: 'For two years of my life I went through it, and I've come out of it now.' Chloe, whose health has recovered, added that at her lowest point her anorexic crisis was so severe that she couldn't remember most of the time she was starving herself.

It was another desperately difficult time for Olivia, who admitted that for a while she was in denial about her daughter's problem. 'I have to admit that,' she said, 'because you don't want to think that anything could be wrong – not to say I wasn't frightened, and nervous, and anxious for her.'

Olivia and Matt both rallied round to help Chloe through her problems with the aid of a specialist therapist and a nutritionist. And, like Olivia, Chloe was greatly aided in her recovery by creating music. Perhaps inevitably, Chloe had always wanted to follow in the footsteps of her parents and pursue a career in showbusiness, and her voice was good enough for Olivia occasionally to invite her up on stage to join her at concerts. She has since launched off on a singing career.

* * *

Chloe made her film debut when she was seven in the 1994 film *A Christmas Romance*. Fittingly, Olivia played Chloe's mother and it marked Olivia's return to the screen for the first time since recovering from cancer. Olivia played a penurious widow with two daughters who lives in a rented house in the mountains surrounded by farm animals and decent, caring neighbours. But her happy existence is threatened when a banker arrives to tell her she faces eviction unless she can pay the rent. A snowstorm unexpectedly traps the banker into having to spend a few days with the family and he begins not only to enjoy their life but to fall for Olivia's character Julia.

As Chloe's thoughts increasingly turned to following in Olivia's footsteps, mother and daughter teamed up again in a new family film called *The Wilde Girls*, shot on Queensland's Gold Coast in 2001 and directed by Olivia's long-time friend Del Shores. In a plot which had undertones of her own life, Olivia played a single mother living in Georgia and doing her best to raise her daughter in the most normal fashion while trying to keep secret her past as a famous singer.

The occasional forays into movies that took her fancy was a direct result of a new freedom Olivia felt after her recovery from illness. She was financially secure, she had nothing to prove and now she could make the records she wanted to, often away from the mainstream and without commercial pressures, and appear in the films she thought worthwhile. One of these had been the film *It's My Party* with Eric Roberts, released in 1996.

Another, in 2000, was *Sordid Lives*, in which Olivia's enviable position of being able to pick and choose drew her to playing totally against type. 'A black comedy about white trash', as the film came to be billed, *Sordid Lives*, written and directed by Del Shores, had been a successful play. After seeing it, Olivia told Del that if he ever turned it into a movie, then she would love to play the role of Bitsy-Mae–a gum-chewing, tattooed, foul-mouthed, leather-clad, lesbian ex-con biker who has an affair with a Texas granny.

Del thought she was simply being flippant until Olivia called him on his birthday to pass on her good wishes and ask him what he was up to. Del explained he was chasing big names in a bid to get financial backing to turn *Sordid Lives* into a movie.

Again Olivia suggested that she would like the role of Bitsy-Mae, and again Del wondered if she was joking. But she wasn't – and by signing a letter to confirm she would be in the film, she provided the clout needed for Del to secure the necessary backing.

Sordid Lives was not only a marked change for Olivia, it gave her enormous fun to play the trashy Bitsy-Mae Harling. It allowed her to bleach her hair, but deliberately leave the roots showing, before cutting off clumps of it herself in order to make it spiky. Then she was able to slap on the make-up, apply tattoos to her chest, strut around in the shortest of skirts and cowboy boots, and even play guitar on screen. It was hardly the wholesome Olivia Newton-John image of yesteryear, but she enjoyed herself so much she jumped at the chance to reprise the role of Bitsy-Mae in a spin-off TV series.

During Olivia Newton-John's early career, a joke went the rounds that if white bread could sing it would sound like Olivia Newton-John. Olivia was somewhat irritated, but not overly so, by the squeaky clean, goody-goody image she seemed to have been saddled with. She was only irritated when she was made out to be less than human, which she rightly thought was absurd. Otherwise, she was grateful for any sort of an image – it meant that at least people were sitting up and taking notice of her.

What did irritate her enormously was being assessed as a singer by her looks. She resented anyone who didn't take her singing seriously because they seemed to think she was a model playing at having a musical career. 'Some people don't even bother to listen to you because they assume you can't be pretty and be a good singer at the same time,' she protested.

But undoubtedly Olivia's fresh-faced looks, her winning smile, her pretty appearance, her general 'niceness', her clear voice and her absence from lurid headlines in Sunday newspapers led some to believe that she was uninteresting and bland. Like Cliff Richard, Olivia couldn't, and still can't, understand what is wrong with being nice.

Thirty years ago, Olivia's father Brin was moved to say precisely that in defence of his younger daughter. He told *Woman's Day*: 'It makes me so angry to read in newspapers that because she is not into drugs, alcohol and other people's beds, then she must be dull and stupid. She is a modest, decent, sensible and terribly nice girl. Why can't they accept that? She is also tough, inwardly tough. She's a professional.'

These days the snide critics have been silenced. They accept and applaud Olivia as a woman on a very different journey from the girl who was expected to turn out hit record after hit record in the 1970s and 1980s. The hits may have dried up but no one believed the Women's Guild of Cedars-Sinai Medical Center in Los Angeles got it wrong in 1999 when they gave Olivia the Woman of the 21st Century Award for her devotion to charity work.

Olivia is not a singer who craves the spotlight and needs the applause. She has thought about retiring so many times, but something has always come along to persuade her otherwise. She no longer needs to sell records by the million. Instead she can content herself by recording a Christmas album or release a CD like 2005's *Indigo: Women Of Song* as a salute to singers she's admired. For Olivia, *Indigo* was the fulfilment of an ambition harboured for fifteen years to record an album of oldies. She'd planned such an album back in 1990 but Linda Ronstadt beat her to it and so she shelved the project.

When she eventually felt the time was right to resurrect the idea, Olivia included on the album a cover version of Minnie Riperton's smash hit 'Loving You' because Minnie was the first woman Olivia knew who had died of cancer. The inclusion of 'Rainy Days And Mondays' was a poignant reminder of Olivia's friendship with Karen Carpenter.

As Olivia approached her sixtieth birthday, she revealed that she had fallen in love again. A friendship with handsome Australian health guru John Easterling stretching back fifteen years had blossomed into a romance and friends believe she has finally found the ideal partner.

The two certainly have much in common. Like Olivia, John went through a remarkable life-changing experience following a brush with death through illness. Like Olivia he subsequently regained his health thanks largely to natural medicine. Almost overnight he turned from a dedicated treasure hunter in South America to committed environmentalist and champion of herbal health.

Easterling goes by the nickname of Amazon John, and with good reason. He was a born adventurer, his thirst for exploration and travel fired at school by a story he read about a young boy living in the show-capped mountains of the Andes. After college he sold his car to buy a ticket to Ecuador and set off in search of treasures.

He subsequently made more than a hundred and fifty trips to South America, criss-crossing the Andes many times armed with a machete and some provisions, looking for lost cities and pre-Colombian civilisations. For several years he made a good living dealing in his finds, which ranged from gemstones to ancient artefacts.

But his life changed for ever on a journey of exploration up a tributary of the Amazon in the Peruvian jungle when, desperately weak and stricken with fever, he ditched his dugout canoe on a riverbank and stumbled into a Shipibo village, where he collapsed. Too weak to get up, he was cared for by the villagers, who fed him herbal tea and other local botanical preparations, which broke the fever overnight. Ten years earlier John had encountered a near-death experience in a north Carolina hospital after contracting hepatitis and Rocky Mountain spotted fever, which left him, he says, operating at only 60 per cent of his health capacity.

But after ten days of using the herbal mixtures the natives gave him, John's fever had not only long gone but he felt a flow of energy and a mental clarity he had never experienced in his entire life. 'This life-changing experience in my own health using Amazonian herbs was the watershed experience of my life,' he said. 'After all these years of treasure-hunting in the jungle, I finally realised the real treasure of the rainforest was the life-giving properties of the rainforest itself. I was standing in the highest concentration of life energy on the planet.'

Easterling later met Nicole Maxwell, the author and explorer who spent forty years in the Amazon conducting research into medicinal plants. At the age of eighty-three, Nicole accompanied Easterling back into the Peruvian jungle to help him further his knowledge of the healing potential of rainforest plants. 'I found the purpose and meaning of my life – to bring these life-saving herbals to people throughout the world,' he says.

Since then, Easterling has established the Amazon Herb Company, a thriving business in which the herbs are ecologically harvested from the jungle by hired tribal members. The company's financial support of the tribes has enabled them to cancel some of the logging contracts that otherwise would have resulted in rainforest destruction. A portion of the money from each product sold goes back to the native Indians to support their culture and help save the rainforest.

With a mutual concern for the planet, it is easy to see why Olivia was so drawn to John Easterling. And despite past disappointments in her love life and no closure on the mysterious disappearance of Patrick McDermott, she claimed she felt perfectly at ease in taking her friendship with John to another level.

'It just felt very natural with John,' she explained. 'And if I've learned anything, it's that you have to open your heart. It's easy to shut down after disappointments, but love is the most important thing out there, and always will be, whether you choose to be open to it or not.'

In April 2008, five months before her sixtieth birthday, Olivia set off to walk the Great Wall of China to raise money for the Wellness cancer centre in Melbourne due to open in her name in 2010. Olivia has long advocated that treatment of cancer should focus on the whole person not just the disease itself. The plan, therefore, is for the new centre to provide patients with complementary therapies and to support them by treating the mind and spirit as well as the body.

The idea of a sponsored walk along the wall to Beijing was first mooted four years before and involved months of precise planning as well as lengthy negotiations with the Chinese government before permission was granted. Olivia's trek represented a million steps towards finding a cure for cancer, and she completed the 228km walk in just over three weeks. It involved striding across rough terrain, up steep gradients and camping out often in freezing temperatures.

Olivia spent several months building up her fitness and regularly raising her heartbeat before setting out. She was accompanied on various stages of the walk by a number of celebrities including Sir Cliff Richard, Danii Minogue and Didi Conn, who played Frenchy in *Grease* and who had recently lost both her parents to cancer. Comedienne Joan Rivers turned up for the walk in red high heels and announced Olivia had lured her to China under false pretences. Joan humorously complained that she thought she was being invited to the Great Mall of China and had brought with her a number of credit cards only to find there wasn't a single shop in sight.

In addition to the celebrities, Olivia was joined by a number of cancer survivors or 'thrivers,' as she prefers to call them. The mood of the walkers was upbeat and positive. They wore wristbands bearing the words Hope, Courage and Faith, and at night they all gathered round and sang songs together from *Grease* led by its female star.

Typically, Olivia even managed to save the life of a kitten along the way. She found the tiny little animal, thought to be just one day old, in a freezing pond where it had been left to die. Olivia rescued it and helped nurse it back to life by feeding it milk from a syringe. She named it Magic after her own hit song and spent several sleepless nights getting up every two hours to feed it. 'I was sure it would die when I found it,' she said. 'It was freezing cold and very weak. But with constant love and care we helped him grow.' Magic became the walkers' mascot and even attracted its own sponsors.

To swell the funds for her cancer centre, Olivia also released the CD *The Great Walk to Beijing: A Celebration in Song*, which featured duets with various artists including Keith Urban, Richard Marx, and Barry Gibb. Fittingly, Olivia recorded one of the duets with Cliff Richard, the British pop idol who had given her such an important break almost forty years before, right at the start of her career. It was a further reminder of how far she had come.

Olivia's happiness was finally complete when, on 21 June, 2008, she wed John in Peru in a secret ceremony. A second, equally private, marriage ceremony followed a week later on Jupiter Island, Florida, and the newlyweds broke their happy news to family and friends at a barbecue held at Olivia's Malibu home on 4 July.

Guests thought they were being invited to an American Independence Day party. Instead, they were asked to raise their glasses to John and Olivia, Mr and Mrs Easterling. Now cancer-free, fulfilled, in love and happy to become a bride again at the age of 59, it is an indication of how far Olivia has come on her life's journey.

Proudly Olivia sported for all to see a beautiful symbol of herself and John and their deep love for each other – a 5.1 carat natural intersecting twin diamond set in platinum.

'I've found someone who is my soul mate, companion and life partner,' she declared with girlish glee. 'My life is on a wonderful path and it's flowing beautifully.'

Three months later, when she celebrated her sixtieth birthday, Olivia was still in the first flush of newlywed bliss and no one doubted her when she said: 'I'm the happiest and healthiest I've ever been, and I feel very fortunate to reach sixty.'

In John she had found a husband who commanded respect in his own right. He was never a man likely to be referred to as Mr. Olivia Newton-John. Nor, as she had found among boyfriends in the past, was he a man out to compete with her. As if to emphasise his masculine standing, Olivia was only too pleased to be known as Mrs. Olivia Newton-John Easterling.

And, as a dutiful wife, she was content to accompany John and put in personal appearances with him on a 10-city lecture tour of America to support his drive to promote health benefits associated with the preservation of the Amazon Rainforest. The tour was also a chance for the couple to introduce Zamu, a revolutionary organic Rainforest blend of ingredients scientifically recognized for their beneficial health properties.

While Olivia was eager to follow her path as an environmentalist, it was *Billboard* who provided an opportune reminder of her standing as a singer. To celebrate 50 years of its pop charts from August 1958 to July 2008, the much-respected music trade magazine published *Billboard's* Hot 100 All Time Top Songs. Olivia's 1981 hit 'Physical' came in sixth place in the list, beating even The Beatles, who came eighth with 'Hey Jude'.

Fully twenty seven years on, the irony of the accolade was not lost on Olivia. 'Physical', she could laugh to herself, was the one single she had never wanted released. In a blind panic fearing 'Physical's' suggestive lyrics might wreck her career, she had fought hard to block its release.

Billboard's salute was a timely boost for the singer, coming as it did when Olivia was planning a short series of concerts for which the climax would be an appearance at Nashville's revered Ryman Auditorium, known as 'The Mother Church of Country Music.'

Built by Thomas Ryman, a former riverboat captain, it first opened in 1892 as a Union Gospel Tabernacle. But the Ryman acquired a proud country music history when it became the venue for the Grand Ole Opry broadcasts from 1943 to 1974. It then fell into disrepair before being renovated and becoming a venue which has hosted down the years almost all the greats of country music.

Any bitterness towards Olivia which the country music die-hards might have harboured three decades earlier was forgotten as Olivia bounded on to the stage at the Ryman. She quickly had a full house of 2,362 leaping out of their pews to acclaim her.

But while life appeared to be nothing but blue skies for Olivia, as has happened so often before, a cloud was hovering on the horizon waiting to rain on her parade.

Olivia's marriage to John had reminded the media of the mysterious disappearance of her previous beau Patrick McDermott. And in January, 2009, America's NBC broadcast on the current affairs programme *Dateline* a documentary which claimed that McDermott was alive and on the run after staging his own vanishing act.

Philip Klein, a Texas investigator whose agency specializes in tracking down kidnap victims and people who do not wish to be found, was hired to look into McDermott's case.

Klein claimed that the day before he disappeared, McDermott had turned up at Olivia's a house with roses.

Klein went so far as to set up a high-tec website called findpatrickmcdermott.com which secretly showed the investigation team the locations of people accessing the site.

According to the website, there had been 16 sightings of McDermott in Mexico over the past 20 months. And Klein revealed that he suspected McDermott had regularly been logging on to the 'spider' site with the team tracking website hits from what he reckoned was a boat travelling along the Mexican coastline as far as south America.

'When you're running, you always are looking over your shoulder and we're going to catch him looking at us,' said Klein. 'The most interesting hits have come directly from Cabo San Lucas (in Mexico), the last place anybody saw Patrick McDermott.'

Filmography

1965: *Funny Things Happen Down Under*
A group of children in the small village of Wallaby Creek in the Australian outback are set to lose the wool shed they meet to play in unless they can come up with $200 before Christmas. While trying to raise the cash they accidentally stumble across a formula which turns sheep's wool different colours and they try to sell the formula to foreign buyers. Olivia has a small role and sings 'Christmas Time Down Under'.

1970: *Toomorrow*
Sci-fi musical centred around four students attending the London College of Arts and living in Chelsea, with Olivia as the 'den mother'. To pay their way through college they form a pop band and create an original and stimulating musical sound, which subsequently brings them into close contact with alien visitors from a world called Alphoid. The dying aliens kidnap the group as they need the band's 'vibrations' to survive. Co-stars included Roy Dotrice, Roy Marsden. With Karl Chambers, Vic Cooper and Ben Thomas as Olivia's Toomorrow bandmates.

1972: *The Case (TV)*
A co-production between the BBC and the Swedish broadcasting authorities starring Cliff Richard in a comedy-drama about the singer trying to get rid of a stolen suitcase full of money he had inadvertently picked up on his way to Sweden. Olivia and comedian Tim Brooke-Taylor find themselves caught up in the caper.

1978: *Grease*

John Travolta and Olivia star as Danny and Sandy, two teenagers who enjoy a summer holiday romance then meet again unexpectedly as students at Rydell High School. But true love runs far from smoothly for prim cheerleader Sandy and Danny, greasy leader of the college T-Birds gang, as they attempt to rekindle their romance. Co-stars in the most successful movie musical of all time included Stockard Channing, Jeff Conaway, Eve Arden, Edd Byrnes, Frankie Avalon and Sid Caesar.

1980: *Xanadu*

Olivia stars as Kira, a heavenly muse who comes down from Mount Olympus to Earth to inspire frustrated artist Sonny (Michael Beck) and an old-time jazz musician Danny (Gene Kelly) to follow their dreams to open a roller-skating disco and musical pleasure dome. But Sonny and Kira's love for each other is complicated by her being only a temporary Earthling.

1983: *Two Of A Kind*

Fantasy romantic comedy starring John Travolta as Zack, a bumbling, unsuccessful inventor who tries to rob a bank to pay off his debts and thereby avoid the thugs chasing him to pay up. Olivia plays the devious bank teller Debbie who, despite being held up at gunpoint, cleverly sends Zack away with a bag full of worthless paper and runs off with the real loot herself. Zack sets out to track her down and, when he finds her, the two villains have the chance to redeem themselves and an opportunity to save the world by embarking on a romance. Co-stars included Oliver Reed, Beatrice Straight and Charles Durning.

1990: *A Mom For Christmas* (TV)
A little girl called Jessie, whose mother died when she was three, and who is largely neglected by her workaholic father, wins a free wish in a department store. Her wish for a mother to be with her over the Christmas period is fulfilled when a shop mannequin called Amy (Olivia Newton-John) comes to life.

1994: *A Christmas Romance*
Olivia stars as Julia, a single mum struggling to raise two daughters while living in the mountains surrounded by farm animals and good neighbours. A city banker (Gregory Harrison) brings the grim news that she will be forced out of her house unless she can pay the rent. But when he is caught in a snowstorm and forced to spend a few days with the family, he starts to appreciate their way of life and falls for Julia. Olivia's daughter Chloe plays Deenie, one of Julia's daughters.

1996: *It's My Party*
Eric Roberts stars as a gay man facing death who gathers all his friends together for a final farewell party, before engaging a medical professional to help him end his days with dignity. Olivia plays Lina Bingham, one of the dying man's friends and a woman who is in the throes of divorce and with a son who is coming out. Co-stars include George Segal, Roddy McDowall, Lee Grant, Sally Kellerman and Marlee Matlin.

2000: *Sordid Lives*
Black comedy about white trash in a Texan town, based on Del Shores's hit play. An eccentric cast of characters includes Beau Bridges as a love rat Vietnam vet with

wooden legs, Bonnie Bedelia as a mother in denial over her gay son, Delta Burke as a bitter, gun-toting, cheated wife out for revenge, and Olivia as Bitsy-Mae Harling, a tattooed lesbian ex-con. Olivia reprises the role in a spin-off *Sordid Lives* TV series.

2001: *The Wilde Girls*

Family film with Olivia starring as Jasmine Wilde, a single mother living quietly in a small town in Georgia. Jasmine is desperate to keep secret the fact that she was once a famous singer, but her secret past is revealed when her daughter Izzy (Chloe Lattanzi) herself shows special singing talent and attracts the interest of a Los Angeles record producer.

Discography

ALBUMS

1970: *Toomorrow* (soundtrack)
1971: *Olivia Newton-John*
1972: *Olivia*
1974: *Music Makes My Day*
1974: *Long Live Love*
1974: *If You Love Me Let Me Know*
1975: *Have You Never Been Mellow*
1975: *Clearly Love*
1976: *Come On Over*
1976: *Don't Stop Believin'*
1977: *Making A Good Thing Better*
1977: *Greatest Hits*
1978: *Grease* (soundtrack)
1978: *Totally Hot*
1980: *Xanadu* (soundtrack)
1981: *Love Performance – Olivia Live In Japan*
1981: *Physical*
1982: *Greatest Hits Volume II*
1983: *Two Of A Kind* (soundtrack)
1985: *Soul Kiss*
1988: *The Rumour*
1989: *Warm And Tender*

1992: *Back To Basics: The Essential Collection*
1994: *Gaia: One Woman's Journey*
1998: *Back With A Heart*
2000: *One Woman's Live Journey*
2001: *Sordid Lives* (soundtrack)
2001: *The Christmas Collection*
2002: *2*
2005: *Indigo: Women Of Song*
2005: *Stronger Than Before*
2006: *Grace And Gratitude*
2008: *Olivia's Live Hits*
2008: *The Great Walk to Beijing: A Celebration in Song*

(Note: Some albums were released in different forms in different countries.)

SINGLES

| | CHART POSITIONS | | |
	UK	US	AUS
1971: If Not For You	7	25	14
1971: Banks Of The Ohio	6	94	1
1972: What Is Life?	16	–	–
1973: Take Me Home, Country Roads	15	119	–
1973: Let Me Be There	–	6	16
1974: Long Live Love	11	–	15
1974: If You Love Me (Let Me Know)	–	5	2
1974: I Honestly Love You	22	1	2
1975: Have You Never Been Mellow	–	1	12
1975: Please, Mister, Please	–	3	28

	CHART POSITIONS		
	UK	US	AUS
1975: Something Better To Do	–	13	–
1975: Let It Shine	–	30	54
1976: Fly Away (with John Denver)	–	13	–
1976: Come On Over	–	23	62
1976: Don't Stop Believin'	–	33	–
1976: Every Face Tells A Story	–	55	–
1977: Sam	6	20	74
1977: Making A Good Thing Better	–	87	77
1977: I Honestly Love You (re-release)	–	48	–
1978: You're The One That I Want (with John Travolta)	1	1	1
1978: Summer Nights	1	5	8
1978: Hopelessly Devoted To You	2	3	4
1979: A Little More Love	4	3	4
1979: Deeper Than The Night	64	11	71
1979: Totally Hot	–	52	96
1979: Dancin' Round And Round	–	82	–
1980: I Can't Help It (with Andy Gibb)	–	12	–
1980: Xanadu	1	8	–
1980: Magic	32	1	2
1980: Suddenly	15	20	26
1981: Physical	7	1	1
1982: Landslide	18	52	42
1982: Make A Move On Me	43	5	15
1982: Heart Attack	46	3	–
1983: I Honestly Love You (re-release)	–	48	–

	CHART POSITIONS		
	UK	US	AUS
1983: Tied Up	–	38	–
1983: Twist Of Fate	57	5	17
1984: Livin' In Desperate Times	–	31	–
1985: Soul Kiss	–	20	12
1985: Toughen Up	–	–	69
1986: The Best Of Me (with David Foster)	–	–	80
1988: The Rumour	–	62	25
1990: Grease megamix	5	–	–
1992: I Need Love	75	96	–
1992: No Matter What You Do	–	–	30
1995: Had To Be (with Cliff Richard)	22	–	–
1998: Grease megamix	4	–	–
1998: I Honestly Love You (remix)	–	67	–

(Note: Some of the above singles were not released in different countries and therefore do not register in the charts.)

Sources: *The Guinness Book of Hit Singles, Billboard* magazine, *Australian Encyclopaedia of Rock*

Index